# UNVEILING ADMIRAL YI SUN-SIN AND THE TURTLE SHIP

## Historical Evidence and Scientific Verification

Kwangsoob Ko

Bookorea

**Unveiling Admiral Yi Sun-Sin and the Turtle Ship**
Historical Evidence and Scientific Verification

© 2025. Kwangsoob Ko
All rights reserved.

No part of this book may be reproduced, stored in a retrieval system, or transmitted in any form or by any means — electronic, mechanical, photocopying, recording, or otherwise — without the prior written permission of the author, except for brief quotations in reviews, critical articles, or scholarly work.

| | |
|---|---|
| This edition printed | August 10, 2025 |
| This edition published | August 15, 2025 |
| Author | Kwangsoob Ko |
| Cover Design | Doyle Ko |
| Editor | Anna Ko |
| Publisher | Bookorea |

Printed in Bookorea Publications Ltd.
Chankyu Lee
Pubulished by Address Woorim A-1007, 14, Sagimakgol-ro 45beon-gil, Jungwon-gu,
　　Seongnam-si, Gyeonggi-do, South Korea
ZIP 13209
TEL 02-704-7840
FAX 02-704-7848
E-mail ibookorea@naver.com
Homepage www.북코리아.kr

ISBN 979-11-94299-54-7 (93990)

₩25,000

The Representative Portrait of Admiral Yi Sun-sin

The Depiction of Admiral Yi Sun-sin Constructing the Turtle Ship

The Statue of Yi Sun-sin in Gwanghwamun Square, Seoul, the Capital of South Korea

The 18th-century Turtle Ship(above) reprpducted by the Korea Naval Academy in 1999. The Turtle Ship(below) reproduced by theNaval Academy in 2022, and it is considered the closest to the Turtle Ship used during the Imjinwaeran. It has been on display at the Naval Academy since 2022.

*This book is dedicated to my beloved family
and
to all who hope for peace on the Korean Peninsula*

# Preface

If a foreigner visiting Korea for the first time were to ask a Korean on the busy streets of Seoul, "Who is the most respected figure and what is the most important historical invention in Korea's 5,000-year history?" they would likely hear the response, "Admiral Yi Sun-sin and the Turtle Ship."

Although it has been 425 years since Admiral Yi passed away, Koreans still revere him as a heroic figure who transcends generations, social status, and ideology. This admiration is not only because he was a great war hero who defeated over 700 Japanese vessels during the Imjinwaeran (1592-1598), but also because of his just conduct as a public servant, his selfless dedication without expectation of reward, and his symbol of pioneering spirit and challenges. Koreans especially hold in high regard Admiral Yi's creative and innovative leadership, as demonstrated in the development of the Turtle Ship. The Turtle Ship was an incredibly innovative warship for the 16th century. Remarkably, it had the capability to fire cannons simultaneously from the bow, stern, and sides, allowing it to charge into enemy fleets and crush their core with minimal damage.

Admiral Yi and the Turtle Ship were first introduced to the Western world over 100 years ago by foreigners. In 1905, an American, H.B. Hulbert, briefly introduced Yi Sun-sin and the Turtle Ship in his book, and in 1921, a British Admiral, G.A. Ballard, also mentioned Yi Sun-sin and the Turtle Ship in his own work. In the 20th century,

British World War II hero, B.L. Montgomery, along with other generals, admirals, and military historians, slowly began to introduce Admiral Yi to the world. However, these foreign introductions mainly focused on Admiral Yi's mythical naval victories, and mentions of the Turtle Ship remained superficial.

Around 50 years ago, in 1970, Professor Jo Seong-do of the Korean Naval Academy published the first English book on Admiral Yi in Korea. In 1976, interpreter Park Yeon-hee published another English book on Admiral Yi in Korea. While these two English books contained more in-depth content compared to earlier foreign introductions, their influence on the Western world was quite limited since both were published domestically in Korea. Through my own research on Yi Sun-sin and the Turtle Ship, I have carefully examined both domestic research efforts and the foreign introductions of Yi. I have come to realize that most of the information about Yi Sun-sin and the Turtle Ship known to the Western world stems from brief introductions made by foreigners in the early 1900s, and at best, from the two English books published in the 1970s. Unfortunately, the latest research findings from the past half-century have not been reflected. I believe the reason for this is the lack of professional books or scholarly research written in English, as well as the insufficient international academic activity by Korean researchers over the past 50 years.

In this context, I often recall the evaluation of Admiral G.A. Ballard, a British naval historian and admiral, from 100 years ago. In the second chapter of his book *The Influence of the Sea on the Political History of Japan*, titled "The Korean War of the 16th Century" (1921), Ballard assessed Yi Sun-sin and the Turtle Ship as follows:

> *"Yi Sun-sin's name is not well known to Western historians, but he deserves to be regarded as one of the greatest naval commanders in the world. It was providence that Korea produced Admiral Yi Sun-sin. He is*

*no less than Admiral Nelson, and his extraordinary talent in developing the Turtle Ship surpasses Nelson's. However, it is unfortunate that his fame has not spread beyond Joseon to the Western world due to the small size of the nation."*

As a graduate and proud officer of the Korean Naval Academy, and later a professor at the Naval Academy and Naval College, I have dedicated my career to educating future generations as a successor to Admiral Yi. However, after reviewing research and materials on Yi Sun-sin and the Turtle Ship from abroad, I have realized that not much has changed even in the 21st century. As Admiral Ballard lamented 100 years ago, Yi Sun-sin and the Turtle Ship remain largely unknown in the Western world and have not received the proper recognition they deserve. This unfortunate reality has given me a heavy sense of responsibility and mission.

The book is based on the seven-year war diary Yi Sun-sin left behind, official documents he sent directly to the king, and the historical records from the Annals of the Joseon dynasty. It also incorporates the latest research findings from Korean scholars over the past 50 years. The book consists of seven chapters, with each chapter covering the following topics: Chapter 1 discusses the domestic and international situation during the Imjinwaeran, Yi Sun-sin's life, and the Turtle Ship. It includes newly revealed information on the Turtle Ship and its tactics and armament capabilities. Chapter 2 covers the battles Yi Sun-sin participated in, along with their analyses.

The book uniquely includes a detailed map of combined Turtle Ship and Panokseon naval battles, drawn by the author on Google Maps, to help readers visualize the course of the battles. Additionally, it presents a simulation-based reconstruction of the *Battle of Jeolido*, often forgotten due to lack of records. Chapter 3 describes how, despite losing half his troops due to a combination of plague and famine during protracted negotiations between China and Japan, Yi Sun-sin led his forces to victory. It also highlights his foresight and leadership in preparing for future battles, anticipating a second Japanese invasion. Chapter 4 details Yi Sun-sin's trials and difficulties, the destruction and revival of the Korean Navy, and the temporary leadership of Admiral Won Gyun, who led the navy to destruction before Yi's reinstatement. This chapter includes recent research correcting the historical error that Yi Sun-sin was removed from his post for disobeying royal orders. Chapter 5 focuses on the miraculous Battle of Myeongryang, where Yi Sun-sin led 13 vessels to victory against over 130 Japanese vessels, and the rebuilding of the Korean Navy. Chapter 6 deals with battles during the period of the Korea-China allied fleet operation. It covers Yi Sun-sin's skillful management of his relationship with Chinese Admiral Chen Lin, which led to the successful Battle of Noryang, where Yi was killed in action. This chapter also summarizes Yi Sun-sin's strategies and tactics, comparing them to modern-day military guidelines. Chapter 7 highlights Yi Sun-sin's legacy as both a soldier and a public servant. It also emphasizes his humanity, demonstrated by his deep filial love and devotion to his parents, even amidst the chaos of war.

It took about 10 long years to complete this book. I would like to express my deepest gratitude to Dr. Jusik Kim, Dr. Jongpyung Park, a researcher on Yi Sun-sin and the author of *Nanjungilgi*, and my former student, Dr. Joomi Park. Without their support and guidance, this research would not have been completed. I also extend my sincere thanks to the scholars and colleagues in Korea who have shown great interest in my research. Their support and collaboration have significantly contributed to the completion of this book. Moreover, without the unwavering support of my wife, In-Ok Kim, and my family, who stood by me through this long Joourney, it would have been difficult to publish this book. My wife accompanied me in exploring and surveying remote islands in the southern part of the

Korean Peninsula to uncover hidden historical sites related to Yi Sun-sin during the early stages of my research. I also want to thank my eldest son, Do-Yle, for designing the book cover, my second son, Min-Seok, for his uplifting suggestions, and my second daughter-in-law, Anna, for reviewing the manuscript. I also wish God's blessings upon my beloved family members: Eun-Young, Gun-Woo, Ye-Ri, and Gun-Ho.

June 2025

**Kwangsoob Ko**
Emeritus Professor
Korea Naval Academy

# Contents

Preface / 9

## Chapter I. Imjinwaeran (Imjin War), Yi Sun-sin and Turtle Ship (Geobukseon)

| | |
|---|---|
| **The Outbreak of the Imjinwaeran (Imjin War)** | **20** |
| Domestic Situations before the Imjinwaeran (Imjin War) | 20 |
| **Who is Yi Sun-sin?** | **29** |
| **Life of Yi Sun-sin** | **31** |
| Evaluation of Admiral Yi Sun-sin's Life | 37 |
| War Preparation of Yi Sun-sin prior to Imjinwaeran | 42 |
| Turtle Ship Cannon Firing Test | 48 |
| **The Turtle Ship and the Panokseon** | **50** |
| The Turtle Ship | 50 |
| Construction Background, Structure and Function of the Turtle Ship | 52 |
| Effective Range of the Cannon Mounted on the Turtle Ship | 59 |
| Tactics of the Turtle Ship | 69 |
| Main Battleship Panokseon | 72 |
| Weapons of the Korean Navy | 76 |
| Weapons and Ships of the Japanese Navy | 78 |
| An Episode about the Miracle of the Turtle Ship in the 1970s | 80 |
| Battle Scenes of the Turtle Ship | 83 |

## Chapter II. Glorious Naval Battles of Admiral Yi Sun-sin

**The 1st Campaign: The Battle of Okpo, Happo, and Jeokjinpo** — 86
  The Japanese Army's Capture of Seoul and Advance North — 86
  The Battle of Okpo — 87
  The Battle of Happo — 92
  The Battle of Jeokjinpo — 94
  The Lessons of the 1st Campaign — 94

**The 2nd Campaign: The Battle of Sacheon, Dangpo, Danghangpo and Yulpo** — 97
  The Battle of Sacheon: Participation of the Turtle Ship — 98
  The Battle of Dangpo — 101
  The Battle of Danghangpo — 104
  The Battle of Yulpo — 107
  The Significance of the 2nd Campaign — 107

**The 3rd Campaign: The Battle of Hansan and Angolpo** — 110
  Ground Combat and Sea Control Situation — 110
  The Battle of Hansan by the *Hakikjin* — 113
  The Battle of Angolpo — 121
  Outcomes and Significance of the 3rd Campaign — 126

**The 4th Campaign: The Battle of Busanpo** — 127
  Background of the Battle — 127
  Processing and Engagement of the Battle — 129

## Chapter III. Yi Sun-sin's Battles and Preparations for Future Naval Warfare: During China-Japan Negotiations in 1593-1596

**The 5th Campaign: The Battle of Ungpo** — 138
  King's Order and Preparations for the Naval Expedition — 138
  Battles and Challenges at Ungpo (The naval battle and landing operations) — 139
  Surveillance Activities and Consideration on Farming — 144
  Characteristics and Significance of the Campaign — 145

| | |
|---|---|
| **The 6th and 7th Campaigns:** <br> **The Battle of Danghangpo and the Jangmunpo Landing Operation** | **148** |
| Yi Sun-sin Becomes the Supreme Naval Commander | 148 |
| The 6th Campaign: The Battle of Danghangpo | 149 |
| Geumtopaemun (Document Prohibiting the Conquest of Japan) | 152 |
| Comparison of the 1st and 2nd Battles of Danghangpo | 154 |
| The 7th Campaign: The Jangmunpo Landing Operation | 155 |
| **Preparations for Future Warfare by Yi Sun-sin During Negotiations** | **162** |
| Negotiations and Yi Sun-sin's Response | 162 |
| Securing Stable Military Supplies and Establishing Military Discipline | 164 |
| Admiral Yi Sun-sin's Command Challenges | 166 |
| Efforts to Resolve Manpower Shortages and Secure Command Authority | 167 |
| Admiral Yi Sun-sin's Leadership amid Crisis: <br> Struggles and Devotion in Command | 168 |
| Resolute Leadership Despite Limited Resources and Internal Challenges | 170 |

### Chapter IV. Yi Sun-sin's Dismissal, Won Gyun's Naval Defeat, and Yi Sun-sin's Return

| | |
|---|---|
| **Dismissal and Rankless Service (Baekuijonggun)** | **184** |
| **The Tragic Battle of Chilcheonryang** | **188** |
| Leadership Confusion and Prelude to the Battle of Chilcheonryang | 188 |
| The Catastrophe of Chilcheonryang and Devastation: <br> Collapse of the Korean Navy | 189 |
| Evaluation and Lessons of the Battle of Chilcheonryang | 193 |
| King's Regret and Yi Sun-sin's Return to Tongjesa | 195 |
| Immediate Actions for Reorganization and Battle Preparations | 197 |
| Movement to the Myeongryang Strait for Decisive Fight | 200 |
| **The Truth About Yi Sun-sin's Claimed Disobedience** | **202** |
| The Outbreak of the Jeongyu War and the Impeachment of Yi Sun-sin | 202 |
| Misunderstandings about Admiral Yi Sun-sin's Disobedience | 203 |
| Reassessment of Historical Evidence and Misconceptions | 204 |
| Discovery and Analysis of Yi Won-ik's Reports | 204 |
| Correction on Yi Sun-sin's Historical Errors | 205 |

## Chapter V. The Miraculous Battle of Myeongryang and Rebuilding Navy

**The Battle of Myeongryang: Miraculous Victory** — 212
   Battle Progress and Results — 214
   Evaluation and Significance of the Battle of Myeongryang — 219

**Rebuilding the Devastated Korean Navy** — 221
   Yi Sun-sin's Suffering after the Victory in the Battle of Myeongryang — 221
   Plans for Strengthening Forces at an Unknown Island — 225
   Efforts to Rebuild the Destroyed Navy at Gohado — 229

## Chapter VI. The Last Victory of Yi Sun-sin and the End of the Imjinwaeran

**The Truth about the Battle of Jeolido** — 236

**Korean-Chinese Allied Naval and Ground Operations** — 241
   The 4 Routes for Simultaneous Land-Sea Campaign — 241
   Blockade Operations by the Korean-Chinese Allied Fleet — 242

**The Battle of Noryang and the Death of Yi Sun-sin** — 247
   The Naval Battle Process and Engagement — 247
   Achievements and Significance — 253
   Descendants of Chinese Admiral Chen Lin in Korea — 254
   Yi Sun-sin's Fleet Operation Concepts and Naval Operational Principles in Imjin War — 256
   Admiral Yi Sun-sin's Main Battle Fleet Operation — 256
   Review of Yi Sun-sin's Naval Battles Applying Naval Operation Principles — 258

## Chapter VII. Lessons from Yi Sun-sin and His Deep Love for Mother

**The Five Spirits of Chungmugong Yi Sun-sin**   262

**The Lessons of Chungmugong Yi Sun-sin**   264
   One Example of Lessons of Yi Sun-sin   264
   The Last Party for His Mother   266

Bibliography / 272
Chronology of Admiral Yi Sun-sin and Imjinwaeran / 276
Index / 285

# Chapter I

Imjinwaeran (Imjin War),
Yi Sun-sin and Turtle Ship
(Geobukseon)

# The Outbreak of the Imjinwaeran (Imjin War)

**Domestic Situations before the Imjinwaeran (Imjin War)**

In 5000 years of Korean history, the Joseon dynasty was founded by King Taejo, Yi Seong-gye, who established the dynasty using military power and the support of the aristocrats, in 1392 and ruled Korea for over 500 years. He began to develop a governance system in collaboration with these aristocrats. The fundamental philosophy of governance was based on Confucianism. During the early Joseon period, the concept of the royal politics, which involved ruling with virtue, acknowledging others, and providing a political system beneficial for not only the aristocrats but also the common people, was crucial in Confucian thought. However, they could not fully establish political systems and governance based on Confucian philosophy in the early days of Joseon, because the focus was on stabilizing the country and strengthening royal authority. Confucian politics in the Joseon era were developed during the reign of King Sejoong, who established local and military systems and intended to conduct politics grounded on Confucian philosophy. Through various compilation projects, Sejoong communicated and completed the essential political systems. He taught scholars Confucian values through the Jiphyeonjeon (Ideological tendency & the administration of the Royal Academic Institute). He set up a bureaucratic system, creating the foundation for Confucian politics, which became the leading political philosophy of Joseon. In the meantime, the aristocrats, who were central to royal authority from the early days of Joseon, became nobles by acquiring government positions and evolved into either civil or military officials. The aristocrats, who were of the Yangban class, ultimately dominated not only the political sphere but also Joseon's economic and cultural aspects. The Yangban class became a hereditary system, receiving various tax exemptions, which intensified class discrimination and caused increasing damage to Joseon's politics, economy, and society.

### Factional Party and Political Confrontation

The aristocrats, bureaucrats, and scholars who helped King Taejo exert political power and establish the dynasty led royal court society. In the early days of the dynasty, they created a governance system through their leadership. However, the Hoongoo faction's increase and misuse of power deepened, leading to clashes with the Silhak faction, which argued that Neo-Confucianism must serve as the foundation of the overall social order.

Ultimately, the Hoongoo faction suppressed the Silhak faction by instigating the factional fightings uprisings in 1498 (Muosahwa) and 1504 (Gabjasahwa) during King Yeonsan-gun period. Later, the Hoongoo faction incited the factional fightings such as the Gimyosahwa (1519) and Eulsasahwa (1545) uprisings during King Jungjong and King Myeongjong periods, respectively. Joseon confused significant political, economic, and social turmoil as it continually faced frequent uprisings, even before the reign of King Seonjo. In other words, societal order was disrupted by the collapse of the caste system, the imbalance in military service, the misuse of official authority to expand farmland, and the upheaval of the public tax system. Following the reign of King Myeongjong, the Sarim faction, led by the Silhak faction, took the political power. However, it split into the Dongin and Seoin groups, with the Dongin faction further dividing into the Namin and Bukin factions, deepening divisions in politics and academia.

After the establishment of the Joseon dynasty, one of the most urgent tasks was to reform the military system and reorganize it into a centralized structure. In the early days of Joseon, the military system was not well-established. Still, as the stability of the dynasty was solidified, King Sejong took steps to reorganize it into three main branches: Royal Military, Central Military, and Provincial Military.

Within the provincial military, both the army and the navy were established. The army, known as Byeongyeong (the army headquarters), was led by a commander known as Byeongmajeoldosa (the commander of the army headquarters in the provinces) or Byeongsa. The navy, known as Suyeong (the naval headquarters), was commanded by Sugunjeoldosa (the commander of the naval headquarters in the province) or Susa.

Each province had a chief administrative officer known as Gwanchalsa who held dual responsibilities for the army and the navy. However, dedicated commanders were stationed in these positions to ensure effective leadership in the main army and navy bases. In most cases, each province had one army and one navy base. However, in regions like Hamgyeong Province, Gyeongsang Province, and Jeolla Province, where defense against the Jurchen people and Japanese pirates was crucial, two army and navy headquarters were established. Within the army and navy, there were large and small units known as Jinyeong (military base). In some cases, local officials exercised command over these units. The soldiers serving in these local units were typically peasants who took turns serving in the military and working as farmers during the agricultural season.

From Korea's founding until the Imjinwaeran in the late 16th century, many changes were happening in Europe. During this time,

Europe was going through a period called the Renaissance. This was a time when there was a lot of change in culture, art, politics, the economy, and society. The Renaissance, which happened around the 15th century, was a time of learning and exploring new ideas. The printing press's invention helped to spread new ideas about art, science, and other subjects. Also, the advanced navigation helped Europeans explore the world. In the 16th century, Europe began to expand its influence around the world. This started with the discovery of the New World by Columbus in 1492, followed by Vasco da Gama's trip to India in 1497, and Ferdinand Magellan's Journey around the world in 1519. During this time, Europe also began to explore and take over parts of Africa and South America. This led to Europe becoming very wealthy. By 1600, England had even created the East India Company to trade with the East.

### Diplomacy with China (Ming dynasty) and Japan

Meanwhile, in Asia, the Ming dynasty in China underwent changes. After it was founded in 1368, the Ming dynasty focused on strengthening its power at home and abroad. Since the founding of the Joseon dynasty, there has been a friendly relationship with Ming China. From the start, Joseon pursued a policy of close ties with Ming until its fall. Joseon would send tributes to China, and in return, China would endorse the kings of Joseon. This was necessary for a small country to reduce political and military tensions and coexist. Every year, Korea sent a tribute envoy to China, and China dispatched an envoy to endorse the crowning of a new king in Joseon. This relationship between Korea and China provided a reason for China to participate in the Japanese invasions of Korea, and accordingly, Ming sent troops to Korea.

Since its establishment, Korea did not establish formal relations with Japan, but pursued a Gyorin policy based on appeasement and diplomacy to counter Japanese pirates, known as Waegu. The Waegu were a group of Japanese pirates who routinely attacked and looted the coasts of the Korean Peninsula and China. The damage caused by the Waegu was one of the main factors leading to the fall of Goryeo dynasty of Korea.

After the founding of Joseon, the core of its southern policy was the Waegu issue. Especially, King Taejo Yi Seong-gye had a lot of experience dealing with the Waegu before establishing Joseon. Even after the establishment of Joseon, the Waegu's invasion of the Korean coast continued. Especially, the Japanese from Tsushima couldn't give up their pirate habits as they couldn't meet their needs with the food produced on their land. In 1419, during Sejong's first year, Korea dispatched General Yi Joong-mu to punish Tsushima and clean up the Waegu's base. The lord of Tsushima sent an envoy to Korea to express his apology. Korea allowed them to trade and set up *Waegwan* (an official residence was built in Joseon to communicate with the Japanese) in Ungcheon, Dongrae, and Ulsan, but in 1510, during King Jungjong's 5th year, the Japanese living in Sampo (Ungcheon, Dongrae, and Ulsan) caused a riot and Korea had to close Waegwan and open some places, implementing a carrot and stick policy. Other than dealing with Japanese pirates, there were no significant official exchanges with Japan. Joseon had no major wars for over 200 years after its founding in 1392, until the Imjinwaeran in 1592. Korea and Japan didn't interact much during this period. Meanwhile, Japan was changing fast. In 1543, Portuguese sailors, led by Mendes Pinto, visited Japan, bringing Western culture. They introduced modern weapons, including guns, which Japan learned to make. In 1549, a Catholic priest named Francisco Xavier visited Japan, and Catholicism began to spread. After more than a hundred years of civil war, Toyotomi Hideyoshi unified Japan. He dreamed of taking over the whole continent with his new military technology.

## Chapter I. Imjinwaeran (Imjin War), Yi Sun-sin and Turtle Ship (Geobukseon)

In 1585, Toyotomi Hideyoshi wanted to conquer China, India, and the Korean Peninsula. He even asked the Portuguese to bring two war vessels to help conquer China. Meeting with overseas monks and merchants who knew a lot about foreign cultures, Hideyoshi's desire to conquer China and the wealthy Joseon dynasty grew.

In 1589, King Seonjo sent Hwang Yun-gil, Kim Seong-il as envoys to Japan. They arrived in Kyoto on July 22, 1590. They could not meet Toyotomi Hideyoshi right away because he was away. They finally met him on November 7, 1590. Hwang Yun-gil told the Korean government that Toyotomi Hideyoshi planned to invade. Kim Seong-il, however, didn't agree with Hwang's warning. He told the government that Toyotomi Hideyoshi wouldn't invade. The government couldn't agree on what to do. King Seonjo sided with Kim Seong-il, promoted him, and stopped preparing for war. Meanwhile, Toyotomi Hideyoshi was preparing his soldiers and setting up a headquarters in Nagoya.

The Korean government argued about telling China what happened in Japan. Ultimately, they decided to hide that they had talked to Japan. They said they had learned about Hideyoshi's plans from a captured person and then let go. In November 1591, Kim Eung-nam was sent to China as an envoy and returned with a letter from the Chinese emperor.

In December 1591, four months before the Imjinwaeran, King Seonjo told his officials not to build defensive walls and embankments to avoid hurting the people. This was to prepare for a possible Japanese invasion. But, in February 1592, when generals Yi Il and Shin Rip returned from checking the country's military readiness, they reported to the government without expressing any worries. These decisions showed that the government was not ready for the coming threat. In the end, the Korean government was too caught up in internal politics to react properly to the crisis, leading to the people being dragged into the war.

## Japan's Invasion of Korea

In January 1592, Toyotomi Hideyoshi issued orders to his troops for the invasion of Korea. The main points of his orders were as follows:

Firstly, those who flee from the expeditionary force and those associated with them will be executed. Secondly, sailors will be conscripted to prepare vessels for the expedition, and all imperial family members in Kyoto should return to their territories to prepare for the expedition. Thirdly, General Kato Kiyomasa and General Konishi Yukinaga will be rewarded and appointed as commanders of the vanguard force. Other orders included preparing maps and vessels for communication, supporting ports to be used in the expedition, residency of generals and their children in Osaka, and repairing and maintaining roads and bridges throughout the country.

On January 5, 1592, Toyotomi Hideyoshi organized the invasion force, which consisted of 16army divisions, 29,000 direct command troops, 30,000 reserve troops, and 9,200 navy troops, with a total of approximately 330,000 troops. The vanguard force departed from Nagoya on March 1 and headed for Tsushima Island. Each general across the country led their troops to gather in Nagoya on the designated date as per with Hideyoshi's orders. On March 18, 1592, Toyotomi Hideyoshi ordered to organize the expeditionary force, consisting of nine divisions with a total of 158,700 troops, and the domestic standby force of 118,300 troops. The first vanguard force to attack Busan consisted of Konishi Division with 18,700 troops, Kato Division with 22,800 troops, Kuroda Division with 11,000 troops, and a total of 52,500 troops. On March 18, 1592, Hideyoshi's general order included the following operational instructions:

Firstly, all expeditionary forces should depart to Korea in the designated order. However, if there is no favorable wind, choose a clear day and cross the sea along the coast. If one soldier or horse is lost due to rash navigation in bad weather, or if they do not cross the sea even when the weather is good, they will be punished. Secondly, horses should cross the enemy coast after building a bridgehead. Thirdly, each division should appoint one person responsible for managing the ship and send them to Tsushima after landing in Korea to perform support missions for subsequent support troops. Fourthly, if the King of Korea approves the landing, follow the order of rank to land. However, if the approval is not granted, temporarily land on the coast and firmly establish a fortified construction after securing a bridgehead. In this case, subsequent troops and navy will be mobilized simultaneously. Toyotomi Hideyoshi prepared vessels that could transport the invasion force in one and anchored these vessels at various ports including Tsushima, Iki Island, Shimoneseki, Hakata, and Nagoya. The landing force planned to secure a foothold at the Busan landing site until the arrival of the follow-up forces and construct a fortification there. Toyotomi Hideyoshi believed that the success of the operation relied on the acquisition and operation of the vessels. He appointed a naval staff to oversee the construction, deployment, and operation of the vessels.

He also called upon naval forces such as Kuki Yoshitaka, Wakisaka Yasuharu, Dodo Takadora, and Kato Yoshiaki to participate in the naval operation to protect the transport fleet. He emphasized that military provisions were crucial to winning the war and planned to supply weapons, ammunition, and gunpowder from the homeland. On the other hand, he planned to procure food for the soldiers locally after occupying the area. To this end, he appointed Japanese officials in each region of Korea to implement local governance. He appointed Korean administrators in the eight provinces of Korea in preparation for the occupation of Korea as the commanders of the invading forces. Toyotomi Hideyoshi finished his preparation and instructions for the invasion operation and commanded the overall national affairs and operations from the Nagoya War Headquarters.

On April 13, 1592, the Japanese forces launched their invasion with a total strength of 200,000 troops and under the command of Ukida Hideie's son-in-law, Konishi Yukinaga. The vanguard, led by Konishi Yukinaga, consisting of 18,700 troops, landed in Busan, and additional follow-up forces arrived by around 700 vessels.

This marked the beginning of the Imjinwaeran, a seven-year conflict. After landing in Busan, the Japanese troops spent the night at sea, and on the morning of the 14th, Konishi's troops successfully captured Busan Castle.

Despite the strong defense and resolve of Jeong Bal and his forces, they were all defeated. Park Hong, the navy commander of Gyeongsang Left Province, chose to flee rather than engage in battle. On the 15th, Konishi's forces captured Dongrae Castle and swiftly advanced towards Seoul.

# Who is Yi Sun-sin?

Admiral Yi Sun-sin is one of the most celebrated heroes in Korean history. Despite 430 years having passed since his death during a naval battle that ended Japan's invasion war, Koreans' love and respect for Yi Sun-sin remain unwavering. On his birthday, April 28, various organizations, including government agencies, hold commemorative events to honor the noble spirit and lessons left by Admiral Yi Sun-sin. Furthermore, Yi Sun-sin is a prominent figure in various genres of Korean society, including movies and dramas. Military educational institutions, including the Naval Academy, have long offered regular courses on Yi Sun-sin. Civilian universities have recently established doctoral programs in *Yi Sun-sin Studies*. This phenomenon indicates that the tangible and intangible assets left by Yi Sun-sin have reached academic domains.

During the 16th century East Asian international war, known as the Seven-Year Imjinwaeran, Admiral Yi Sun-sin led numerous naval battles to victory, comparable to any war hero in world maritime history. Koreans admire Admiral Yi Sun-sin beyond a typical war hero due to his exceptional morality and practice of fairness and justice, which are rare in everyday war heroes. Moreover, despite being branded a traitor by the absolute monarch and suffering hard vessels, he demonstrated a spirit of sacrifice as a public servant by leading the final battle to victory, which ended the war at the cost of his life. This book is based on the war diary *Nanjungilgi* written by Yi Sun-sin himself and the battle reports he submitted to the king. It also corrects some serious errors related to Yi Sun-sin's legacy from his death to the present day and includes new facts revealed through scientific research and historical evidence.

# Life of Yi Sun-sin

Yi Sun-sin was born on April 28, 1545 (lunar calendar March 8) in Geoncheondong, Seoul. He died in the Battle of Noryang on December 16, 1598 (lunar calendar November 19) at the age of 54. He was a soldier of the Joseon dynasty of Korea. Admiral Yi Sun-sin led the Korean Navy during the Imjinwaeran, an international war of the 16th century. He created the world's first wooden armored ship, the Turtle Ship (*Geobukseon*), and used it in naval battles. Through this, he defeated hundreds of Japanese war vessels and won every naval battle. He is recognized as a war hero and regarded as one of the few great naval commanders in world naval history.

Confucianism heavily influenced the Korean society during Yi Sun-sin's time. Politicians fought for the king's favor, and scholars held higher status and power than soldiers. While society seemed peaceful during Yi Sun-sin's childhood, the political situation was unstable. Yi Sun-sin was born as the 12th descendant of the Deoksu Yi clan. He was the third son of Yi Jeong.

Like most parents, Yi Sun-sin's parents hoped he would succeed as a scholar-official. When Yi Sun-sin was young, his family moved from Seoul to Asan in Chungcheong Province (Chungcheongdo), his mother's hometown. Despite his parents' hopes of him becoming a successful scholar, Yi Sun-sin wanted to be a soldier. He married at the age of 20 and had his first son at 23. His wife, the daughter of Bang

Jin, the magistrate of Boseong County in Jeollado(Jeolla Province), was as wise as Yi Sun-sin from a young age. A short story tells of how, at the age of 12, when a thief broke into their home and her father had fired all his arrows to chase the thief away, she shouted, *"Here are more arrows, Father! We have plenty of arrows!"* while throwing noisy objects on the floor, making the thief mistake the sounds for arrows and flee. Her wisdom is believed to have significantly contributed to shaping Yi Sun-sin's future.

Yi Sun-sin began his military career after passing the military examination in 1576. Until he was appointed Jeolla Jwasusa (the Commander of the Jeolla Left Navy, equivalent to the current commander of the South Sea Fleet of the Republic of Korea Navy in February 1591, he served in various roles in the forces and navy. After being appointed as Jeolla Jwasusa, except for his period of rankless military service (*Baekuijonggun*) he led the Korean Navy until his heroic death in the Battle of Noryang. In July 1580, Yi Sun-sin was appointed as *Manho*, the commander of the coastal defense forces under the Jeolla Jwasusa, located in present-day Goheung County, Jeollado. The position of *Manho* was similar to today's naval commander, overseeing the coastal defense forces. Before he was appointed Jeolla Jwasusa, Yi Sun-sin was also appointed as the magistrate of Jeongeup County in 1589. Although he carried out administrative duties, his term was less than a year.

Yi Sun-sin was appointed as Jeolla Jwasusa approximately 14 months before the Imjinwaeran began on April 13, 1592. Anticipating the threat of invasion, he devoted himself to military training, tactical drills, and weapon development, including the construction of the Turtle Ship. His efforts proved successful when, on May 7, 1592, he achieved his first naval victory against the Japanese at Okpo Bay in Gyeongsang Province. Following this, Admiral Yi Sun-sin led the Korean Navy to numerous decisive victories until his heroic death at the Battle of Noryang.

On August 15, 1593, about 16 months after the outbreak of the Japanese invasion in 1592, Yi Sun-sin was appointed as *Tongjesa*, commanding the navies of Jeolla (Jeollado, Jeolla Province), Gyeongsang (Gyeongsangdo, Gyeongsang Province), and Chung cheong (Chungcheongdo, Chungcheong Provinces). While Yi Sun-sin served as *Tongjesa*, tedious peace negotiations were conducted between China and Japan, excluding Korea. As the war dragged on, the Korean land was devastated by Japanese atrocities, epidemics, and crop failures, making it increasingly difficult to maintain regular military operations. With no support from the central government, the navy was reduced to half its size compared to the beginning of the Imjinwaeran. Despite these adversities, Yi Sun-sin secured military supplies on his own and dedicated himself to resisting the Japanese invasion for his country.

In late 1596, with the expectation of a large-scale second invasion by the Japanese, King Seonjo appointed Yi Won-ik as *Chechalsa* and sent him to the southern front of the Korean Peninsula to oversee war operations. Yi Sun-sin occasionally consulted with Yi Won-ik to prepare for the Japanese attack. On January 12, 1597, Kato Kiyomasa led a large military force to invade Busan. This Japanese attack is known as Jeongyu War (Jeongyujeran). The term, Imjinwaeran, which began in 1592, generally includes the Jeongyujaeran (Jeongyu War) of 1597.

In January 1597, Yi Sun-sin was punished and held responsible for failing to prevent the enemy's invasion in advance as *Tongjesa*. He was dismissed from his position, and his command was handed over to Admiral Won Gyun. On February 26, Admiral Yi was sent to Seoul and imprisoned. Yi Sun-sin barely escaped death and was released on April 1, assigned to serve as a soldier without rank in Hapcheon, Gyeongsang Province, under the *Tongjesa* system. While moving south from Seoul, Yi Sun-sin's mother passed away, but due to his *Tongjesa* status, he could not complete her funeral and had to leave.

On July 18, 1957, Yi Sun-sin learned that the Korean Navy, commanded by Won Gyun, had been destroyed in a surprise attack by the enemy during the Battle of Chilcheonryang on July 16. Many commanders, including Admirals Won Gyun and Yi Eok-gi, were killed. Yi Sun-sin grieved for their deaths all night. After consulting with his superior, General Kwon Yul, Yi Sun-sin, still a soldier without rank under *Baekuijonggun*, went to Noryang Strait to evaluate the situation. He arrived at Noryang Strait on July 21 and found the remaining commanders mourning the severe defeat. They discussed strategies throughout the night, and Yi Sun-sin developed an eye infection from the extreme stress and lack of sleep.

King Seonjo reappointed Yi Sun-sin as *Tongjesa*. Yi Sun-sin received the king's order at Son Kyung-rae's house. This reappointment restored Yi Sun-sin's rank and showed how desperate King Seonjo and the government were, understanding the seriousness of the situation. Soon after being reappointed as *Tongjesa*, Yi Sun-sin began his mission to address the critical condition of the Korean Navy. Admiral Yi Sun-sin moved to Hoeryeongpo in Jangheung, Jeollado.

At Hoeryeongpo, after the devastating defeat at the Battle of Chilcheonryang, where over 200 vessels were destroyed and tens of thousands of naval soldiers were killed, only 12 vessels awaited Yi Sun-sin. Despite his heartache and sorrow, *Tongjesa* Yi Sun-sin had no Choice but to recognize the harsh reality. On August 20, Admiral Yi Sun-sin, determined to fight to the death, boarded his flagship and began sailing towards Myeongryang Strait (also known as *Uldolmok*, located near Haenam and Jindo in Jeollado). Departing from Hoeryeongpo, while fending off the pursuit of the Japanese Navy, Yi Sun-sin passed through several ports in Jeollado and arrived at Usuyeong in Haenam on September 15, 1597. During his Journey to Usuyeong, he secured one more ship, bringing the total number of vessels participating in the Battle of Myeongryang on September 16 to 13.

In the Battle of Myeongryang, with a small military force, he achieved a significant victory against the Japanese Navy. In the Battle of Myeongryang, Yi Sun-sin's fleet of 13 vessels defeated 31 out of 133 Japanese vessels. Just before the Battle of Myeongryang, Yi Sun-sin gave a famous speech to his soldiers as follows:

*"Those who are determined to die will live; those who seek to live will die."*

After the victory at the Battle of Myeongryang, Admiral Yi Sun-sin had no time for rest and consolation for his exhausted soldiers. After the battle, Yi Sun-sin moved the Korean fleet northwest, passing through the waters of Mokpo, and spent the first night after the victory at Dangsado Sinan County. After their defeat, the Japanese fleet retreated southward following the southeast current, but a significant number of enemy forces remained in the southern waters of Jindo. Yi Sun-sin's fleet repositioning was a strategic decision considering the enemy's movements.

From that day on, Admiral Yi Sun-sin's fleet sailed or anchored along the west coast and islands of the Yellow Sea for more than 40 days, eventually landing and settling on Gohado (Island in Mokpo) on December 29, 1597. During this period, Yi Sun-sin spent about 18 days on Anpyeondo, an island recorded in Yi Sun-sin's war diary, *Nanjungilgi*, which had long been unidentified in Korea's island naming convention, and was presumed to be Palmido or Jangsando in Sinan County. In 2018, research by the author confirmed it as the current *Anjwado* in Sinan County. It was here that Yi Sun-sin formulated the future direction and rebuilding strategy of the Korean Navy. *Anjwado* inspired Yi Sun-sin's strategic insights. Particularly at the temporary naval headquarters on *Anjwado*, Yi Sun-sin developed plans for the Joint creation and strengthening of a Korean and Chinese naval fleet.

After planning on *Anjwado*, he left on October 29 and landed on Gohado. At the Gohado Headquarters, Yi Sun-sin strengthened communication with the central government and local officials and dedicated himself to rebuilding the Korean Navy. As a result, during the 106 days spent on the southwestern islands and coastal areas, he secured public sentiment and built new vessels, forming a basic force for the Joint Fleet with the Chinese Navy. By the time he left Gohado, the number of Korean naval vessels had increased from 13 to 53. During the 106 days, about 40 vessels were built, primarily centered around Jeolla Province. This was the result of the tireless efforts of Admiral Yi Sun-sin, the Korean Navy, and coastal residents.

On February 17, 1598, Yi Sun-sin moved to Gogeumdo and established the Korean naval headquarters, laying the foundation for a Joint naval force. Strategically, Admiral Yi Sun-sin's relocation of the Korean fleet to Gogeumdo in Wando, near Gyeongsang Province, which was dominated by the Japanese Navy, was to block Japanese naval activities and to consider it as a strategic base for Joint operations with the Chinese Navy. Gogeumdo had wider farmland and more civilian houses than Gohado, making it easier to procure local military supplies. At Gogeumdo, Admiral Yi Sun-sin continued to push for the strengthening of naval forces.

Despite the efforts made with local residents to rebuild the exhausted navy while staying in Gohado, the force was still not as powerful as before. To form a Joint Fleet with the Chinese Navy, it was crucial to have at least an equal or superior naval force to the Chinese Navy.

On July 16, 1598, the main Chinese naval force of 5,000 men, led by Admiral Chen Lin, arrived at Gogeumdo. At Gogeumdo, Admiral Yi Sun-sin faced conflicts between Chinese and Korean commanders but overcame them with outstanding leadership. Admiral Yi Sun-sin, along with Admiral Chen Lin, participated in the final battle of the war, the Battle of Noryang, which took place on December 16, 1598. After a fierce battle, they destroyed over 200 enemy vessels and won the Joint Fleet's victory, but Admiral Yi Sun-sin was killed in this battle. He was shot and severely bleeding during the battle, and he shouted as follows:

*"The battle is ongoing. Do not let my death be known."*

The battle continued until noon after Admiral Yi Sun-sin's death. The enemy retreated, and while the battle continued, Konishi's troops stationed in Suncheon fled along the coast. They eventually retreated from Namhae to Geoje. By late November 1598, the Japanese forces, which had illegally invaded and devastated Korea since April 1592, completely withdrew. This ended the painful seven-year war.

## Evaluation of Admiral Yi Sun-sin's Life

Human history can be described as a history of war. Throughout countless wars, there have been many great military commanders like Genghis Khan, Napoleon, Frederick, Hannibal, and Nelson, who led their countries to victory in battles. However, even these great commanders did not always win every battle. Among these great generals, it is rare to find someone like Admiral Yi Sun-sin who participated in and won many wars. Admiral Yi Sun-sin fought in 26 naval battles and won every one of them. Notably, while many globally renowned commanders received extensive support from their countries and citizens with military equipment and supplies, Admiral Yi Sun-sin's situation was different. He had to be self-sufficient without the full support of the state and had to overcome disgrace and hard vessels, such as being dismissed twice. Admiral Yi Sun-sin led the final battle to victory and died on the ship during the battle.

In the 16th-century East Asian international conflict involving Korea, China, and Japan, Admiral Yi Sun-sin emerged from a small Eastern Country During the seven-year war, Admiral Yi Sun-sin led 26 major battles to victory and destroyed over 700 Japanese naval vessels. This record is vividly preserved in historical Korean documents such as Yi Sun-sin's diary *(Nanjungilgi)* and the Annals of the Joseon dynasty *(Sillok)*, representing a rare wartime achievement in world naval history. He lived his entire life as a soldier and died heroically on the battlefield. Let's examine the domestic and international evaluations of this unparalleled hero, Admiral Yi Sun-sin.

Son Won-il, who led the establishment of the Korean Navy and served as the first Chief of Naval Operations, emphasized in the book of his memoirs as follows:

*Admiral Yi Sun-sin was not only a military strategist but also a loyal public official who dedicated himself to the national interest through actions, not words. Admiral Yi Sun-sin will always be respected as one of the greatest patriots by all Koreans.*

Yi Eun-sang, who translated the war diary *Nanjungilgi* from classical Chinese to Korean, said as follows:

*Admiral Yi Sun-sin is not only the sole model of a bright, righteous, prosperous, and vibrant path in our history but also the source of life. Therefore, we should not regard him merely as an abstract or conceptual symbol of patriotism or as a mere idol. We must recognize him as a philosophical path that should be alive and practiced in our daily lives through modern and scientific methods.*

The importance of Yi Sun-sin becomes clear when looking at the evaluation of Professor Jo Seong-do, who led the study of Yi Sun-sin's spirit and interacted with Yi Eun-sang. Professor Jo Seong-do of the Naval Academy, who led Yi Sun-sin studies in Korea from the early 1970s for over 20 years, evaluated Yi Sun-sin in his book *Chungmugong Yi Sun-sin* as follows:

*Chungmugong Yi Sun-sin was born into a humble scholar family, fought through various adversities, and ultimately sacrificed his life righteously for his country and people. He remains a 'legacy' and 'lesson' in the hearts of not only Koreans but also people around the world. Living by the principles of fairness and justice between good and evil, justice and injustice, joy and sorrow, love and betrayal, he resisted all conspiracies and sorrows. His footsteps will never be erased, now or in the future. He is gone, but his spirit will live forever.*

Two evaluations by people who closely observed Admiral Yi Sun-sin during the Imjinwaeran are introduced. These are *Yeonguijeong* (equivalent to today's Prime Minister) Yu Seong-ryong, who recommended Yi Sun-sin as Jeolla Jwasusa, and Chinese Admiral Chen Lin, who fought alongside Yi Sun-sin in the last battle of the Imjinwaeran. These evaluations are particularly meaningful and impressive because they come from people who saw Yi Sun-sin up close during the war. Below is Yu Seong-ryong's evaluation of Yi Sun-sin in the book of *Jingbirok*.

*Admiral Yi Sun-sin was a general who fought a hundred battles and could support a collapsing sky with one hand. He had a hundred talents but was unlucky enough not to display even one. Thanks to Yi Sun-sin, the country survived and existed, and without him, it would have perished.*

Admiral Chen Lin was the commander of the Chinese Navy who fought alongside Yi Sun-sin in the last battle of the Imjinwaeran. The two admirals fought against the Japanese Navy, risking their lives. After winning the battle, Admiral Chen Lin learned of Yi Sun-sin's death. He was deeply saddened and wrote a letter to King Seonjo of Korea. In the letter, Admiral Chen Lin said that *"Admiral Yi Sun-sin was a great leader who could command both heaven and earth."* He also mentioned that Admiral Yi Sun-sin made a significant contribution to Korea's recovery after the war.

Japanese Admiral Sato Tetsutaro, who served as a major general during the Russo-Japanese War, wrote in his 1902 book, *Theories on National Defense*, as follows:

*Historically, it is extremely rare for generals to truly master the art of war. When thinking of naval commanders, one must mention Admiral Yi Sun-sin of Korea in the East and Admiral Nelson of England in the West. Unfortunately, because he was born in Joseon, Yi Sun-sin's bravery and wisdom are not widely recognized in the West. However, looking at the records of the Imjinwaeran, he was an outstanding naval commander. To find someone equivalent in the West, only Admiral Michiel de Ruyter of the Netherlands comes to mind. Admiral Nelson falls short of Yi Sun-sin in terms of character and personal virtues. Admiral Yi Sun-sin was the inventor of the Turtle Ship and a war commander who fought with excellent naval tactics 300 years ago.*

The evaluation of Admiral Yi Sun-sin by Admiral Togo, who led Japan to victory in the Russo-Japanese War, is also widely known in Korean society. After winning the Battle of Tsushima, Admiral Togo was praised as a great general comparable to Admiral Nelson at a celebratory banquet. However, he humbly replied as follows: *Nelson was not that great. Admiral Yi Sun-sin of Joseon is the only naval commander genuinely deserving to called a great general.*

British war hero Bernard Law Montgomery in his book, *A History of Warfare*, described as follows:

*Admiral Yi Sun-sin designed a ship that could withstand any attack and had excellent defensive capabilities. The ship (Turtle Ship) had an iron-clad deck to prevent bullets from penetrating and iron spikes to prevent enemies from boarding. The ship was equipped with cannons on both sides of the hull. The Japanese Navy could not resist Admiral Yi Sun-sin's ironclad warship. Korea's maritime victory paralyzed Hideyoshi's land offensive.*

British naval historian G.A. Ballard in his book, *The Influence of the Sea on the Political History of Japan*,
 evaluated Yi Sun-sin as follows:

*Admiral Yi Sun-sin's name is not well known to Western historians, but his achievements will position him as one of the great naval commanders. He possessed broad and accurate strategic judgment, the skills of an excellent naval tactician, and outstanding leadership and relentless offensive spirit, the fundamental essence of war. He pursued victory in all battles he commanded until the end. In contrast, his brave attacks were never reckless adventures. Admiral Nelson did not hesitate to attack the enemy whenever an opportunity arose, but he did not neglect meticulous attention to ensure success. Admiral Yi Sun-sin had one advantage over Admiral Nelson, which was his excellent talent for inventing the Turtle Ship. He destroyed the enemy's battle fleet, disrupted their supply lines, annihilated their transport fleet, destabilizing the enemy's positions on land, and completely collapsing their ambitious plans. Nelson, Blake, or Jean art could not have accomplished as much as this commander from a small country suffering from foreign oppression. It is unfortunate that Admiral Yi Sun-sin's fame is not widely recognized outside his country.*

## War Preparation of Yi Sun-sin prior to Imjinwaeran

On February 13, 1591, Yi Sun-sin was officially appointed as Jeolla Jwasusa (the Commander of the Jeolla Left Navy), about 1 year and 2 months before the outbreak of the Imjinwaeran. The Jeolla Jwasusa was a position that referred to the commander of the navy in the left region of Jeolla Province. As a third-rank officer, Jeolla Jwasusa was in charge of five naval bases (Bangdap, Sado, Nokdo, Balpo, and Yeodo) and five administrative districts (Suncheon, Boseong, Nagan, Gwangyang, and Heungyang). While serving as Jeolla Jwasusa, Yi Sun-sin anticipated the invasion of the Japanese forces and strengthened his military preparations.

At the time when Yi Sun-sin was appointed as Jeolla Jwasusa, the domestic political and social situation in Korea was highly chaotic. The factional fight in the central government spread throughout the country, putting the country in political instability. Public sentiment was driven away by the ruling class's exemption from military service, unfair tax benefits, and unfair appointment of officials. This social atmosphere spread to the military community responsible for national security, and military discipline was highly disordered. The central government established a strong defense plan by establishing *Bibyeonsa* to prepare for Japanese military invasion. Minister of National Defense Yi Yul-gok insisted on training 100,000 troops to King Seonjo, but this was not achieved. The incompetence and corruption of the central government also extended to front-line commanders, both navy and army, at the time. Even military commanders were virtually neglecting national security.

As mentioned earlier, even the perception of urgent national security collapsed due to a false report on the situation of the invasion of Japan by a representative who went to Japan as an envoy. The defense policy of the incompetent government was inconsistent. The central government also withdrew its policy to strengthen some defense facilities, saying not to incite the people. Some army generals even argued that we should abolish the navy and focus all our efforts on land warfare. Yi Sun-sin argued in his report *(Janggae)* to the king as follows:

*When it comes to stopping Japanese invaders by sea, there is nothing better than the navy. It is something that neither the navy nor the army can eliminate.*

Yi Sun-sin foresaw Japan's invasion early on and had the strategic idea that enemies coming by sea must be destroyed at sea. His records of the military preparations in Jeolla Province are documented in his war diary. Yi Sun-sin kept a war diary from January 1, 1592, to November 17, 1598, two days before he died in the Battle of Noryang. Yi Sun-sin's war diary, *Nanjungilgi*, was registered as a UNESCO Memory of the World on June 18, 2013. It contains valuable records of his combat experiences, strategies, and daily life. This diary is considered an essential document for understanding Korean history and culture.

Although it is unknown why he started writing his diary on that day, it is clear that he continued to write it until the Battle of Noryang, where he served as *Tongjesa*. Yi Sun-sin's diary records are essential for understanding his life and military achievements. Let's focus on Yi Sun-sin's diary to explore how he managed his naval forces and prepared for war from the time he assumed the position of the Jeolla Jwasusa until the outbreak of the Imjinwaeran.

In the year of Imjin (1592), Admiral Yi Sun-sin celebrated

the New Year's Day in Yeosu, Jeolla Province. His mother and wife resided in Asan, so he spent the holiday with his younger brother, nephews, and sons in the naval base. Celebrating the New Year in the naval base was not an ordinary affair. From the early morning, he inspected the military and focused on managing the naval bases in Jeolla Left Province. He had holes drilled in stone pillars to transport them to the Yeosu area, inspected the sea defenses, and engaged in archery with military officers whenever he had a spare moment. His daily routine was no different from any other day. The stone pillars with holes were used to moor vessels or tie chains installed to defend against enemy vessels. Due to the severe winter in January, he handled military tasks related to land-based operations, ship maintenance and preparing for potential external threats instead of maritime training. Before the outbreak of the Imjinwaeran, Admiral Yi Sun-sin's military preparations in Jeolla Province included creating the Turtle Ships, building warvessels, conducting mock command exercises, and, above all, inspecting the 5 naval bases under his command. Admiral Yi Sun-sin's inspection of the five naval bases under his command in Jeolla Province to confirm the state of readiness was a series of measures taken to enhance combat readiness by emphasizing the importance of being a hands-on commander and verifying the defense conditions.

The naval base inspections by Admiral Yi Sun-sin commenced on February 19th and continued for about ten days. These actions were taken less than two months before the outbreak of the Imjinwaeran. On the first day, he arrived at Yeodo base and inspected the state of readiness. An official named Hwang Ok-cheon guided him. The naval base inspections by Admiral Yi Sun-sin commenced on February 19th and continued for about ten days. These actions were taken less than two months before the outbreak of the Imjinwaeran. On the first day, he arrived at Yeodo base and inspected the state of readiness. An official named Hwang Ok-cheon guided him. Hwang Ok-cheon was an official who was captured before being executed just before the Battle of Okpo. After inspecting various defenses, war vessels, and weaponry, Admiral Yi Sun-sin confirmed that they were relatively well-prepared. Following the official duties, he enjoyed drinks with the on-site commanders and local officials.

On the 22nd, en route to the Nokdo base, Admiral Yi Sun-sin stopped at Heungyang's shipyard to inspect weapons and war vessels. He then proceeded to Nokdo, climbed up the newly constructed watchtower to survey the surroundings and praised the commander's readiness. He also observed a naval artillery demonstration, and in the evening, he hosted commanders and staff officers, sharing drinks and expressing gratitude for their hard work. On the 23rd, they left late. The strong wind stopped them near the shore when they reached to the Balpo base, strong wind made them stop near the shore. It was hard for them to get off the ship. After they landed, they had to walk through tall grass to reach the Balpo base. They arrived there in the evening. On the way from the ship to the fortress, everyone got wet in a light rain. Even in the rain, Admiral Yi Sun-sin liked the beauty of the southern land. He saw flower petals blowing in the wind. For a moment, he forgot about the upcoming invasion by Japanese pirates' descendants.

On the next day, the 24th, it kept raining in spring. They rode horses to Sanyang below Mabuk Mountain in Godomyeon, all soaked in rain. Then, they took a boat to the Sado base. When they got to the fortress, they checked the warvessels and weapons. Unlike other naval bases they visited, the Sado base wasn't prepared well. Yi Sun-sin punished not just the high-ranking officers but also lower-ranked ones, including the commander of the Sado base. Because the inspection results were terrible, Yi Sun-sin didn't seem to cheer up the commanders or officers by having drinks with them. This shows his way of leading with rewards and punishment. On the morning of the 26th, they left Sado and reached Geaido (Chudo, Sari Island). There, they got on a

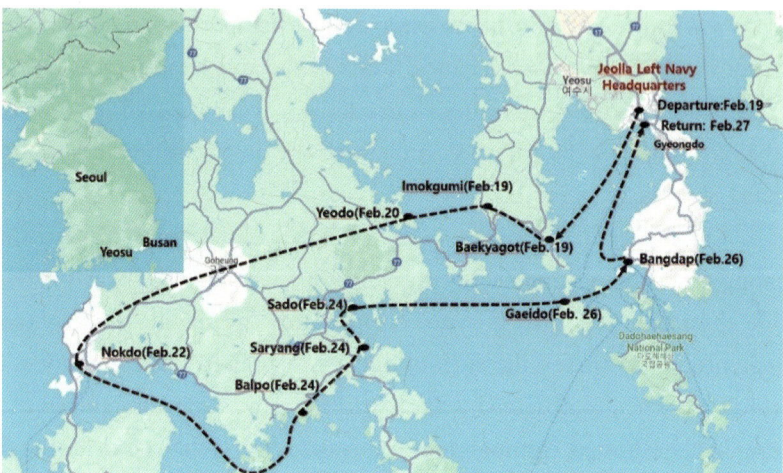

Figure 1: Admiral Yi Sun-sin's Inspections of the Naval Bases in Jeolla Province prior to the Imjinwaeran.

welcoming ship at the Bangdap base (Gunnaeri, Dolsaneup, Yeosu) and went to the Bangdap base in Dolsan Island for an inspection. The inspection showed that the warvessels and weapons were good, but the arrows were in bad shape. On the morning of the 27th, after finishing the inspection, they went up to Bukbong and looked at the maritime landscape. Admiral Yi saw that the Bangdap base was far from the mainland and easily accessible to enemies because it was open around. The Bangdap base was very important strategically. It helped detect Japanese pirates coming into Jeolla Province's waters from Gyeongsang Province. But it was farthest from the mainland. Also, the Bangdap base was where Korean Navy built the famous Turtle Ships. Admiral Yi Sun-sin thought the Bangdap base was very important among all the bases he managed. After checking the bases, Admiral Yi Sun-sin gave advice to the commanders and staff at the Bangdap base. When they got to Gyeongdo (Hwayangmyeon, Yecheongun), they talked about the inspections while having drinks with the group already there. Then, they went back to the Jeolla Left Navy Headequaters in Yeosu.

As explained earlier, Admiral Yi Sun-sin directly visited the five naval bases under his headquarters to inspect their state of readiness for war, knowing that in the event of war, they would be summoned to the headquarters and dispatched to the battlefield. During that time, people were unhappy with the corrupt military system and unfair treatment in society. This affected the soldiers' morale at remote bases and naval stations. Admiral Yi Sun-sin knew about the situation in these bases. He often sent letters, called commanders to the main base for guidance, and sometimes scolded them when needed. However, Yi Sun-sin knew that seeing things for himself was the best way to be sure. Moreover, he anticipated that the Japanese forces would invade soon. Therefore, he visited his subordinate units directly to inspect the commanders' war preparations, check the soldiers' discipline and morale, and devise appropriate measures. In preparation for war, Admiral Yi Sun-sin spared no effort in inspecting not only the naval bases but also the headquarters. To get ready for war, Admiral Yi Sun-sin worked hard inspecting naval bases and the headquarters. Starting in early March, he looked over both the regular and irregular troops. He made the castle walls in the Jeolla Left Navy Headquarters higher and dug deeper traps. He gave tasks to the *Seunggun*, a group of Buddhist monks trained for combat, and punished leaders who didn't perform well. The headquarters needed strong defenses against enemy attacks by sea or land. He made sure the people in charge of weapons like bows, armor, helmets, and swords did their jobs properly. By late March, he made the headquarters even more secure by checking new castles and digging deeper traps outside the walls. Yi Sun-sin also checked if chains were tied to stone pillars on both sides of the harbor to stop enemy vessels from entering.

## Turtle Ship Cannon Firing Test

Generally, after a warship is built, it is equipped with all necessary equipment and weapons. It then goes through sea trials, maneuver training, and live-fire drills to prepare for combat. No matter how exceptional a warship may be, if the performance of its weapon system is inadequate, the warship is meaningless. Therefore, it is essential to test the performance of a warship at sea before it is deployed in actual combat. Consequently, Admiral Yi Sun-sin's cannon demonstration on the Turtle Ship on March 27 was significant. This was the first training exercise with weapons mounted on the Turtle Ships built at the headquarters and the naval yard in the Bangdap base. After testing the Turtle Ship's cannons on March 27, 1592, they raised sails for the first time on April 11. The next day, the 12th, they practiced firing the *Jija* cannon and the *Hyeonja* cannon at sea. On the day of the Turtle Ship's gunnery practice, the Japanese had finished preparing to invade Korea and left for Busan the next day. It was remarkable that the Turtle Ship cannon demonstration occurred just one day before the Japanese invasion. Later, the Turtle Ship played a significant role in defeating Japanese naval vessels.

The cannons mounted on the Turtle Ship at that time were the same as those installed on the Panokseon, which was active during the naval battles of the Imjinwaeran alongside the Turtle Ship. It is assumed that Admiral Yi Sun-sin was well aware of the strengths and weaknesses of the cannons mounted on the existing Panokseon. The cannons on the Panokseon were fired from the deck, making the crew vulnerable to arrows and weapon systems fired from enemy vessels. Therefore, Yi Sun-sin devised the construction of the Turtle Ship to reduce friendly casualties and aggressively charge at enemy fleets for close-quarters combat. As explained later, the Turtle Ship is a special combat vessel with a roof built over the existing Panokseon, creating unique structure. It resembles a turtle and is equipped with 14 cannons: one each at the bow and stern, and six on each side. This secret weapon could fire cannons in all directions, even when surrounded by enemy fleets. After the outbreak of the Imjinwaeran, Yi Sun-sin first deployed the Turtle Ship in the Battle of Sacheon, achieving a great victory, and subsequently reported the existence of the Turtle Ship to the king for the first time. Yi Sun-sin had kept the construction of the Turtle Ship a secret, even from the king, to maintain security.

Even before the outbreak of the Imjinwaeran, Admiral Yi Sun-sin's foresight and leadership in preparing for war were impressive. Unlike the central government and King Seonjo, who were passive in preparing for war, Yi Sun-sin anticipated the enemy's invasion and devoted himself to preparations. On April 15, 1592, Admiral Yi received reports from Admiral Won Gyun, the Commander of the Gyeongsang Right Navy, that the enemy had landed in Busan on April 13. Eventually, war broke out. This proactive preparation helped him win naval battles during the Imjinwaeran, where he defeated over 700 enemy vessels and won every naval battle.

# The Turtle Ship and the Panokseon

**The Turtle Ship**

The Turtle Ship is a special ship designed to allow all crew members, including the bridge, combat personnel, and ship operating personnel, to conduct operations inside the hull without being exposed to the outside world. The Turtle Ship is a cultural heritage that shines along with Yi Sun-sin in Korean history. In 2016, an American military company selected it as one of the world naval history's seven most luxurious war vessels.

It played a decisive role in Yi Sun-sin's victory in numerous naval battles during the Japanese invasions of Korea. The battle Turtle Ship is the world's first wooden armored combat ship. The most reliable sources about Yi Sun-sin's battle Turtle Ship during the Japanese invasions of Korea are Yi Sun-sin's direct records and the *Yi Chungmugong Haengrok* written by Yi Sun-sin's nephew. In particular, the expression below in the book written by this person indicates whether the battle Turtle Ship is an ironclad ship or not. According to the *Yi Chungmugong Haengrok,* the battle Turtle Ship is the same size as the Panokseon. The top is covered with wooden planks, with narrow cross-shaped paths for people to walk through, and the rest is studded with knives and awls. As recorded by this person, the battle Turtle Ship was *a wooden armored battleship* that was remodeled from a wooden ship called Panokseon and covered with a roof on the deck with planks, which were wide pieces of wood. It is often said that the battle Turtle Ship was an ironclad ship or that the turtle's back was covered with iron because it was misinformed in the Western world by foreigners or by repeating uncertain Japanese and domestic sources.

In the naval battle of the Imjinwaeran, the Turtle Ship was deployed at the forefront of the Korean naval attack formation, firing threatening shots with cannons, charging into the enemy camp, and performing a direct strike on the enemy ship's hull within the effective range of the cannons. There are still unclear parts about the Turtle Ship's hull structure that participated in the Japanese invasions of Korea because the exact blueprint for the Turtle Ship has not been handed down. It was only recently that the true nature of the effective range of the cannon mounted on the Turtle Ship was revealed through scientific simulation, and based on this, Yi Sun-sin's Turtle Ship operation tactics were systematically reexamined.

The history of the Korean Turtle Ship first appears in records in 1413, approximately 180 years earlier than the outbreak of the Imjinwaeran in 1592. After 1413, there are no records of the construction and operation of the Turtle Ship until Yi Sun-sin mentioned it in his diary in February 1592. On February 8th, 1592, there is a record about the fabric used to make the sails of the Turtle Ship. On March 27th, there's a mention of a cannon firing test, and from April 11th, there are records of sail production. On April 12th, a day before the start of the Imjinwaeran, Yi Sun-sin set out to sea on his newly built Turtle Ship for live-fire training. Based on Yi Sun-sin's diary entries, it's believed that he had anticipated Japan's invasion about 1 year and 2 months before the start of the war and built the wooden-armored Turtle Ship soon after his appointment as the commander of the Jeolla Left Navy. Although Yi Sun-sin could not deploy the Turtle Ship in the first campaign of the Imjinwaeran, from the second campaign, he integrated the Turtle Ship into battles, employing Joint tactics with the primary battleship, Panokseon, leading every naval battle to victory.

## Construction Background, Structure and Function of the Turtle Ship

The Turtle Ships that exist in Korean history include the Turtle Ship of the late 16th century during the Japanese invasions of Korea, also known as the Turtle Ship of Yi Sun-sin, who made great contributions in naval battles during the Japanese invasions of Korea. In addition, there were several types of Turtle Ships, including the Turtle Ship of the 18th century. In the history of the Turtle Ship in Korea, except for the period of the Japanese invasions of Korea, there were no naval battles with Japan for hundreds of years after the end of the Japanese invasions of Korea, so there was no case of the Turtle Ship engaging the enemy in a naval battle until it disappeared from Korean history. Moreover, the size and appearance of the Turtle Ship during the Japanese invasions of Korea changed or changed over time, so it is not known whether the Turtle Ship after the Japanese invasions of Korea was able to maintain the same function as the Turtle Ship during the Japanese invasions of Korea in actual combat.

Therefore, this book focuses on the Turtle Ship's tactical operation capabilities during the Japanese invasions of Korea, which were verified based on the records of Yi Sun-sin, who directly participated in the naval battle, and the records of the Japanese Navy that participated in the naval battle. The most credible description of the Turtle Ship during the Imjinwaeran can be found in a report written by Admiral Yi Sun-sin himself and presented to the king.

The details of *Geobukseon*, the battle Turtle Ship, as reported by Yi

Sun-sin to the king on June 14, 1592, are as follows:

*Anticipating a potential invasion by the Japanese, I specially constructed the Geobukseon, the battle Turtle Ship. At the front, a dragon's head was crafted and attached, from which cannons could be fired. The roof was studded with iron spikes. From inside, one could see out, but from outside, it was impossible to see in. Even if surrounded by hundreds of enemy vessels, it has the capability to break through and fire its cannons.*

Admiral Yi Sun-sin's records are brief, so it's hard to imagine exactly how the battle Turtle Ship looked based only on them. Nevertheless, what stands out in the record is the clear purpose and function of the battle Turtle Ship. Specifically, the passage:

*Even if surrounded by hundreds of enemy vessels, the battle Turtle Ship can penetrate the enemy vessels and fire its cannons.*

The above mentions confirmed in every naval battle the battle Turtle Ship participated in. In essence, the battle Turtle Ship, during naval battles, led the offensive formation, advancing at full speed while firing its cannons, and approached enemy vessels to strike directly warship's hull and destroy them. In addition, the record *"anticipating a potential invasion by the Japanese, I specially constructed the battle Turtle Ship."* clearly states that Yi Sun-sin coolly assessed the power of the Korean Navy at the time. When Yi Sun-sin took office as commander, he recognized that the battle vessels and weapon systems of the Jeolla Left Naval Forces as well as the morale of the soldiers were degraded and their will to fight was low. Yi Sun-sin, who predicted that Japan would invade, found out the reality of the Jeolla Left Navy's weapon system and began building the battle Turtle Ship, which could complement the Panokseon, the main battleship of the Korean Navy.

Compared to Japanese battle vessels, the Panokseon is a battleship with a sturdy hull and powerful guns, but since the combatants are exposed to the outside during battle, it is risky to charge into the enemy fleet in the early stages of an engagement. The Turtle Ship was an armored combat ship that had the advantage of being able to approach the enemy fleet early in the battle and directly attack the hull of the enemy ship because its combat personnel were not exposed to the outside when engaging the enemy. Yi Sun-sin came up with an ingenious idea to compensate for the weaknesses of the Panokseon and built the Turtle Ship in preparation for the Japanese invasion.

The Turtle Ship first participated in the Battle of Sacheon and began to demonstrate its power. The function of the Turtle Ship was revealed as assault and close combat in the report of the battle results reported by Yi Sun-sin to the king below. In this fight, the assault leader first rode the Turtle Ship and rushed into the enemy fleet, firing cannons such as *Cheonja cannon, Jija cannon, Hyeonja cannon, and Hwangja cannon.*

Throughout all times and times, the close combat was evaluated as a high-risk tactic with the characteristics of a desperate battle. The Panokseon can be seen as an advantage in securing visibility and subduing enemies that are approaching the ship because the combat personnel operate on a high deck, but it also has the disadvantage of being easily exposed to the enemy and becoming the target of the enemy's concentrated attack. Therefore, even though the Panokseon was the main battleship of the Korean Navy, it was difficult for her to engage in assault or close combat at great risk. To make up for the shortcomings of the Panokseon, Yi Sun-sin built a wooden armored Turtle Ship that was a modified version of the Panokseon and sent it into battle, thereby improving its combat effectiveness and leading to victory in all naval battles.

The Turtle Ship record written by Yi Sun-sin's nephew, Yi Bun, along with the record written by Yi Sun-sin himself, is considered the most reliable source of information about the Turtle Ship during the Japanese invasions of Korea. Yi Bun's record mentions the hull structure, mounted weapons, and functions of Yi Sun-sin's Turtle Ship in more detail. Based on these two records *(Yi Sun sin's diary and Yi Bun's book, Haengrok)* the characteristics of Yi Sun-sin's Turtle Ship during the Japanese invasions of Korea can be summarized as follows:

Figure 2: Depiction of Turtle Ships in Yi *Chungmugongnseo*

*The size of the Turtle Ship's hull is the same as that of the Panokseon, the main battleship at the time. The roof of the Turtle Ship was covered with boards and an iron knife or awl was installed to prevent enemies from climbing up. A dragon's head was attached to the bow, and the dragon's mouth served as a hole through which the cannon could be fired. The stern is shaped like a turtle tail, and there are gun holes underneath it to fire cannons. There are 6 cannon holes on the port side of the hull and 6 cannon holes on the starboard side, for a total of 14 cannon holes. There are 16 oars in total, 8 on the port side and 8 on the starboard side. The Turtle Ships were equipped with cannons such as Cheonja, Jija, Hyeonja, and Hwangja, and when fighting, she advanced into the enemy fleet from the vanguard and fired cannons forward, backward, left, and right to suppress the enemy.*

Except for the above explanations, there is no reliable historical information about Yi Sun-sin's battle Turtle Ship during the Japanese invasions of Korea. There are several types of battle Turtle Ships from the Joseon dynasty of Korea including the 18th-century Turtle Ship, in addition to the 16th-century Turtle Ship from the time of Yi Sun-sin, which was explained above. Due to a lack of historical records regarding Yi Sun-sin's battle Turtle Ship, most research and restoration efforts concerning the vessel rely on the accounts recorded in the 18th century. While there is still controversy over the hull structure of Yi Sun-sin's battle Turtle Ship, the one restored in 2022 by the Naval Academy, known for its advanced research and experience in the Geobukseon restoration in Korea, is garnering attention. This restoration is considered the closest to Yi Sun-sin's original battle Turtle Ship to date. While there are historical records of Yi Sun-sin and his nephew regarding Yi Sun-sin's Turtle Ship, there are no reliable drawings of it. Therefore, for the study of Admiral Yi's Turtle Ship's shape and hull, many often refer to the Tongjeyeong Turtle Ship drawing included in *Yi Chungmugong Jeonseo* from the 18th century.

Figure 3: The Restored 16th Century Turtle Ship in 2022

Therefore, since this painting of the Turtle Ship is about 200 years different from the 16th century when Admiral Yi Sun-sin was active, so it cannot be concluded that it is the same as the Turtle Ship of

Admiral Yi Sun-sin. This book introduces two representative types of Turtle Ships recently restored by the Republic of Korea Naval Academy, which has the most outstanding experience and expertise in Turtle Ship restoration. One is the Turtle Ship restored in 1999, which is considered to resemble an 18th-century Turtle Ship closely.

Figure 4: The Restored 18th Century Turtle Ship in 1999

The other is the Battle Turtle Ship restored in 2022, which is highly regarded as the closest replica of the Turtle ship Admiral Yi Sun-sin deployed in battle during the 16th century. According to recent information from the Naval Academy Museum, the Turtle Ship constructed in 1999 is 34.2 m long, 10.3 m wide, 6.4 m high, has a displacement of 150 tons, and can carry 130 people. However, it was revealed that the structure of the ship's head does not allow cannons to be fired. On the other hand, the Turtle Ship constructed in 2022 is 24.3 m long, 9.64 m wide, 5.67 m high, with a displacement of 92 tons, and can carry 125 people. Notably, unlike the 18th-century model, the 2022 version can fire cannons from its head. This significant difference is one of the main reasons.

Based on the analysis of domestic research on Yi Sun-sin's Turtle Ship to date, the consensus is that the internal structure of Yi Sun-sin's Turtle Ship includes three levels:

The main deck, the upper deck (or a modified upper deck) and the lower deck. In other words, the first floor is below the main deck, the second floor is between the main deck and upper deck, and the third floor is above the upper deck. The Turtle Ship reconstructed by the Naval Academy also falls within this category. In addition to the structure of Yi Sun-sin's Turtle Ship, the placement of cannons within the Turtle Ship, whether they were positioned on the main deck (2nd layer) or the upper deck (3rd layer), is highly significant. Since the Turtle Ship was derived from the Panokseon, it makes sense to examine how cannons were placed on the Panokseon to infer where they might have been positioned on the Turtle Ship. In historical records like the *Gakseondo* from the late Joseon period, illustrations of Panokseon do not show cannon ports on the main deck (2nd layer). It is unclear whether this omission is due to the actual absence of cannon holes on the main deck or if they were present but not depicted in the illustration. On the other hand, there are records from 1633, such as the *Haeyu* document by Choe Jin-rip and records from 1778, such as *Pungcheon Yuhyang*, which mention firing cannons from both the main deck (2nd layer) and the upper deck (3rd layer). Additionally, in a document from the late Joseon period called the *Sugun Joryeondo*, cannon holes are marked on the 2nd layer (where the main deck would be). Some argue that based on such records, on Panokseon, cannons may have been fired from the 2nd layer and small arms from the 3rd layer. These historical records are also used to make reasonable estimates regarding the positioning of cannons within the turtle shp. The cannons mounted on the battle Turtle Ship of Admiral Yi were of the same type as those on the Panokseon. And the cannons were so heavy that soldiers could not adjust them during firing. As a result, military personnel fired the cannons while they were fixed in place on their mounts.

The Gebukseon's cannon was mounted inside a wooden cart, and while the cart is fixed to the deck, the cannon's barrel is exposed to the outside through a gun hole outside the Turtle Ship's hull.

Therefore, the cannons, fixed on their carts, fired at a consistent elevation angle, making it difficult to adjust the firing angle freely towards the target. The trajectory of the projectiles is primarily determined by the physical position of the cannon, including the firing height and the elevation angle. In essence, targets located geometrically below the trajectory of projectiles could generally be out of hitting line, and only those along the trajectory line created by the cannon's elevation angle could be hit.

## Effective Range of the Cannon Mounted on the Turtle Ship

### Effective Range of the Cannon

In the first naval battle of the Imjinwaeran, Admiral Yi Sun-sin did not deploy the battle Turtle Ship. As mentioned earlier, considering that Admiral Yi Sun-sin had just completed the construction of the battle Turtle Ship and conducted practical training one day before the outbreak of the Imjinwaeran.

It seems impractical to have immediately employed it in combat. However, starting from the second campaign, Admiral Yi Sun-sin deployed the battle Turtle Ship, placing it in the vanguard of the Panokseon formation for ramming and close combat missions.

Admiral Yi Sun-sin effectively employed Joint tactics, harmonizing the advantages of both the Panokseon and the battle Turtle Ship, leading to victories in all naval battles. The Turtle Ship would charge towards enemy vessels, closing in for close-range cannon fire, while the main combat vessel, the Panokseon, would follow up with subsequent tactics.

Therefore, the effective range of the large cannons on the Turtle Ship, which were used to engage and fire upon enemy vessels at close quarters directly, holds significant importance. Understanding the actual effective range of the cannons mounted on the Turtle Ship is a crucial element, not only for comprehending Turtle Ship tactics but also for analyzing how Admiral Yi Sun-sin leveraged the advantages of both the Panokseon and the battle Turtle Ship in all the naval battles in which the battle Turtle Ship participated. It is imperative to distinguish the concepts of *maximum range and effective range*. The term *maximum range* refers to the distance that a weapon system can reach and is often called the *firing range*. On the other hand, *effective range* indicates the accuracy of the weapon system and means the distance at which the weapon can be effectively used or the distance at which a target can be hit with an average probability of 50%. Even if a target is within the maximum range, the effective range at which the target can be hit varies depending on the characteristics of the target, terrain, shooting conditions, and ballistic properties.

As mentioned earlier, the effective range of the Turtle Ship's cannons has not been revealed in past Korean history, so explanations of Admiral Yi Sun-sin's naval tactics or Turtle Ship tactics did not incorporate the concept of effective range.

The primary mission of the battle Turtle Ship was confirmed through direct records from Admiral Yi Sun-sin. Its mission was to charge at the forefront of the Korean naval formation, engage in close combat near the enemy, and directly attack enemy vessels with its cannons. Apart from the fact that the battle Turtle Ship was constructed based on existing Panokseon design, no special measures were taken to increase its speed, assuming its role as an assault vessel.

Admiral Yi Sun-sin's naval diaries and reports to the king often mention that in addition to the Turtle Ship's preemptive attacks, the main combat vessel, the Panokseon, also charged together and struck the enemy vessels. Furthermore, as the Turtle Ship was a modified armored combat vessel based on the Panokseon, there is no evidence to suggest that its speed was significantly faster than the Panokseon, given the possibility of increased hull resistance. The term *charge* in the context of the Turtle Ship refers to swift movement at full or combat speed to carry out aggressive operations.

Explicit and specific records from Japanese naval commanders who participated in the Imjinwaeran and Admiral Yi Sun-sin's writings confirm that the Turtle Ship engaged in assault and close combat when confronted with enemy vessels. Documents authored by a Japanese naval commander who took part in the Imjinwaeran contain records indicating that the distance between Japanese war vessels and the Turtle Ship was approximately 10m. Furthermore, from the casualty records of the Turtle Ship oarsmen, as mentioned in Admiral Yi Sun-sin's battle outcome reports, it is evident that the Turtle Ship engaged in close combat with enemy vessels during actual battles.

The numerical gap mentioned in the Japanese commander's records between the Turtle Ship and enemy vessels during the Imjinwaeran battles holds significant importance, as it provides the only available data for estimating the effective range of cannons on both the Turtle Ship and the Panokseon during that time.

Scientifically determining the effective range of the Turtle Ship's cannons is crucial for reevaluating the tactics employed during the early stages of the Imjinwaeran battles. Before the author's research, there was only one study on the firing range of the cannon, which was used as the primary offensive weapon on the Turtle Ship. In 1989, Professor Park Hae-il conducted simulations applying ballistic equations to study the cannon's trajectory. There are also documented cases of live firing tests of the cannon undertaken at the Naval Academy.

The results of both Park Hae-il's cannon trajectory simulations and the live firing tests consistently indicated that the cannon's range was approximately 50% of what was mentioned in historical documents. The reason for these results falling significantly short of the documented cannon range in both tests appears to be inaccuracies in representing factors such as the initial velocity of the cannon projectile.

During the Imjinwaeran, the cannon used on the Turtle Ship was essentially a linear cannon aimed at its target within its line of sight. When mounted on the Turtle Ship and fired at a fixed angle during naval battles, the projectile likely followed a trajectory, eventually falling at a horizontal distance similar to what is described in historical records.

From the perspective of engineering ballistic equations, the projectile departing from the cannon's muzzle exhibits both linear and curved motion. Considering the Turtle Ship's tactics, which involved approaching enemy vessels closely and directly hitting them at close range, it can be inferred that the projectile hit the enemy vessel during its initial linear motion after being fired. The cannonball's trajectory after firing is greatly influenced by factors such as the projectile's initial velocity, mass, and firing angle. Therefore, whether through simulations or live firing tests, predicting the range or adequate range of the cannon used during the Imjinwaeran is challenging due to the lack of specifications and uncertainties surrounding this historical artifact.

**Analysis of Effective Range of Battle Turtle Ship Cannon**

Before scientifically examining the effective range of the large cannons mounted on the battle Turtle Ship, let's first explore the historical records that can help estimate the maximum range and practical range of cannons during the Imjinwaeran, as well as the geometric significance of the firing angles of these cannons.

According to historical records, about 150 years before the Imjinwaeran, in the *Sejong Sillok* Volume 107, on March 30, 1445, it is documented that improvements were made to the maximum range of various cannons. Specifically, the *Cheonja cannon* had a maximum range of 1,300 bo, *the Jija cannon* had a maximum range of 900 bo, and the *Jija cannon* had a maximum range of 600 bo, leading to a significant increase in accuracy.

Additionally, approximately 100 years before the outbreak of the Imjinwaeran, in a record from May 28, 1493, during the reign of King Seongjong, it is noted in the *Sejong Sillok* that in defending fortresses, they would use cannons to target distant enemies. As the enemy approached, they would switch to using bows, and when the enemy got even closer, they would resort to throwing stones, outlining land-based combat tactics.

Moreover, in the 25th volume of the *Myeongjong Sillok*, dated June 6, in the 14th year of King Myeongjong's reign, during a discussion at the secret council, there is a record indicating that large firearms were used at distances where enemy projectiles could potentially reach them. Around 11 years after the conclusion of the Imjinwaeran, in 1609, according to the advice of Yi Hang-bok, it was made clear that the effectiveness of large cannons was a matter of concern, not only in land-based battles but also in naval engagements. Based on these historical sources, it can be estimated that the maximum range of cannons was approximately 1,000 bo, which would roughly translate to a distance of around 1,000 m in today's terms. Among the mentioned historical records, the record by Yi Hang-bok, 11 years after the end of the Imjinwaeran, holds unique significance due to its distinct perspective on the utilization of cannons in both land and naval warfare. Yi Hang-bok pointed out a significant issue concerning cannons such as the *Cheonja cannon* and *Jija cannon*. Despite their considerable size and the substantial amount of gunpowder they consumed, resulting in powerful and fierce firepower, these cannons had the fatal drawback of their projectiles not maintaining a consistent trajectory. The reason for paying particular attention to the statement *"projectiles do not travel straight"* in Yi Hang-bok's record lies in ballistic engineering. When a cannon is fired, the projectile's path follows an irregular trajectory, characterized by unpredictable curves or frequent misfires.

This inherent unpredictability makes it exceedingly challenging to predict cannon's range and effective range of cannons accurately. In essence, Yi Hang-bok's record indicates a substantial deviation from the cannon ranges commonly cited in historical documents, highlighting the unpredictable nature of cannon range as a critical factor influencing accuracy. This unpredictability likely had a significant impact on the naval tactics of Admiral Yi Sun-sin during the Imjinwaeran.

### Effect of Cannon Axis and Elevation Angle on Projectile Range

To explore the geometric basis of the Turtle Ship's cannon's effective angle, let's start by examining the impact of the cannon's trajectory and firing angle on the range, as explained in past U.S. Navy Gunnery Manuals. According to the U.S. Navy Gunnery Manual (Fire Control Fundamentals, 1953, Bureau of Naval Personnel, Navpers 91900), naval artillery fire control before the 19th century primarily relied on gunners visually confirming targets to enhance accuracy. It was considered more of an art than a science, and accuracy was

Figure 5: Cannon Firing Techniques Before the 19th Century

limited without sophisticated aiming systems, except for close-range engagements Furthermore, the manual notes that after a projectile is fired with its initial fixed velocity, its range depends primarily on the angle, known as the firing angle, between the horizontal plane and the direction of the shot. In other words, when the firing angle increases, it takes more time for gravity to overcome the projectile's vertical speed.

During this time, the projectile travels a greater distance from the gun, increasing range as shown in Figure 5. The above explains how pre-modern cannons were operated in the U.S. Navy before modern artillery and fire control systems were developed. Although there are differences in time periods, this method is similar to how Korea's naval cannons were thought to be used during the Imjin War.

As shown in Figure 6, if the velocity of the projectile departing from the cannon exit increases, it can be predicted that not only the linear motion but also the range can increase, even without applying the ballistic motion equation at the same angle. In this context, it is noteworthy that both the simulation results from Park Hae-il's past research and the range observed during the cannon's live-fire test at the

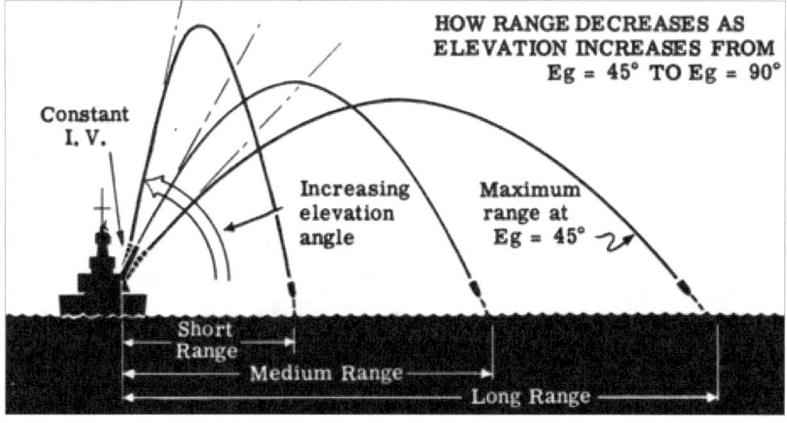

Figure 6: Projectile Trajectory Based on Changes in Firing Angle

Naval Academy are only around 50% when compared to the literature. In both cases, under the same conditions, if the projectile's speed leaving the cannon increases significantly During firing, the projectile's linear motion and range can increase substantially. The range of the cannon listed in historical literature could not be realized in both past simulation results and live fire results because the cannon specifications during the Japanese Invasion of Korea were not met. As a result, the projectile's speed was not realized when firing the cannon, and the range of the cannon could not be reproduced.

In the Battle of Imjin, the cannon's hits on the enemy vessels were not the result of impacts from irregularly falling projectiles after firing. Instead, they occurred during the linear motion phase of the projectiles leaving the cannon exit. The reason is that the cannon mounted and used on the Turtle Ship or Panokseon was a direct-fire cannon.

### Cannon Axis Line and Elevation Angle of Hull-mounted Cannons

During the Imjinwaeran, cannons on the Panokseons or the Turtle Ships were carried on the cart and placed in the ship's cannon hole for use. The cannons mou nted on the Turtle Ships, or the Panokseons, are so heavy that people cannot carry them and fire, and the hull and cannon are rigid. Therefore, if roll and pitch occur on the Turtle Ship or the Panokseon and the hull attitude changes, the cannon's gun axis line also changes. While no clear historical evidence specifies the exact firing angles of these ship-mounted cannons during the Battle of Imjin, some research studies have suggested a minimum firing angle of 17 degrees. Additionally, during ballistic simulation analyses of the cannons, significant results were obtained by applying a firing angle of 20 degrees.

### Turtle Ship Cannon Projectile Trajectory

Here, it is worth noting that since the Turtle Ship cannon is

Chapter I. Imjinwaeran (Imjin War), Yi Sun-sin and Turtle Ship (Geobukseon)

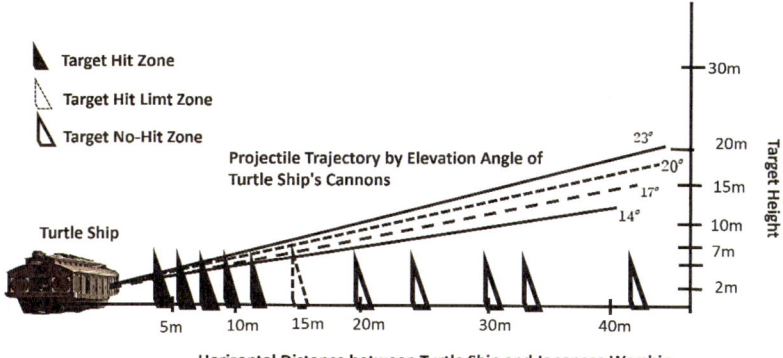

Figure 7: Effective Range of the Turtle Ship's Cannons

a direct firing gun, the Turtle Ship's strike against the enemy ship occurs in the process of straight-line motion, that is, the trajectory of the projectile, which is governed by geometric factors such as the elevation of the gun barrel and the horizontal movement distance of the projectile. In addition, it is necessary to recall that the Turtle Ship's cannon, a direct-firing gun, has several additional physical characteristics as follows. First, the initial motion of the projectile is linear; second, as the initial speed of the projectile increases, the linear motion rises at the same elevation angle; third, the horizontal movement distance of the projectile is governed by the elevation angle of the barrel; fourth, both the hull and the barrel, being steel structures, have the characteristic of the gun axis of the cannon fixed to the hull being affected by the movement of the hull. Therefore, the trajectory that can directly hit the enemy ship can be limited to straight motion among the projectile trajectories of the cannon fired from the Turtle Ship.

Thus, the Turtle Ship applied the trigonometric principle, which is a function of the cannon's elevation angle, the projectile's horizontal movement distance, and the projectile's altitude to analyze the trajectory of the cannon's projectile. In the figure 7*(referred to https// doi.org/10.31818/KNST2024.3.7.)*, the solid and dashed lines represent the flat trajectory of the projectile in a straight-line motion when fired from a Turtle Ship gun at a given elevation angle. The horizontal axis represents the distance between the Turtle Ship and the enemy ship, and the vertical axis represents the height of the target. As can be seen in this figure, the boundary of the targetable hull of the large Japanese ship selected as a target is around 15 meters away.

Table 1: Effective Range of Turtle Ship's Cannons

| Cannon Angle (degree) | Turtle Ship-Target Horizon Distance | | | | | |
|---|---|---|---|---|---|---|
| | 5m | 10m | 15m | 20m | 30m | 40m |
| | Projectile Altitude (m) | | | | | |
| 14 | 3.4 | 4.7 | 6.1 | 7.4 | 10.1 | 12.8 |
| 17 | 3.6 | 5.1 | 6.6 | 8.2 | 11.3 | 14.4 |
| 20 | 3.8 | 5.6 | 7.4 | 9.2 | 12.8 | 16.4 |
| 23 | 4.1 | 6.2 | 8.3 | 10.4 | 14.6 | 18.8 |

Referencing the data in Table 1, it can be seen in more detail that even at a distance of 15 meters, if the elevation angle of the cannon is 14 degrees or 17 degrees, the height of the projectile trajectory of the Turtle Ship cannon is 6.1 meters or 6.6 meters, respectively. Therefore, the enemy large ship with a height of 7 meters can collide with the projectile and the Turtle Ship cannon can hit the enemy ship's hull. However, the height of the projectile trajectory at an elevation angle of 20 degrees or 23 degrees is 7.4 meters or 8.3 meters, respectively. Therefore, the projectile passes over the height of the enemy large ship of 7 meters, so there is no mutual collision, and the enemy ship' hull cannot be hit.

On the other hand, if the horizontal distance between the Turtle

Ship and the enemy ship is narrowed to within 10 meters, the height of the projectile is below 7 meters in any case of the four elevation angles, so the Turtle Ship cannon can hit the hull of the enemy ship. However, suppose the boundary distance of the strike, which is the distance exceeds 15 meters and exceeds 20 meters.

In that case, the projectile trajectory height is always greater than 7 meters, so the projectile of the Turtle Ship passes over the enemy large ship. Therefore, it can be seen that this area is a blind area. Based on the results of this study, by recalling the characteristics of the engagements in which the Turtle Ship participated, we can guess why the Turtle Ship penetrated deep into the enemy ship and hit the hull of the enemy ship, and why the Panokseon vessels that followed the Turtle Ship rushed in unison and hit the hull of the enemy ship while entering the enemy fleet. Also, we can understand why the Turtle Ship had to approach the Japanese fleet to within 5 to 9 meters to fire its guns, as stated in the Japanese historical records, *Goryeoseon Jeongi*.

## Tactics of the Turtle Ship

### Close Combat within Effective Range: Direct Strikes on Enemy Hulls within Effective Range

The excellence of cannons is cited as one of the factors contributing to the victory in the naval battles of the Imjinwaeran. Additionally, the maximum range of about 1,000 m, as reported in literature, has always been a critical factor in the excellence of the cannon. Nevertheless, when analyzing Yi Sun-sin's naval battles, it is difficult to find examples or instances where the enemy was subdued by long-distance strikes as reported in literature. Instead, it can be confirmed that most engagements took place within the range of bows or effective range. In actual combat, cannon attacks from the Panokseon or the Turtle Ship were often carried out in coordination with bow attacks within this range. Although it was difficult to directly strike the enemy hull from outside the effective range of the Turtle Ship's cannons, firing from this range could still inflict significant psychological damage on the enemy. Therefore, there were often instances where the Turtle Ship would fire from outside its effective range while charging into the enemy formation. The easiest way to estimate the effective range of cannons among the naval tactics of the Japanese Invasion of Korea is through the core tactics of the Turtle Ship, which involve charging and close combat. As mentioned earlier, the Turtle Ship charged deep into enemy territory at the forefront of the Korean naval formation and directly struck enemy hulls with cannons. This tactical form of the Turtle Ship is clearly shown in Yi Sun-sin's diary and reports on the results of naval battles.

As seen in the author's research results, a proper understanding of the effective range of the cannons mounted and used on the Turtle Ship during the Japanese invasions of Korea is significant. This is because the effective range of the Turtle Ship's cannon in actual combat has a considerable impact on the Turtle Ship's engagement method and the overall tactics of the Korean Navy, including the Panokseon. The battle Turtle Ship approached the enemy ship and directly struck the hull because the cannon's effective range was limited to about 15~20 meters based on the enemy ship. As shown in the simulation results, it was difficult for the Turtle Ship to directly hit the enemy ship's hull from more than 20 meters away.

In particular, it was challenging to attack enemy vessels with low hull heights using the Turtle Ship's guns. Therefore, Yi Sun-sin wisely utilized the Joint tactics of the Panokseon and the Turtle Ship by leveraging their strengths, leading the naval battles to victory.

### Joint Tactics with the Panokseon

It is difficult to find records of the Turtle Ship operating alone in the naval battles of the Imjinwaeran. The patterns of the Turtle Ship's charging and close combat were observed in the context of Joint operations with the Panokseon. This indicates that the Turtle Ship enhanced the synergy of combat power by forming a complementary combat system with the main combat ship, the Panokseon. The tactics and engagement methods of Yi Sun-sin's fleet in the naval battles of the Imjinwaeran varied depending on the location and size of the enemy fleet, the maneuvering of the enemy fleet, the size of the Korean fleet, the size of the engagement area, and tidal conditions. Despite these variations, the author's research identifies representative stage-specific attack characteristics of the tactics in the naval battles involving the Turtle Ship during the Imjinwaeran.

In the early stages of engagement, the Turtle Ship advanced at the forefront of the Korean fleet, firing threatening shots with its cannons, while the Panokseons following behind primarily used bows and small firearms to kill enemy personnel and sometimes fired cannons in conjunction with these weapons.

At this stage, cannon fire from the Panokseons behind the Turtle Ship was likely more psychological and threatening, serving as cover fire for the Turtle Ship's vanguard rather than aiming to strike enemy hulls directly. It is presumed that the firing was conducted considering a safe firing zone to minimize friendly casualties among the advancing vanguard, including the Turtle Ship.

In the middle stages of engagement, as the Turtle Ship entered the range where it could strike enemy hulls, it conducted destructive fire with its cannons, followed by the Panokseons also closing in and killing enemy personnel with bows and small firearms while advancing to within effective cannon range to conduct destructive cannon fire on enemy hulls. Yi Sun-sin's representative tactics involved the Turtle

Ship first approaching and striking the enemy fleet, disrupting their formation, followed by the main combat vessels, the Panokseons, also closing into effective range to attack the main enemy fleet. In the final stages of engagement, the battle proceeded with capturing and boarding enemy vessels, suppressing enemy personnel, or setting enemy vessels on fire, with variations depending on each naval battle. Admiral Yi Sun-sin maximized the strengths of the armored Turtle Ship by minimizing friendly casualties while approaching deeply into enemy fleets to strike enemy hulls directly. After the Turtle Ship focused on striking enemy command vessels early in the engagement, the numerous main combat vessels, the Panokseons, also approached the enemy fleet to within effective cannon range and concentrated their fire, leading to the collapse of the enemy fleet.

Readers will find it easier to understand Yi Sun-sin's naval tactics, particularly those involving the Turtle Ship, in this book than in any other book published to date. To explain Yi Sun-sin's naval tactics and the tactics of the Turtle Ship more clearly, the author has created all the battle diagrams in this book based as much as possible on Yi Sun-sin's own recorded materials.

## Main Battleship Panokseon

The Panokseon was the main battleship of Yi Sun-sin's fleet during the Imjinwaeran. Maengseon, which was used as a military ship in the early Joseon dynasty, was discarded during the reign of King Jungjong and Myeongjong, and the newly developed ship was the Panokseon. The reason why Panokseon appeared was during Sampowaelan (Japanese pirate invasion), which occurred in the 5th year of King Jungjong (1510). In this rebellion, Japanese pirates invaded Korea with hundreds of vessels, killed Busan *Cheomsa*, occupied Jepo, and kidnapped Jepo

*Cheomsa.*

The Japanese pirates then surrounded Ungcheon fortress, set fire to it, and committed riotous acts. Afterwards, the Japanese invaded Jeolla Province and Hwanghae Province in the 17th and 18th years of King Jungjong's reign (1522, 1523), and invaded Saryangjin, Gyeongsang Province with about 20 battle vessels in May of the 39th year of King Jungjong's reign. During this period, the first person to advocate the development of a new battleship was Seo Hu, who invented the wall-loading artillery for naval warfare. In the 16th year of King Jungjong's reign, he said to King Jungjong,

*Nowadays, only small vessels are used in the navy, but small vessels, no matter how agile they are, are useless in close combat. He declared, we must look down on the enemy from above and subdue the enemy with a tall ship that the enemy cannot jump into with his sword drawn.*

In the 39th year of King Jungjong's reign, Song Heum also repeatedly reported on the development of large vessels. In May and June of the 10th year of King Myeongjong's reign (1555), Japanese pirates invaded Dalryang Port, Haenam, Jeolla Province with about 70 vessels, killed Jeolla soldiers and Jangheung magistrate, and invaded Yeongam. Although Japanese pirates continued to invade like this, Korean war vessels could not fight them off, so the development of a new type of ship was required. The size of the Panokseon is approximately 140.3 tons in weight, 8.74 m in width, 5.56 m in height, and 32.16 m in length. An upper deck was added on top of the main deck to resemble a two-story house. In particular, the newly created Panokseon was taller than the existing *Maengseon*, making it difficult for Japanese pirates, who were excellent at close-quarters battle tactics, to use their tactics. The upper deck is flat like the rooftop of a house, and a structure was installed around it to create a shield plate.

The upper deck was a space for combat personnel and command staff, and the space between the main deck and the upper deck was used for rowing to protect the troops. Panokseon was developed into the main battleship of the Joseon dynasty as its size and combat efficiency increased compared to the existing *Maengseon*. The Panokseon's hull was also strong, so it caused significant damage to enemy vessels when it came into contact with them during a melee during a naval battle.

In the Imjinwaeran, which broke out 37 years after the development of the Panokseon, the Korean Navy was able to fight the war by taking advantage of the leading battle vessels Panokseon and the Turtle Ship, which was created by modifying the Panokseon, and Yi Sun-sin was able to achieve a decisive victory in the naval battle. There is no record of the exact size of the Panokseon during the Japanese Invasion of Korea, but each ship had more than 125 soldiers on board, and there is a record of having as many as 180 Panokseons. There is a view that the Panokseon has the advantage of attacking the enemy while looking down from above because the hull is high. However, this advantage applies to personal weapons such as bows and small guns, but cannot be said to be an advantage for heavy weapons such as cannons. This is because large naval guns are heavy and cannot freely adjust their elevation, and the higher the gun's position, the larger the blind zone area becomes, so there is a disadvantage in directly attacking the enemy hull. It is necessary to mention the records based on vague assumptions hat the cannon fired from the Panokseon could attack enemy vessels from a distance by using the range of the cannon. There is no record of firing a cannon from a distance of about 1,000 m, which is the range of the cannon mentioned in the literature, and causing damage to the enemy ship in Yi Sun-sin's battle diary or report. As mentioned earlier, Yi Sun-sin's cannons operated on vessels were direct-fire cannons that could destroy enemy vessels on a linear trajectory. Also, the projectiles used at the time were mostly damaged by colliding with enemy vessels rather than by exploding to damage enemy vessels.

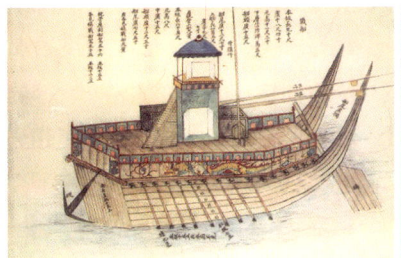 

Figure 8: The Panokseons depicted in the *Gakseondobon* of Historicalrecord (left) and the Panokseon featured in the movie 'Hansan: RisingDragon (right)'

In addition, the possibility of hitting an enemy ship with a cannon mounted on a Turtle Ship or Panokseon was determined by the horizontal distance between the firing point and the enemy ship and the relative height between the enemy ship and the Korean ship. Because the height of the enemy's large ship was less than 7 m, the effective range of the cannon mounted on the Panokseon that could hit the enemy ship was significantly shorter than the range of about 1,000 m. Therefore, the attack on the enemy ship's hull by the primary warship, the Panokseon, was carried out close to the enemy fleet after the Turtle Ship made a preemptive attack to maintain the effective range. In *Joseongi*, written in 1663 by Okawachi, who participated in the Japanese invasions of Korea, there is an article describing the Battle of Chilcheonryang in which Won Gyun was defeated. The description is as follows:

*The Panokseon is incomparably larger than a Japanese ship. It clung to the bottom of the Panokseon, but its hull was so high that even a long spear with handle as long as 2 gan (approximately 3.64 m) could not reach it, so jumping into the enemy ship was out of the question. We barely won by firing muskets to prevent the oars from rowing and firing fiery arrows.*

From this record, the Panokseon hull was so high that the Japanese Navy could not board Korean war vessels and engage in close combat. Instead, it can be seen that they fought after getting close to the Panokseon and killing the oarsmen with rifles to weaken the power of the Panokseon. The Panokseon during the Japanese Invasion of Korea became increasingly enlarged as she reached her later generations. The Panokseon during the Japanese Invasion of became increasingly enlarged as she reached the later generations.

## Weapons of the Korean Navy

In the naval battles of the Imjinwaeran, Korean war vessels relied on a combination of powerful cannon called *Chongtong* and traditional bows, while the Japanese Navy focused primarily on firearms known as *teppo*, an early type of musket. Both sides also utilized swords and spears for close-quarters combat. There were Korean *Chongtongs* came in various sizes, some of which were truly impressive.

*Cheonja-Chongtong (Heaven Cannon):* This colossal cannon was the largest and heaviest, weighing a staggering 300 kg (661 lbs). It fired lead balls and large arrows, reaching targets over 1,000 meters (3,300 ft) away.

*Jija-Chongtong (Earth Cannon):* The second-largest cannon, weighing about 92 kg (203 lbs), it fired a projectile called *Janggunjeon*, hitting targets up to 1,010 meters (3,314 ft) away. Its dimensions were 89 cm (35 in) in length and 96 mm (3.8 in) in width.

*Hyeonja-Chongtong (Black Cannon):* A popular Choice for Admiral Yi Sun-sin's fleet, these cannons were often mounted on the dragon heads of the famous the Turtle Ship They fired lead balls and bundles of

Figure 9: Cannon (*Chongtong*) displayed inside the Turtle Ship at the Korea Naval Academy (right), *Cheonja Chongtong (Heaven Cannon)* loaded with a *Daejangjeon* (projectile) displayed at the Korea Naval Academy Museum (right)

large arrows, with a range similar to the *Jija-Chongtong*.

This medium-sized cannon came in different sizes, weighing between 75 and 85 kg (165 to 187 lbs) and measuring 79 to 95.5 cm (31 to 37.6 in) in length and 56 to 73 mm (2.2 to 2.9 in) in width. Its maximum firing range was 1,010 meters (3,314 ft).

*Hwangja-Chongtong (Yellow Cannon):* This cannon fired lead balls and special arrows with wings for added stability. In addition to these larger cannons, the Koreans also had a smaller personal firearm called *Seungja-Chongtong (Victory Cannon)*.

Overall, the Koreans employed a combination of long-range cannons and traditional weapons, while the Japanese focused on firearm technology. This difference in weaponry played a significant role in the naval battles of the Imjinwaeran.

The effective range of *Chongtongs* described above is unclear, as to whether they were measured in an actual battle or obtained through experimentation on land. However, research suggests that when mounted on vessels and used as direct-fire guns, the effective range for destroying an enemy ship's hull is significantly shorter than the listed ranges. For more information on this, please refer to the Turtle Ship

Figure 10: Various Cannons (Chongtong) Displayed in National Museums (left), The Firing Scene of Cannons

description chapter in this book.

## Weapons and Ships of the Japanese Navy

The Japanese Navy primarily used muskets known as *Teppo*, which had range of approximately 100-200 m and a maximum effective range of about 50 m. Japanese warvessels included the Adakebune (large ship), Sekibune (medium ship), and Kobaya (small ship). The Adakebune served as the flagship and primary combat vessel of the Japanese naval fleet during the Imjinwaeran, leading squadrons of smaller war vessels like the Sekibune and Kobaya. These vessels were also used for troop transportation, escorting transport fleets, and carrying military supplies. The Adakebune was designed by the prominent Japanese naval commander Kuki Yoshitaka during the Imjinwaeran. It was a large ship with a length of approximately 33 m, a width of about 12 m, and could carry around 180 crew members.

Figure 11: Adakebune (above) and Sekibune (below)

The Adakebune typically featured two or three tiers of decks and was equipped with various weapons, having a similar size and shape to the Korean Panokseon. The Sekibune was a medium-sized warship following the Adakebune, with a crew of 40 to 80 and around 80 to 140 rowers. It was mainly used for combat and fast travel.

The Kobaya, known for its speed, was used for reconnaissance and communication. Japanese warvessels had a V-shaped or prow shape in cross-section and placed one person per rowing oar, while Korean war vessels typically had 4 to 5 people per rowing oar. Japanese war vessels had relatively weaker hulls than Korean naval flagship, the Panokseon.

## An Episode about the Miracle of the Turtle Ship in the 1970s

If one were to ask any Korean above elementary school age walking the streets of Seoul who the most respected figure in Korean history is, and what the proudest legacy is, it would not be difficult to hear the answer, *"Admiral Yi Sun-sin and the Turtle Ship."* Koreans, in particular, take great pride in the fact that Yi Sun-sin built the world's first armored warship, the Turtle Ship, and created a legendary naval victory. Here, I would like to introduce an interesting story related to the Turtle Ship and the establishment of a shipyard during Korea's industrial development in the 1970s. South Korea, now a global powerhouse in the shipbuilding industry, is home to world-renowned shipbuilding companies. Hyundai Heavy Industries, established in 1972, was the first large-scale shipbuilding company in Korea and has represented Korea's shipbuilding industry for more than half a century. The founder of Hyundai Heavy Industries, the late Chung Ju-yung (1915-2001), was a prominent entrepreneur representing Korea. This intriguing story about the Turtle Ship, the Hyundai Ulsan shipyard, and Chung Ju-yung dates back to 1971. Chung Ju-yung had an ambitious plan to build a shipyard at that time. He tried to get funding in the United States and Japan with only a business proposal, a black-and-white photo of the Mipo Bay beach where the shipyard would be built, and a map. However, as Korea was still a developing country and Hyundai was an unknown company, no country was willing to lend a large amount of money. In September 1971, Chung Ju-yung contacted Barclays Bank in the UK. The bank presented several prerequisites for lending money. Among these, the top priority was a business proposal and a recommendation letter from a reputable British shipbuilding consultancy firm. Chung Ju-yung had a business proposal prepared by the British shipbuilding consultant firm A&P Appledore, but obtaining a recommendation letter from Charles Longbottom, the chairman of A&P Appledore, proved challenging. Chairman Longbottom stated, *"There's no one willing to buy vessels yet. I am not confident in Hyundai Construction's repayment ability and potential, so I cannot write a recommendation letter."*

In response, Chung Ju-yung asked, *"Would it be possible if the Korean government provided a guarantee?"* Longbottom replied, *"To my knowledge, the Korean government also cannot repay such a large amount,"* thus rejecting the request. At this point, Chung Ju-yung showed Longbottom a 500-won banknote issued by the Bank of Korea, which featured the Turtle Ship.

He said, *"The Republic of Korea built an ironclad ship 300 years before Britain did,"* asserting that Korea could build a shipyard and construct vessels, thereby possessing the potential to repay the loan. Chung Ju-yung's persuasive argument convinced Chairman Longbottom, who agreed to write the recommendation letter. Based on this recommendation, Chung Ju-yung approached George Livanos,

Figure 12: The 500-won Bill Issued by the Bank of Korea in the 1970s

the brother-in-law of Greek shipping tycoon Aristotle Onassis, and secured a contract to build two oil tankers. This success allowed him to borrow a significant sum from Barclays Bank, leading to the miraculous construction of Korea's first large-scale shipyard in Ulsan. Since the establishment of the Hyundai Ulsan shipyard, Korea's shipbuilding industry has continued to develop, eventually becoming the strongest shipbuilding nation in the world. Many in Korea refer to this fascinating real-life story involving Chung Ju-yung, the shipyard, and the Turtle Ship as the *"Miracle of the Turtle Ship."*

## Battle Scenes of the Turtle Ship
### Turtle Ship's Functions as Recorded by Yi Sun-sin (Source: The Movie 'Hansan')

Figure 13: The Scenes of the Turtle Ship Leading the Charge (Source: The Movie 'Hansan')

The Turtle Ship Firing Cannons (Chongtong) from the Dragon's head

Figure 14: The Scenes of the Turtle Ship Firing (Source: The Movie 'Hansan')

# Chapter II

## Glorious Naval Battles of Admiral Yi Sun-sin

# The 1st Campaign: The Battle of Okpo, Happo, and Jeokjinpo

## The Japanese Army's Capture of Seoul and Advance North

On April 18, as Konishi's troops moved towards Miryang through Yangsan, Kato's army of about 22,800 soldiers landed in Busan, and Kuroda's army of 11,000 soldiers landed at Jukdo, south of Gimhae. Konishi's troops advanced through the central route, Kato's troops through the eastern route, and Kuroda's troops through the western route, all moving toward Seoul. The commander, Kim Myung-won, who was guarding the Han river, fled to the Imjin river, causing the capital's defense line to collapse. Twenty days after landing in Busan, on May 3, Konishi's troops entered through the East Gate, and Kato's troops entered through the South Gate of Seoul. Soon after, Kuroda's and Mori's troops also entered Seoul without any fighting. After capturing Busan and Dongrae Castles, the Japanese forces defeated the Korean army in Sangju and Chungju, entered Seoul on May 3, and advanced to Pyongyang by June 13. King Seonjo, who had not prepared for the invasion or strengthened the city's defenses, abandoned the capital, Seoul, on April 30 and fled to Pyongyang on May 7. After capturing Seoul in just 20 days, Konishi's troops crossed the Imjin river on May 27 and advanced towards Pyongyang, while Kato's army marched toward Hamgyeong Province and Kuroda's army moved

Chapter II. Glorious Naval Battles of Admiral Yi Sun-sin

Figure 15: The Japanese Troops' Attack Route

towards Hwanghae Province.

## The Battle of Okpo

Admiral Yi Sun-sin received a letter from Won Gyun, Gyeongsang Right Naval Commander, at twilight on April 15, 1592, stating that approximately 90 Japanese vessels had entered the waters near Busan.

Simultaneously, he received a message from Park Hong, Gyeongsang Left Naval Commander, reporting that around 350 Japanese vessels had invaded Busan harbor. At the time, major commanders were required to send copies of their reports (*Janggye*: report to King) to neighboring commanders. Upon receiving this news, Admiral Yi Sun-sin informed the neighboring commanders about the Japanese incursion and requested that the commanders in Gyeongsang Province provide information about the enemy's movements.

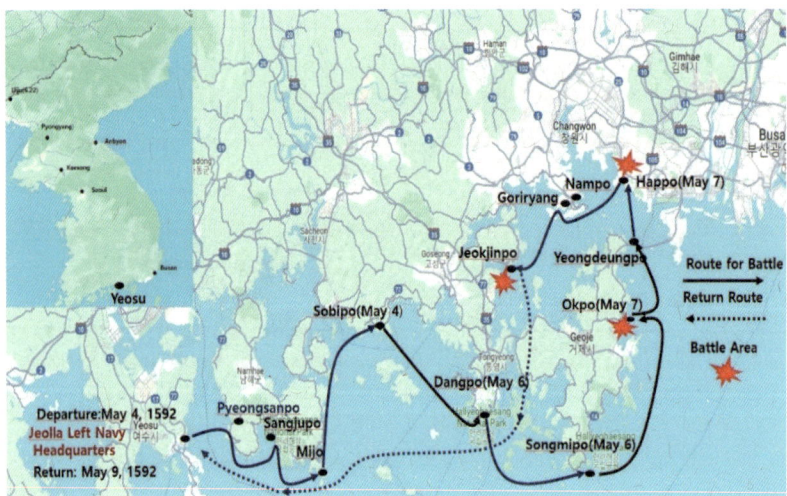

Figure 16: The 1st Campaign Route of Admiral Yi Sun-sin (Battles of Okpo, Happo, and Jeokjinpo)

Yi Sun-sin immediately called in the regional generals and staff officers for preparations. Admiral Yi Sun-sin requested the King to allow him to participate in the Gyeongsang sea, which was outside the jurisdiction of the Jeolla Left Naval Forces.

On April 27th, King Seonjo permitted Admiral Yi Sun-sin to deploy in the Gyeongsang Province waters. Yi Sun-sin, upon receiving this order, sent a report to the King, stating,

## Chapter II. Glorious Naval Battles of Admiral Yi Sun-sin

*As the enemies advancing inland are soon to invade the capital, there is no one who does not exert themselves. If we obstruct the enemy's return route and annihilate the Japanese vessels as they may be worried about their rear, they might immediately stop advancing north and retreat. Therefore, on May 4, when the first rooster crows, I will set sail toward Gyeongsang Province.*

On May 4th, the day after the Japanese forces occupied the capital, Seoul, Yi Sun-sin set out to the Busan Sea area in the early morning with 24 war vessels (Panokseons), 15 support vessels, 46 small vessels, and a total of 85 vessels. Yi Sun-sin's fleet left Yeosu port and continued sailing toward Busan while searching for the enemy. When the Jeolla Left Naval Fleet arrived at Hansan Island on May 6, Won Gyun, Gyeongsang Right Naval Commander, appeared with a ship. Subsequently, three vessels from the Gyeongsang navy and two support vessels joined Yi Sun-sin's fleet. On that day, they anchored at Songmipo in Geoje Island. Out of over a hundred vessels held by the Gyeongsang navy, only four managed to join Admiral Yi Sun-sin's fleet, evading the Japanese Navy. It was indeed a truly pitiful situation.

On the morning of May 7, as the Korean fleet left Songmipo and approached the waters where the enemy was staying in Gadeokdo, Yi Sun-sin received a report around noon from the scout ship that 30 enemy war vessels were around in Okpo Bay. Admiral Yi Sun-sin calmed the soldiers' hearts and boosted their morale by ordering them to move cautiously like a mountain and not act recklessly without orders. The fleet changed to a battle formation as they sailed along the southwest coast of Geoje Island, rounded the end of Jangseungpo, and headed southwest. At this time, reports from scout vessels came in one after another, stating that the enemy fleet was all anchored off Okpo Bay.

Thick fog covered Okpo Bay, and the Japanese Navy, not anticipating the arrival of Admiral Yi Sun-sin's fleet, did not see them until they reached the bay's entrance. It was then that the six Japanese Navy vessels stationed at the entrance, guarding it, shot warning arrows into the air and fled towards the coast. The enemy fleet was led by the Japanese Navy commander, Todo Takatora. The Korean fleet attacked with various cannons and fire arrows, quickly destroying 26 enemy vessels.

Admiral Yi Sun-sin reported the battle situation to the King in *the Report on the Battle of Attacking and Destroying the Japanese Enemy at Okpo,* as follows:

*The various commanders and their soldiers, with one heart and mind, fought with all their strength, and even the ship's leaders who were not military personals, shared the same determination and fought to the*

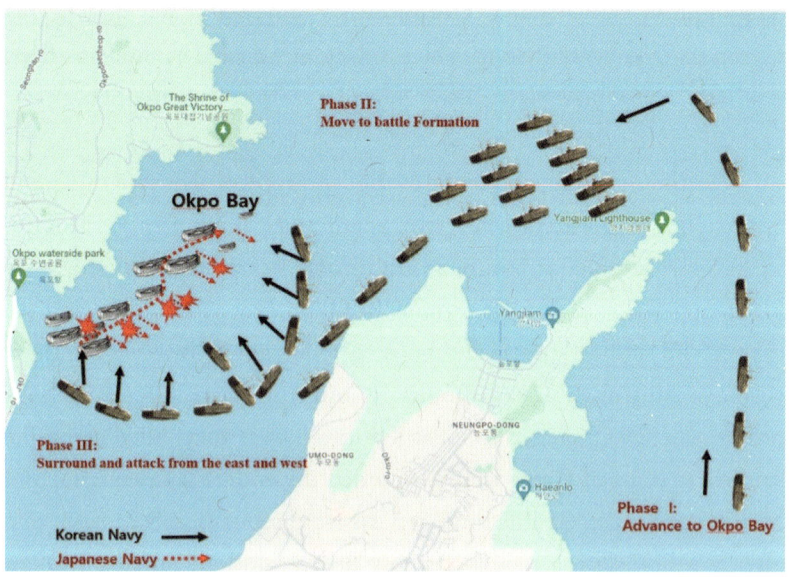

Figure 17: The Situation Map of the Battle of Okpo

*death. We surrounded the enemy from east and west, and the sound of cannons and arrows was like thunder while the enemy also fired and threw things into the water, losing their composure. Our arrows hit some of their high-ranking officers and fell into the water, and we destroyed the enemy completely in a single battle.*

### Analysis of the Battle of Okpo

To understand the situation of the Battle of Okpo, one must pay attention to Yi Sun-sin's record in the Battle of Okpo, which states, *"we attacked the enemy by surrounding them from the east and west, and the sound of cannons and arrows was like thunder, and the enemy lost their composure by firing and throwing things into the water."* If one looks at the figure of the Battle of Okpo published in Korea so far, one can recognize that some didn't include the information mentioned above. Therefore, I would like to introduce a new situation map of the Battle of Okpo based on Yi Sun-sin's records in this book. I considered the geography of Okpo Bay, the direction of the Korean Navy's attack, and the response and escape route of the Japanese Navy. In particular, the situation map was created with an emphasis on the Korean fleet's victory by surrounding and attacking the east and west.

### The Corrected Situation Map of the Battle of Okpo

The figure shown is a battle situation map of the Battle of Okpo, which reinterprets the East-West Encirclement Attack battle situation, taking into account the space of Okpo Bay, the direction of the Korean Navy's entry into the harbor, and the direction of the Japanese Navy's response and escape. As can be seen in the previous battle situation map, it can be seen that the Battle of Okpo attacked with a formation similar to the *Hakikjin (Crane Wing Formation)*, a famous tactic used in the Battle of Hansan Island, which will be introduced later. According to the author's research, Yi Sun-sin preferred the *Hakikjin (Crane*

*Wing Formation)* or a similar encircling attack when the forces were equal or superior and the battle space was relatively wide. Considering the reported accounts after the conclusion of the Battle of Okpo, it is estimated that Admiral Yi achieved victory in the Battle of Okpo, his first naval battle, by utilizing a formation based on the *Hakikjin* formation. Although filled with anxiety, Admiral Yi's troops bravely engaged in fierce combat against the enemy fleet in their first battle.

## The Battle of Happo

Admiral Yi then defeated the enemy at Okpo and proceeded northwards to the northern tip of Geoje Island, in front of Yeongdeungpo. Yi Sun-sin planned to stay in Yeongdeungpo and spend the night securing firewood and water. Around 6 p.m., a scout ship reported that five enemy vessels were sailing in the nearby sea. Yi Sun-sin led his war vessels and moved to the sea in front of Happo.

The enemies abandoned their vessels and fled to land. Commanders of Yi Sun-sin's fleet, including Kim Wan and Eo Yeong-dam, destroyed all enemy vessels with guns and bows and set them on fire.

### Controversy over the Battle of Happo

The naval battle in which Admiral Yi Sun-sin's fleet defeated five enemy vessels near Happo is commonly called the Battle of Happo. However, there is controversy over whether the battlefield of the Battle of Happo was in Jinhae, Ungcheon, or Changwon, Masan. Professor Jo Seong-do, who led early research on Admiral Yi's naval battles in Korea, designated it as Changwon, Masan Port (Happo), but for the past 20 years, there has been an argument that it was in Jinhae, Ungcheon. However, those who claim it was Masan, Happo, refute the argument that it was Jinhae, Ungcheon, stating that the evidence for this claim is uncertain.

The origin of the conflict between the two sides lies in the fact that the evidence for both claims is not entirely clear. Fortunately, the author recently found evidence in Admiral Jeong Un's biography that can determine where the Battle of Happo took place. Admiral Jeong Un was a brave admiral who directly participated as one of Admiral Yi Sun-sin's subordinates in various naval battles, including the Battle of Happo. He strongly advocated for the decision to dispatch forces to the waters of Gyeongsang Province after the outbreak of the Imjinwaeran, despite opposition from other commanders. Furthermore, he was a courageous general who fought at the forefront of the Battle of Busanpo, the largest battle of the Imjinwaeran. He died after being hit by enemy artillery on the battlefield. Admiral Jeong Un's biography clearly states the enemy's departure destination point for the Battle of Happo and accurately records the place names of the time.

### Clarification of Battle Locations

This distinctly contrasts the uncertainty surrounding the enemy's departure and destination points until now. Admiral Jeong Un's biography records, "the enemy vessels came out from Masan Port in Changwon and entered the port of Ungcheon land, Wonpo (currently Jinhae Wonpo-dong Port), where they abandoned their vessels and fled," clearly indicating that the area of the Battle of Happo is the current Jinhae Wonpo-dong Port. The name of the place mentioned by Yi Sun-sin in the records, Ungcheon land Happo is the current Jinhae Ungcheon Wonpo area. The record in Admiral Jeong Un's biography refers to Changwon land Masan Port, which is currently Happo in Masan. At that time, the enemies departed from Masan Happo and moved to Jinhae Wonpo. Therefore, it can be understood that the final battleground at that time was Jinhae Wonpo. Admiral Yi Sun-sin's fleet defeated the enemy fleet at Wonpo Port in Jinhae, sailed in the evening, and anchored overnight in the sea off Nampo, Changwon.

## The Battle of Jeokjinpo

On the morning of May 8th, Yi Sun-sin received news from a scout ship that 13 enemy vessels were anchored in Goriryang, Jinhae. Yi Sun-sin's fleet immediately dispatched the fleet and searched large and small islands, passing Jeodo Island and arriving at Jeokjinpo on the border of Goseong. Thirteen enemy vessels, including large vessels and heavy vessels, were anchored in a row at the entrance to the sea. The enemies were causing trouble, burning the village of the port, and stealing its wealth. When the enemies saw Yi Sun-sin's fleet, they were frightened and fled to the mountains. Yi Sun-sin's fleet destroyed the enemy vessels with his guns and set them on fire, destroying 11 of the 13 enemy vessels. Yi Sun-sin left two vessels behind. He left them behind for the escape of the enemies who were harassing the people on land.

## The Lessons of the 1st Campaign

After the battle, Yi Sun-sin had breakfast and was planning for future battles with Won Gyun and another admiral, when news came that the king had taken refuge in Pyeongando. Yi Sun-sin was so angry and resentful that he held his tongue and cried. On May 9th, Admiral Yi led his fleet back to Jeolla Province and returned to the Jeolla Left Naval Headquarters at noon. In their first campaign at Okpo, Happo, and Jekjinpo, the Korean fleet achieved a significant victory, defeating 42 enemy vessels with a fleet of approximately 30 vessels. Korean troops suffered three injuries.

There were no fatalities or damage to Korean war vessels, resulting in a one-sided victory. After arriving at the Headquarters in Yeosu, Yi Sun-sin submitted a report (*Janggye*) to the king on the outcome of the first campaign on the following day, May 10th. Since King Seonjo had arrived in Pyongyang on May 7th, he received Admiral Yi's report in Pyongyang. After the conclusion of the first campaign (Okpo, Happo, and Jekjinpo), Admiral Yi recognized the following key points.

### Enemy Objectives and Strategies

Firstly, the enemy naval forces aimed to attack coastal regions, specifically to seize logistical supplies, including provisions such as rice, livestock (cattle, horses, chickens, pigs, etc.), to support their troops and other units. They persistently raided the coast, plundering these supplies to provide for their ground forces via sea routes.

### Importance of Sea Control

Secondly, they would advance through the southern sea route towards the western sea to facilitate their logistical support. Consequently, our naval forces needed to safeguard the southern sea and actively impede the enemy's progress into the western sea.

### Comparative Naval Capabilities

Thirdly, *the Teppo* served as the primary weapon for the enemy, while their war vessels were comparatively less robust than our Panokseon. The enemy's vessels had a larger tactical rotation radius, and their V-shaped hulls resulted in significant water resistance during maneuvering. In contrast, our Panokseon featured U-shaped hulls, leading to reduced water resistance, enhanced rotation speed, and a shorter tactical rotation radius compared to the enemy.

### Effective Range of Enemy Weapons

Fourthly, the enemy's matchlock rifles (*Teppo*) possessed a range of approximately 100 ~ 200 meters, with an effective range of about 50 meters.

The victory of Admiral Yi Sun-sin in his first deployment was more than just a victory. Drawing from the confidence and lessons he gained from his first deployment, Admiral Yi went on to win all the naval battles he fought until his final battle.

# The 2nd Campaign: The Battle of Sacheon, Dangpo, Danghangpo and Yulpo

After the first campaign, each base commander returned to their bases. They improved their strategies and inspected weapons using lessons from their previous battles. Meanwhile, Yi Sun-sin's forces of the Jeolla Left Navy were focusing on training. During this time, Won Gyun, the leader of the Gyeongsang Right Navy, frequently alerted Yi about enemy forces entering the western side of Geoje Island, his area of responsibility, and stealing from local homes. Yi Sun-sin figured the enemy was taking food and moving their military supplies and soldiers. They planned to travel along the west coast via the south coast. Even though the Japanese forces defeated the Korean forces in land battles and took over the capital city, Seoul, in just over 20 days since the start of the war, no supply route was better for them than the sea route. Yi Sun-sin was confident he could end the war by defeating the Japanese naval forces and cutting off their sea supply route. To make this plan happen, he asked Yi Eok-gi, the commander of the Jeolla Right Navy, to bring his fleet from Haenam to Yeosu, where Yi Sun-sin's Jeolla Left Navy was stationed, by June 3. The goal was to team up with the Jeolla Right Navy, which hadn't participated in the first campaign. While watching the enemy and getting ready for the fight, Yi received a message from Won Gyun on May 27. The message stated, "Over ten enemy vessels are attacking Sacheon and Gonyang, and ransacking several coastal villages." In response, Admiral Yi Sun-sin quickly informed Yi Eok-gi, *"my fleet is heading to the waters of Sacheon. Let's meet there,"* and prepared for the fight.

## The Battle of Sacheon: Participation of the Turtle Ship

On the early morning of May 29th, Admiral Yi Sun-sin commanded a fleet of 23 vessels, one less than his first campaign, as he set sail for Sacheon.

Figure 18: The 2nd Campaign Route of Admiral Yi Sun-sin (Battles of Sacheon, Dangpo, Danghangpo, and Yulpo)

One ship from the fleet was left behind to defend Yeosu's main base under the command of Admiral Jeong Gyeol. For the second campaign, Yi Sun-sin had secretly prepared the Turtle Ship, intending to employ it in a daring assault tactic to disrupt the enemy formation. As Yi Sun-sin's fleet reached the entrance of Noryang Strait, Admiral Won Gyun, who had retreated to Hadong, led three battle vessels and joined Yi Sun-sin's fleet. He informed Yi Sun-sin that the enemy fleet was converging on Sacheon. Yi Sun-sin's fleet proceeded through the waters of Noryang, turning northward towards Sacheon. At that moment, an enemy reconnaissance ship was spotted sailing from Gonyang toward Sacheon. Leading the fleet, Admiral Yi Sun-sin ordered the pursuit and successfully destroyed the enemy reconnaissance vessel. When the Korean fleet reached the waters in front of Sacheon Harbor, they observed a mountain range extending for 3,000 m behind the harbor, with numerous enemy troops on the ridgeline displaying various flags and banners. Below the ridgeline, twelve Japanese warvessels were anchored in a single line inside the harbor. Due to the shallow water during low tide, Yi Sun-sin's fleet couldn't approach the enemy fleet closely. Yi Sun-sin adopted a strategy of luring the enemy into open waters to engage and defeat them.

When Yi Sun-sin turned his ship and pretended to retreat about 400 m back, about 200 enemy soldiers came down from the base on the mountain, half guarding the ship and the other half jumping up and down for joy, firing artillery and guns from under the hill. As the tide began to rise and the water level deepened, Yi Sun-sin's fleet adapted their formation for a counterattack. Admiral Yi Sun-sin ordered the entire fleet to make a 180° turn, positioning the Turtle Ship at the forefront. The Turtle Ship, which was the first to participate in the war, rushed from the vanguard of the Korean fleet to the enemy fleet and fired the *Cheonja, Jija, Hyeonja, and Hwangja* cannons. The enemies on the mountain, down the hill, and on the ship mercilessly fired their guns and artillery. There were Koreans mixed in with the Japanese soldiers in the enemy lines, and they also attacked the Korean Navy. Yi Sun-sin became even more indignant and charged forward, attacking and destroying the enemy vessels. Several war vessels of

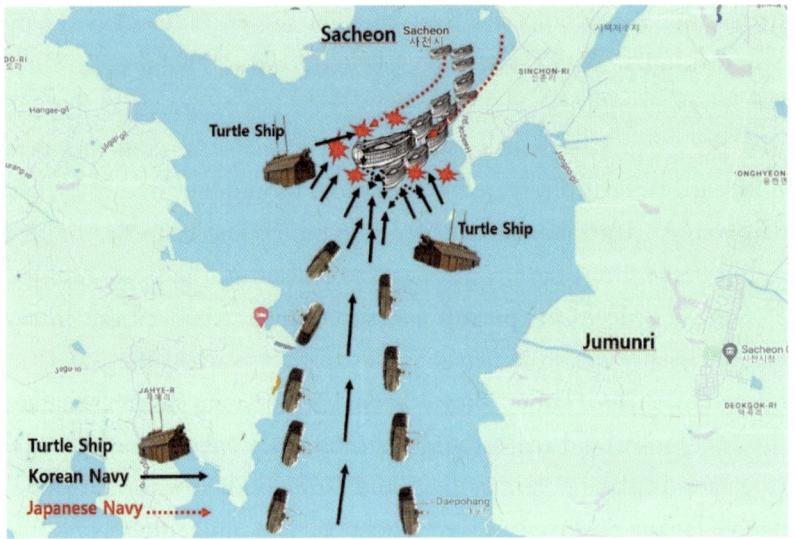

Figure 19: The Situation Map of the Battle of Sacheon

the Korean fleet rushed in, firing their bows and firing various types of projectiles with cannons. The sound of naval cannons shook the heavens and earth, and the enemies retreated to their camp on a high hill, suffering injuries and collapsing. The enemies were stamping their feet and crying from afar, not knowing what to do. Throughout the battle, the Japanese troops on land, aboard vessels, and on the hills relentlessly shelled Yi Sun-sin's fleet. The battle was fierce, resulting in the Korean fleet killing hundreds of enemy soldiers and either burning or sinking 13 enemy vessels. During the intense fighting, Admiral Yi Sun-sin was hit by an enemy bullet on his left shoulder, while Na Dae-yong and Yi Seol-do, both on the Turtle Ship, were struck by enemy arrows. Admiral Yi wanted to land immediately and kill all the enemies, but as it was evening, he left behind a few small vessels, turned around to move to Mojarangpo in Sacheon and spent the night on May 29th. As previously mentioned, the Turtle Ship was the world's first armored ship, made of wood, and it served at the forefront of the Korean fleet, launching daring close-quarter attacks on the enemy vessels using cannons.

## The Battle of Dangpo

On June 1st, Admiral Yi Sun-sin moved his fleet to a resting spot between two small islands near Goseong to allow his soldiers to recuperate and repair their weapons. The following day, June 2nd, at approximately 8 AM, he received a message from a scout ship reporting, "enemy vessels are anchored in Dangpo Harbor." Without delay, Yi Sun-sin set sail towards Dangpo. By around 10 AM, his fleet arrived at the waters before Dangpo and assessed the enemy's activities. The opposing force comprised 9 large vessels and 12 medium and small vessels. Meanwhile, the enemy fired cannons from land at Yi's fleet. The enemy commander was directing the battle from a pavilion above the enemy ship. Yi Sun-sin told the captain of the Turtle Ship to attack. The Turtle Ship moved toward the enemy commander's ship and shot its cannon. The Turtle Ship had various cannons like *Jija* and *Hyeonja* and it fired them as it got close to the enemy command's ship. The enemy command ship's pavilion was destroyed and its hull suffered significant damage.

After the Turtle Ship's attack, Yi Sun-sin ordered all his Panokseons to attack. The enemy's leader, even though he was bleeding from his head, was still calmly directing his vessels. At that moment, a Korean officer named Kwon Jun ran to the enemy's leading ship, shot the enemy leader with a bow, and made him fall. Admiral Jin Mu-sung jumped onto the enemy's ship and hit the enemy leader's neck. Killing the enemy leader with a weapon directly didn't happened often during the war. The Korean Navy's main plan was first to use the Turtle Ships to confuse the enemy and then get close to attack the enemy's vessels directly. After that, the Panokseon vessels would charge the enemy, using cannons and bows to attack. They used bows and small cannons to kill the enemy and big cannons to hit the enemy's vessels. With their leader gone, the Japanese soldiers became unsure of what to do and their formation started to break up as they ran towards the coast. The enemy soldiers couldn't even count how many of them got hurt or killed from the Korean vessels' bullets and arrows. All 21 enemy vessels were either burned or beaten. Yi Sun-sin's fleet won a significant victory.

Before engaging in the Battle of Dangpo, Admiral Yi Sun-sin took precautions against a surprise attack from the rear by positioning scout vessels in the open sea. While annihilating the enemy fleet at Dangpo and bombarding the enemy on the land, a report from the scout vessels informed them that *over 20 enemy large vessels are coming with many*

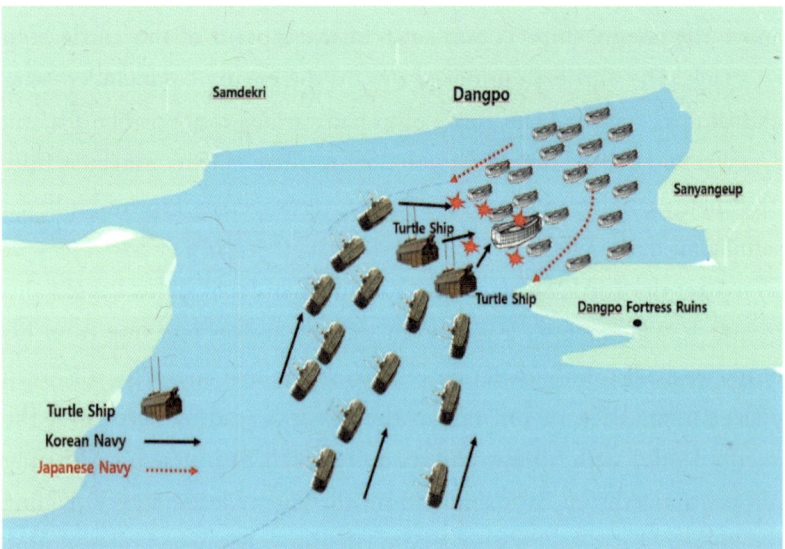

Figure 20: The Situation Map of the Battle of Dangpo

*small vessels from Geoje Island.* Yi Sun-sin intended to pursue the enemy fleet, but the enemy turned around and fled toward Busan upon seeing the Korean fleet. As night fell, Admiral Yi decided to avoid a nighttime battle, let his fatigued soldiers rest, and prepare their firearms. They dropped anchor at Changshindo. On the morning of June 3rd, they searched the waters near Dangpo's western channel but could not locate the enemy. That night, they anchored at Godunpo, Goseong. On June 4th, in the morning, they raised anchor and searched the nearby waters, and when they reached Dangpo's waters, the sun was already high. Numerous vessels were coming from the western sea led by Admiral Yi Eok-gi, the Jeolla Right Naval Commander, made their appearance. Because Admiral Yi Eok-gi, the Jeolla Right Naval Commander, was late in joining with the Yi Sun-sin fleet before the second campaign, Yi Sun-sin's fleet departed Yeosu Port alone on May 1, 1592. The young 32-year-old Admiral Yi Eok-gi brought a fleet of 25 vessels and joined Admiral Yi Sun-sin's forces, forming a Joint Fleet of 51 vessels(Yi Sun-sin with 23 vessels, Yi Eok-gi with 25 vessels, and Won Gyun with three vessels). On that day, the Joint Fleet moved to Tongyeong and anchored. That night, Admirals Yi Sun-sin, Yi Eok-gi, and Won Gyun discussed the strategy and tactics of the Korean Navy late into the night. The main topic of the meeting that night was probably who would be in charge of the combined fleet. Won Gyun might have wanted to be the leader, but because he felt terrible for not fighting when the Japanese attacked and letting his fleet sink, he might not have felt confident enough to say he should be in charge.

The Korean Navy did not have a *Tongjesa* (Commander of the Three Province Naval Forces) position capable of commanding the Joint Fleet, so someone else had to command it. Yi Eok-gi respected Yi Sun-sin, who was 16 years older than him, and highly valued his leadership, so it is presumed that he asked Yi Sun-sin to take command of the Korean fleet. From then on, Yi Sun-sin served as the actual commander of the integrated fleet. The Korean fleet, which met Yi Eok-gi's fleet and formed a Three-Provincial Joint Feet, camped at Chaknyang, the border between Goseong and Geoje, on the night of June 4 and spent the night.

## The Battle of Danghangpo

On the morning of June 5th, Admiral Yi Sun-sin set out towards Geoje, intending to search for and eliminate the enemy vessels. However, thick fog hindered their progress, and while waiting, a messenger, including Kim from Geoje Island, arrived, reporting that many Japanese enemy vessels had entered Danghangpo and were anchored. Admiral Yi Sun-sin led a Joint naval fleet to move north towards Tongyeong Bay and scouted Danghangpo. The entrance of Danghangpo was narrow, about 400 m wide, but it extended for approximately 15 km with a width ranging from 1,000 to 2,000 m, making it suitable for naval operations. Yi Sun-sin ordered the formation of a reconnaissance unit consisting of three of our vessels to enter the port and carefully inspect the area, engaging the enemy and luring them out of the port as they retreated. About an hour after the reconnaissance unit had entered the bay, a report came which stated that *"the enemy fleet, consisting of 9 large vessels, four medium-sized vessels, and 13 small vessels, totaling 26 vessels, is anchored in a line formation. We request a swift entry into the port to defeat the enemy."*

Upon receiving this report, Yi Sun-sin placed four vessels near the entrance of the port to intercept the retreating enemy during the engagement. He organized his formation into a battle-ready line and advanced into the port. In the distance, among the anchored enemy fleet, a large enemy flagship, similar to the one encountered during the

Battle of Dangpo, decorated with three levels of red and gold, came into view. Yi Sun-sin ordered his Turtle Ship assault team to target and defeat the enemy flagship. At this moment, a barrage of enemy bullets rained down on them. The battle was fierce, with over 70 vessels engaged in combat. The thunderous roar of cannons echoed across the narrow waters, and arrows poured down like torrential rain. Yi Sun-sin was the first to surround the enemy fleet, then charged the Turtle Ship into the enemy ship and concentrated on attacking the enemy's vessels with Panokseons. Panokseons took turns maneuvering in and out, firing naval cannons. The Korean fleet fought face-to-face with the enemy for a considerable time. In addition to destroying enemy vessels, Yi Sun-sin wanted to kill all enemy soldiers.

So, Yi Sun-sin pretended to retreat to lure the enemy away.

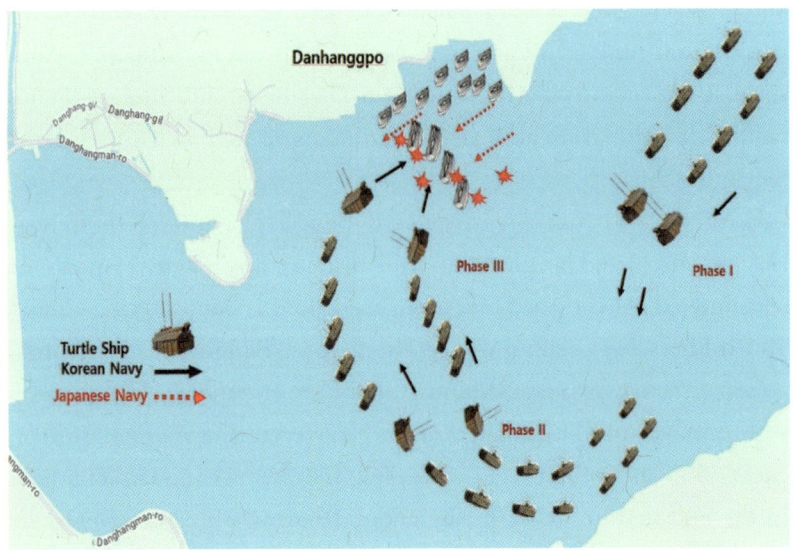

Figure 21: The Phase-by-Phase Situation Map of the Battle of Danghangpo

The enemy fleet came out with escort vessels on both sides. Yi

Sun-sin turned around, surrounded the enemy vessels, and began a quick attack. As usual, he charged the Turtle Ship first into the enemy ship, stabbed below the enemy line, and attacked with naval cannons upward. Subsequently, several Panokseons fired arrows at the sails of the enemy vessels and set them on fire. An enemy commander leading the battle on top of the enemy ship was struck by an arrow and killed. During the fight, four enemy vessels set sail and fled north, and together with the generals under Yi Eok-gi, they surrounded the enemy vessels, defeated them with cannons and bows, and burned all of their hulls. Admiral Yi Sun-sin's fleet successfully encircled the enemy, engaged them in close combat, and destroyed all 26 enemy vessels, leaving only one from the enemy's warship.

The Battle of Danghangpo ended in an overwhelming victory. When the battle ended within Danghangpo, The Korean fleet went out to the entrance of Danghangpo and spent the evening. Early in the morning on June 6th, Bangdap *Cheomsa* reported to Admiral Yi Sun-sin that the enemy who had fled from Danghangpo to the mountains would definitely sneak out of Danghangpo at dawn on the one remaining ship.

Admiral Yi Sun-sin instructed Bangdap *Cheomsa* to wait at the entrance to Danghangpo and destroy any enemy vessels he encountered. As it turned out, a single enemy warship, carrying around 100 soldiers, was sailing out of the harbor. Bangdap *Cheomsa* first attacked the enemy vessels coming out of the entrance to Danghangpo with cannons and bows. The Korean Navy even threw a hook into an enemy ship and pulled it out of the sea. The enemy commander fought to the end despite being hit by about 10 arrows but was eventually decapitated and fell into the sea. Out of about 100 enemies, half of about enemies were killed, and the other half had drowned. When the battle was over, Admiral Yi Sun-sin comforted his soldiers, moved to the Marujang Sea in Goseong on the evening of the 6th and stayed the night. Now, there is a memorial site for Admiral Yi Sun-sin and the Battle of Danghangpo on the shores of Danghang-ri.

## The Battle of Yulpo

On the morning of June 7th, Admiral Yi Sun-sin's combined fleet searched near Siru Island off Wungcheon. While on the way to Yeongdeungpo on the northern tip of Geoje Island around noon, they received intelligence from the scout ship ahead,

*"Five large enemy vessels and two medium-sized enemy vessels are heading towards Busan from Yulpo in Daegeum-ri."* Yi Sun-sin ordered his subordinate commanders to pursue and destroy the enemy vessels. Commanders and officers, including Yi Mong-gu, Kim Wan, Jeong Un, Eo Yeong-dam, Gu Sa-jik, Kim In-young, and Yi Young-nam, destroyed the enemy ship and set it on fire. The enemy fleet's commander, Kurushima Michiyuki, took responsibility for the defeat and committed suicide on shore. The combined fleet anchored at Songjin Port that day. On June 8th, the combined fleet conducted search operations in Masanpo, Angolpo, Jepo, and the waters off Wungcheon, then returned to anchor at Songjinpo. The next day, June 9th, they conducted search operations throughout the day and anchored at Dangpo in the evening.

## The Significance of the 2nd Campaign

On June 10th, after completing the second campaign operation that had lasted for two weeks since May 27th, Admiral Yi Sun-sin returned to his base in Yeosu with the Jeolla Left Navy, while sending Yi Eok-gi's and Won Gyun's fleets back to their respective bases. Admiral

Yi defeated 72 Japanese vessels during the second campaign, including 13 at Sacheon, 21 at Dangpo, 30 at Danghangpo, and 8 at Yulpo.

Although the enemy had 225 casualties, there were 13 deaths and 37 injuries without a destroyed ship on the Korean side. Admiral Yi also sustained injuries during this campaign. The significance of the second campaign operation lies in the blockade of the Japanese naval forces, the first victory of a Joint naval force consisting of Admiral Yi's and Yi Eok-gi's fleets, and the first confirmation of the performance of the Turtle Ship.

Yi Sun-sin sent a report to the king on the results of the battle after the second campaign. In this report, Yi Sun-sin expressed his feelings for not being able to stop the Japanese forces, which had illegally invaded Joseon, from the sea at the beginning of the war. Admiral Yi was angry with the irresponsible and incomprehensible behavior of the commanders of the naval forces of Gyeongsang Province, who had thrown their vessels and weapons into the sea without even fighting the enemy once and ran away, thus making it easy for the enemy to carry out their landing operations. He regretted that if they had fought back with all their might and blocked the enemy's advance from the sea, the Japanese invasion could have been prevented, and the country would not have been in such a terrible state. In this battle, the Turtle Ship, which was Admiral Yi's creation, became a symbol of the Imjinwaeran, and the armored Turtle Ship proved to be very effective in assault and close combat. Also, his leadership and tactical abilities and his creative use of weapons and troops, were evident in his writings on the second campaign.

The following is a summary of the report that Admiral Yi Sun-sin submitted to the king after the second campaign, and it clearly shows Admiral Yi Sun-sin's attitude toward battle and the majesty of the Turtle Ship.

*The war would not have reached this point if well-trained and selected soldiers had been entrusted to brave and wise commanders. If it's a naval battle, all the soldiers are on the ship. Therefore, even if the soldiers want to run away while looking at the enemy fleet, they cannot do so. Moreover, the soldiers must row their oars and beat the drum quickly, and if anyone disobeys orders, military law will be enforced immediately. So how could they not put all their heart and energy into it?*

*The Turtle Ship rushes in first, followed by the Panok ship, firing Jija-Chongtong and Hyeonja-Chongtong, and showering hail like a hail of shot and stone. Then, the enemy's morale will be easily broken and there will be no time for them to respond. This is the easy thing about naval warfare. I was concerned that there would be an invasion by Japanese enemies, so I built a special Turtle Ship. The Turtle Ship can easily rush in and open fire even if there are hundreds of enemy vessels. During this campaign, the assault commander was in charge of the Turtle Ship.*

He expresses regret that if the military had used all its might to stop the enemy coming from the sea, the landing of Japanese troops could have been prevented, and Joseon's territory would not have reached this point. In addition, this article shows that Yi Sun-sin not only had farsightedness as a strategist, but also developed weapons and tactics, creatively operated troops, and was a commander with great skill.

# The 3rd Campaign: The Battle of Hansan and Angolpo

**Ground Combat and Sea Control Situation**

When the Korean Navy, led by Yi Sun-sin, was winning consecutive victories at sea, the Japanese army occupied Seoul, Korea's capital, 20 days after landing in Busan. They swiftly captured Pyongyang and Kaesong, almost occupying Korea's inland regions, prompting King Seonjo to flee near the Chinese border.

Let's take a brief look at the wartime situation on land. The Japanese invaders across the country defeated the Korean army, and King Seonjo left Pyongyang on June 11, arriving in Yeongbyeon on June 14. The Japanese commander Konishi's forces were preparing to attack Pyongyang, gathering at Dongdaewon, south of the Daedong river. Kato's and Mori's forces were advancing towards the eastern coast, including Anbyeon and Wonsan. On the other hand, about 40,000 troops from Jeolla and Gyeongsang Provinces and 10,000 from Chungcheong marched from Onyang on June 4 to attack the Japanese forces stationed at Munso Mountain near Yongin.

However, they suffered a significant defeat in a battle against the Japanese commander Wakisaka's 1,500 troops, and the 50,000-strong Korean army panicked. Leaders like Gwak Jae-woo and Ko Gyeong-myeong stepped up to rescue the struggling nation in chaotic times.

On July 8, 1592, during the Battle of Hansan Island, Ko Gyeong-myeong led about 6,000 guerrilla fighters from Jeolla Province, including Gwangju and Damyang, to join the Battle of Geumsan. Ko Gyeong-myeong was the 10th generation of the Jangheung Ko clan and a former bureaucrat who ranked first in the civil service exam. He was dismissed from his central government position and educated younger students in his hometown of Gwangju. In 1592, during the Japanese invasions of Korea, he raised an army as a leader of the volunteer army and died along with his son while fighting against the Japanese army.

The Korean government built *Pochungsa Memorial Hall* in Gwangju Metropolitan City to commemorate General Ko Gyeong-myeong and his two sons. Notably, Ko Gyeong-myeong's eldest son participated in the Battle of Jinju but was killed. He participated in the Jinjuseong Battle to avenge his father and younger brother who were killed in the Battle of Geumsan. Additionally, Gwak Jae-woo, a guerrilla leader from Gyeongsang Province, defeated the Japanese forces in the battles of Uiryung, Hyunpung, and Yangsan from July 25 to 29. As the Korean army suffered consecutive defeats on land, General Cho Seung-hoon, commander of China's first force, arrived in Korea with about 3,000 Chinese troops. On July 7, 1592, Cho Seung-hoon's troops attacked Pyeongyang Castle, which the Japanese army occupied but was defeated by the Japanese troops.

Admiral Yi Sun-sin departed Yeosu Port on May 29, 1592, defeated 72 enemy vessels in the battles of Sacheon, Dangpo, Danghangpo, and Yulpo, and returned to Yeosu Port on June 10, 1592. However, the Japanese Navy still held control over the crucial maritime areas of Gyeongsang Province, mainly due to the inadequacy of the naval forces under Won Gyun, responsible for guarding Geoje Island, Namhae, and Hansan Island. Although the Japanese Navy had suffered consecutive losses in maritime battles against Admiral Yi Sun-sin and his fleet, they tried to advance into the West Sea while harassing the

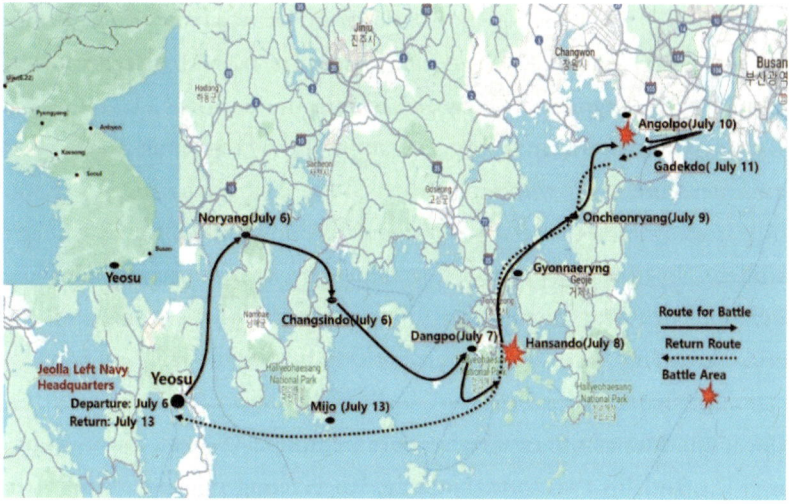

Figure 22: The 3rd Campaign Route of Admiral Yi Sun-sin (Battles of Hansan and Angolpo)

coastal people. After receiving reports of the Japanese Navy's repeated defeats by Admiral Yi Sun-sin's fleet in all naval battles, Toyotomi Hideyoshi ordered his naval commanders, such as Wakisaka Yasuharu, Kuki Yoshitaka, and Kato Yoshiaki, to defeat Admiral Yi Sun-sin's fleet. The Japanese Navy's strategy was to advance into the western sea of the Korean Peninsula, expand supply routes towards Seoul, the capital, and support the ground battles fought by the Japanese army. To achieve this, defeating Admiral Yi Sun-sin and Admiral Yi Eok-gi, who guarded the seas off the western coast of the Korean Peninsula, was essential. Following Hideyoshi's specific orders, Japanese naval commanders, the elite of Japan's naval forces, were determined to annihilate the Korean Navy, making it necessary for Admiral Yi Sun-sin's fleet to confront their aggressive assaults. These three Japanese naval commanders, Kuki Yoshitaka, Wakisaka Yasuharu, and Kato Yoshiaki, were elite naval leaders who had achieved victory by blockading and controlling the seas in the battle of Odawara in 1590 during Hideyoshi's campaign for the unification of Japan. Hideyoshi, as soon as he observed the Korean naval forces stationed in Gyeongsang Province avoiding combat and retreating during the early stages of the Imjinwaeran, decided to engage in ground battles. This was the result of ignoring the combat capabilities of the Korean Navy.

The result of the battle, in which Yi Sun-sin's Korean Navy defeated the Japanese Navy, led Toyotomi Hideyoshi to change his maritime strategy, which had ignored the Korean Navy. Understanding the true capabilities of the Korean Navy, Hideyoshi, unlike in the 1st and 2nd naval campaigns, directly involved these elite naval commanders in naval battles. Wakisaka's fleet, prepared for battle earlier than the Kuki and Kato fleets, departed Wungcheon Harbor in Gyeongsang Province on July 6 and advanced towards the Korean Navy.

## The Battle of Hansan by the *Hakikjin*

### Preparation for Battle and Formation of the National Fleet

After completing the second campaign from May 29 to June 10, 1592, Admiral Yi Sun-sin returned to his headquarters to prepare his vessels and weapons for the upcoming battle. He was also closely monitoring the movements of the Japanese Navy, particularly around Gadeok Island and Geoje Island in Gyeongsang Province, as he had received intelligence about the enemy's activities. On July 4th, the fleet of Yi Eok-gi, commander of the Jeolla Right Naval Force, departed from Haenam, Jeolla Province, arrived in Yeosu, and joined Admiral Yi Sun-sin's fleet. On July 6, they launched their third campaign to block the Japanese Navy in the West Sea. In Noryang, located in the South Sea, they encountered Admiral Won Gyun's Naval Forces and formed a national fleet. The fleet composition included Admiral Yi Sun-sin's fleet, with 24 vessels (including 3 Turtle Ships), Admiral Yi Eok-gi's fleet, with 25 vessels, and Admiral Won Gyun's fleet, with 7 vessels, totaling 56 vessels.

That night, the national fleet anchored in the waters near Changsin Island and used the intelligence they had gathered to analyze and evaluate the enemy navy's strategy. They also discussed the operation and tactics for the upcoming battle to respond to the enemy's tactics.

### The Korean Fleet's Preparations and Operational Planning

First, they emphasized the need for a unified command system under a single commander for the Korean fleet's operations, considering their previous battle experiences. This was proposed with the understanding that arbitrary actions by Admiral Won Gyun had caused significant disruption in previous battles. Second, they discussed communication and signaling needed for operation command. This included fleet movements, fleet progression, weapon selection, visual signals for battle, sound signals, and light signals. On July 7th, a strong east wind made sailing difficult, so the national fleet anchored near Dangpo to restock supplies, food, and weapons. Kim Cheon-son quickly traveled 50 li (about 20 km) from Gyeonnaeryang to Dangpo to deliver critical information to Admiral Yi. Kim reported, *"The enemy fleet, about 70 vessels, has anchored in Gyeonnaeryang after passing Yeongdeungpo around 2 p.m. today."* Upon receiving this report, Admiral Yi Sun-sin dispatched officers to verify the information and urgently summoned Admiral Yi Eok-gi, Admiral Won Gyun, and other commanders. Admiral Yi briefed them on the enemy's situation and instructed them to ready themselves for battle, emphasizing that they would depart the following morning to attack the enemy fleet. He kept planning the operation late into the night, carefully checking the area where it would take place.

### Preparations for Battle and the Enemy's Response

Gyeonnaeryang is a narrow and lengthy strait between Goseong's Yongnam-myeon and Deokho-ri on Geoje Island. It measures approximately 5 km in length, with a minimum width of about 180 m and a depth of 2.8 m.

Because there are many underwater reefs, it's a difficult place for big war vessels like Panokseon and the Turtle Ship to move around, making it a bad spot for naval battles. After carefully considering the waters around Gyeonnaeryang, Admiral Yi concluded, *"the decisive battlefield for tomorrow's battle will be the wide sea in front of Hansan Island"*, and began formulating tactics. First, lure the enemy fleet into the deep waters in front of Hansan Island. Second, a portion of the fleet behind islands like Mirukdo and Hwado should be concealed. Third, if you succeed in luring the enemy, you will form *Hakikjin (crane wing formation)* in front of Hansan Island and engage in battle. After completing the operational plan, Admiral Yi assigned a special mission to the left Turtle Ship commander, Yi Gi-nam, and the right Turtle Ship commander, Park Yi-ryang. The Japanese naval commander Wakisaka, after defeating the Korean army of 50,000 soldiers with his 1,600 troops in the Battle of Yongin on June 6, handed over the defense of the Yongin area to Ukida Hideyoshi. Toyotomi Hideyoshi had Wakisaka, a naval general, participate in land battles in the early stages of the war. Wakisaka won a significant victory in the Battle of Yongin, a land battle. However, when the Japanese Navy lost one battle after another in the naval battle, Wakisaka, a naval general, was sent into the naval battle.

### Commencement of Battle and Victory

On June 19, Wakisaka arrived on the southern coast in Wungcheon and expedited preparations for naval combat. With Hideyoshi's explicit command to annihilate the Korean Navy, Wakisaka did not

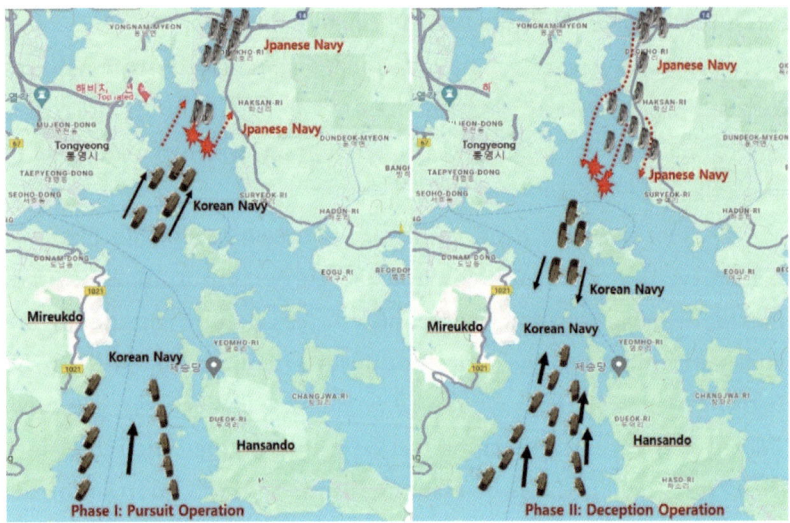

Figure 23: The Phase I and II Situation Map of the Pursuit and Deception Operation in Battle of Hansan

wait for the Kato and Kuki fleets but instead advanced to Yeosu, where the Jeolla Left Navy base was located. He commanded 73 vessels along the front line and set sail on July 6, arriving at Gyeonnaeryang on July 7. In the early morning of July 8, Admiral Yi Sun-sin ordered to depart for the national fleet and stationed as planned in the Hansan Island waters. He directed a few vessels to hide on nearby islands such as Mirukdo and Hwado, while deploying a vanguard of 4-5 Panokseon vessels to advance toward Gyeonnaeryang, where the enemy was anchored. At that moment, two scouting vessels from the Japanese Navy, patrolling in the waters ahead of Gyeonnaeryang, spotted Admiral Yi's vanguard and changed course to return to the enemy's main anchorage in Gyeonnaeryang. The vanguard followed closely behind the enemy, fired its cannons, and initiated the attack. Wakisaka's fleet promptly raised sails and engaged, chasing the Korean vanguard while firing their guns. While observing the nearby terrain and the enemy fleet from

Chapter II. Glorious Naval Battles of Admiral Yi Sun-sin    117

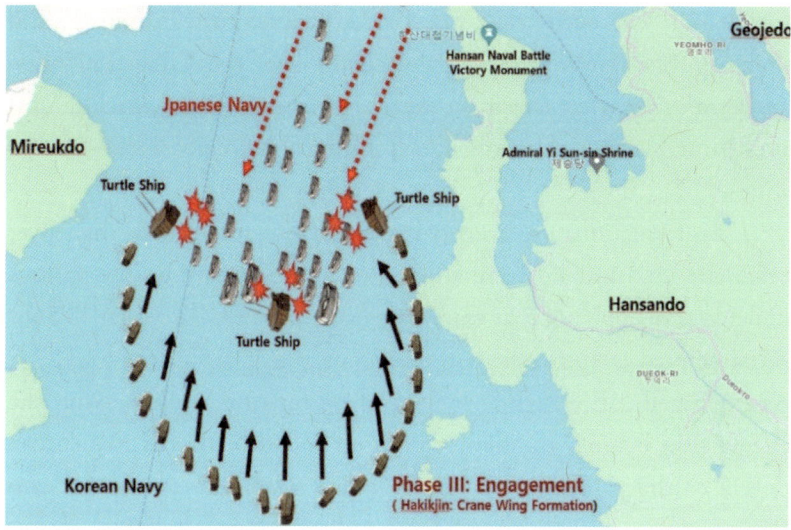

Figure 24: The Phase III Situation Map of the *Hakikjin* Engagement in the Battle of Hansan

behind the scouting unit, Admiral Yi Sun-sin saw that the enemy fleet consisted of 36 large warvessels, 24 medium warvessels, and 13 small warvessels for a total of 73 vessels. Following Yi's orders, the scouting unit engaged the enemy's vanguard fleet and pretended to retreat towards Hansan Island.

The enemy fleet, feeling confident after seeing the scouting unit retreating, pursued the unit while sounding their horns and beating their drums. When the enemy fleet's vanguard passed the western end of Banghwa Island, the Korean main fleet, which was lying in wait, suddenly emerged and joined with Yi Sun-sin's flagship. The Korean fleet advanced towards Hansan Island while firing on the enemy fleet.

When they reached the area in front of Daechuk Island, north of Hansan Island, a signal was given from Yi Sun-sin's flagship by sounding drums and raising the signal flag for the Great Turn

Command. The entire fleet made a 180-degree turn in unison, and then another signal was given by raising the signal flag for *"Form Hakikjin!" (A tactical formation that strikes like a crane's wings.)* Yi Sun-sin's Joint Fleet formed an orderly formation shaped like a crane's wings.

This formation, also known as the *Hakikjin*, is a tactical maneuver originally used in land combat. Unlike land battles, there are various difficulties in applying it at sea. In particular, the *Hakikjin* that Yi Sun-sin attempted in this naval battle was not a normal forward *Hakikjin*. As explained earlier, while maneuvering forward while leaving the enemy fleet behind, the fleet is reversed and maneuvered, which can pose a considerable burden and risk. The *Hakikjin,* meaning *Crane Wing Formation*, is a famous Korean military tactic. Soldiers or vessels are arranged like the outstretched wings of a crane. This strategy was especially successful during the Joseon dynasty when Admiral Yi Sun-sin used it in naval battles. Imagine a horseshoe shape. In the *Hakikjin,* your forces form the curve, with the center slightly pulled back and the ends pointing outwards towards the enemy. This lets you surround them and attack from all sides. The enemy gets confused and scattered, making them easier to defeat. Originally used on land, Admiral Yi Sun-sin cleverly adapted the *Hakikjin* for sea battles. With vessels, the Crane Wing Formation helps them move quickly and use their cannons effectively.

Yi Sun-sin's fleet could overpower them by tricking and outsmarting the enemy. The enemy fleet was trapped within the wings of the Korean fleet's formation. Yi Sun-sin then gave the order to attack:

*"All vessels, open fire!"* Yi Gi-nam, the left assault commander, commanded the battle Turtle Ship and charged toward the right side of the enemy fleet. The right assault commander, Park Yi-ryang, charged

toward the left side of the enemy fleet.

The Turtle Ship captains on the left and right were the first to rush into the enemy fleet and close in, firing their cannons, hitting the enemy hull, and breaking the enemy formation. As the Turtle Ships relentlessly destroyed enemy vessels on the left and right sides of the enemy fleet, the Panokseon captains charged in unison, killing the enemy with their bows and hitting the enemy's hull with various cannons. During the close combat, the Turtle Ships and the Panokseon vessels, and enemy vessels collided. The Korean combat vessels were more extensive and sturdier, so enemy vessels that collided with Korean vessels had their hulls broken. The battle continued from morning until late afternoon. As the battle between both sides intensified, the enemies lost momentum and began to flee. In this battle, the Korean fleet destroyed 35 out of 36 large vessels, 17 out of 24 medium vessels, and 7 out of 13 small vessels, and captured 12 vessels. Considering the enemy's damage and traps, the enemy's death toll is estimated at around 3,000. During the Battle of Hansan, the vice commander of the Japanese Navy, Wakisaka Saeemon, and General Watanabe Shichiuemon were killed.

At the same time, General Manabe fled to Hansando and lamented his defeat before committing suicide. Yi Sun-sin's fleet did not lose a single ship out of 56 vessels;

19 people died, and 14 were wounded. The commander-in-chief of the Japanese Navy, 39-year-old Wakisaka Yasuharu, was the lord of Awaji Island in Shikoku and a renowned military leader both on land and at sea, earning him the nickname *Dragon of the Seas*.

However, he suffered a crushing defeat against Yi Sun-sin and fled disgracefully to Gimhae. After his death, a Japanese scholar named Hayashi Michiharu wrote the following words on the back of his gravestone.

*In the Battle of Hansan, our troops suffered countless casualties, and Wakisaka barely managed to escape to Gimhae. Feeling bitter about his defeat against Yi Sun-sin, Wakisaka led his remaining forces in an attack against Yi and managed to capture one of his vessels.*

The records also describe the battle as follows:

*Upon seeing four or five Korean vessels approaching from within the barrier gate, we fired our cannons and attacked them relentlessly for about half an hour. The Korean vessels began to retreat gradually, but when they reached the open sea after passing through the Strait, they suddenly turned the direction of the fleet into the shape of a "Ki(a sieve used for sifting grain)" formation and surrounded our vessels, launching a fierce attack that inflicted heavy casualties.*

However, some parts of the above text are valid. According to Korean records (reports on the results of Yi Sun-sin's battles), the Japanese Navy never captured or destroyed Yi Sun-sin's fleet in the Battle of Hansan. In the eyes of the Japanese naval commander, the *Hakikjin* looked like a sieve used for sifting grain. The Korean Navy's victory at the Battle of Hansan was a decisive opportunity to change the Japanese Navy's naval battle strategy. The Japanese Navy, which ambitiously and aggressively sought to destroy the Korean Navy, suffered a crushing defeat in the Battle of Hansan and then switched its combat posture to a safe defensive strategy. Let's look at Yi Sun-sin's evaluation of the Battle of Hansan. The following sentence contains a quote from *Jingbirok* written by Yu Seong-ryong that appropriately expresses the significance of the Battle of Hansan Island.

*The enemy had planned to join forces by land and sea and move up to the west, but their plan was failed by the victory at the Battle of Hansan*

*Island, which resulted in losing one of their arms.*

*Although the enemy occupied Pyeongyang, they were unable to advance any further. Therefore, in Korea, we secured the coastal areas from Jeolla and Chungcheong to Hwanghae and Pyongyang, which allowed us to achieve prosperity by supplying military provisions and the delivering orders. All of this is undoubtedly the achievement of the great Yi Sun-sin's victory. Ah! How could it have been possible without the help of heaven?*

G.A. Ballard, a British naval historian, praised Admiral Yi Sun-sin's *Hakikjin* maneuver during the Battle of Hansan Island, saying:

*He turned his entire fleet 180 degrees by tacking a big turn and attacked the Japanese pursuing fleet. A non-expert might think this maneuver is simple, but even naval experts would judge that such a move is only possible for a highly skilled fleet.*

*This turning operation was able to sink many of the enemy's vessels. With this naval victory, Japan's ambition to invade China ended abruptly. This was all thanks to the brilliant strategic expertise of the great Korean naval commander. This is a unique and unprecedented achievement in the history of naval warfare worldwide.*

H.G. Hulbert, a historian, described the Battle of Hansan Island as *Korea's Salami*s. *It was a death sentence for Hideyoshi's invasion of Korea, and it destroyed the plans of the Ming Dynasty conquest that Toyotomi Hideyoshi had planned.*

## The Battle of Angolpo

On July 7, the Japanese naval forces under Admiral Kuki and Admiral Kato, following the Wakisaka fleet, set sail from Busan with around 40 vessels and spent a day at Gadeok Island on July 8. On July 9, they arrived at Angolpo, where vessels like Adakebune and Sekibune anchored outside the harbor, and smaller vessels anchored inside. Admiral Kuki Yoshitaka was a distinguished naval commander who had made significant contributions to naval battles and had become the lord of three provinces. Kato Yoshitaka joined the military at 16 and showed great courage in various battles. Kuki was Japan's top naval commander, responsible for designing and constructing the main battlefront known as the Adake warship.

On July 10, 1592, during the Angolpo naval battle, he barely escaped when Admiral Yi Sun-sin's fleet attacked the Japanese Navy. Angolpo, located near Busan, had a narrow and shallow entrance. Admiral Yi Sun-sin's combined fleet achieved a great victory at the Battle of Hansan, and they anchored inside Geonnaeryang that night. The next day, on July 9, the Korean fleet set sail from their anchorage and while heading towards Gadeok Island, they received a report late in the afternoon from the scout ship that *"the enemy's fleet of about 40 vessels is anchored at Angolpo."*

Admiral Yi Sun-sin intended to attack the enemy. However, due to the fading light and worsening weather, he anchored in Oncheonryang, located northwest of Geoje, and prepared for the operation. In the early morning of July 10, the fleet set sail towards Angolpo. Admiral Yi Sun-sin instructed as follows:

*First, Admiral Yi Eok-gi's fleet is to block the enemy's follow-up support fleet outside Angolpo. When the battle starts at Angolpo, some of the fleet will remain stationed outside for maritime surveillance, and the main fleet will join. Second, Admiral Yi Sun-sin's fleet will form a crane formation (Hakikjin) in the open sea of Angolpo and enter the entrance to Angolpo. Third, Admiral Won Gyun's fleet will follow behind Admiral Yi Sun-sin's fleet.*

Chapter II. Glorious Naval Battles of Admiral Yi Sun-sin    123

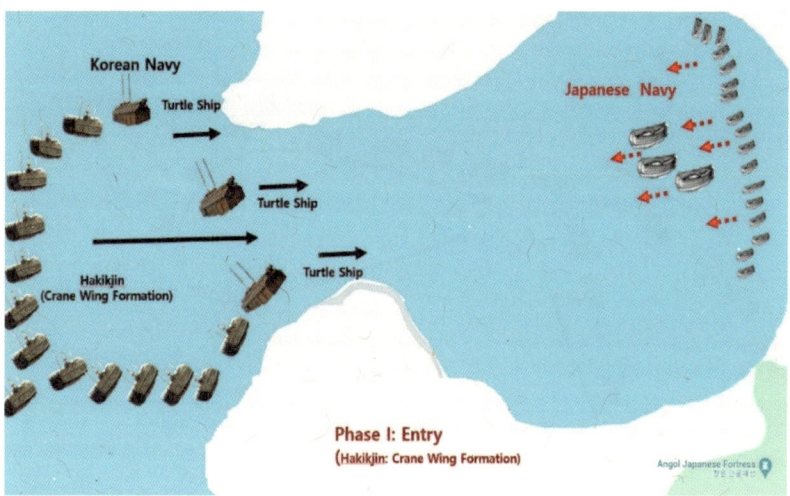

Figure 25: The Phase I (Entry to Angolpo) Situation Map of the Battle of Angolpo

Admiral Yi Sun-sin commanded the Jeolla Left navy and approached Angolpo. The enemy had 42 vessels, with 21 large vessels, 15 medium vessels, and 6 small vessels. Among them, three-level pavilion-style 1 large ship and two-level pavilion style 2 vessels were anchored at the very front facing the outside. Angolpo was so shallow that the land would be exposed when the tide went out. Also, there was insufficient sea space to form the *Hakikjin* formation and enter the port.

Accordingly, Yi Sun-sin's fleet attempted to lure the enemy into the open sea by entering the port in a column-line formation instead of the *Hakikjin* formation. However, the enemy was not fooled because they had been deceived by the Korean fleet's deceptive tactic at the Battle of Hansan a day earlier.

The enemy did not come out and instead attacked with guns and arrows from hiding. Because it was unavoidable, Yi Sun-sin ordered several captains to take turns going in and out and attacking each other.

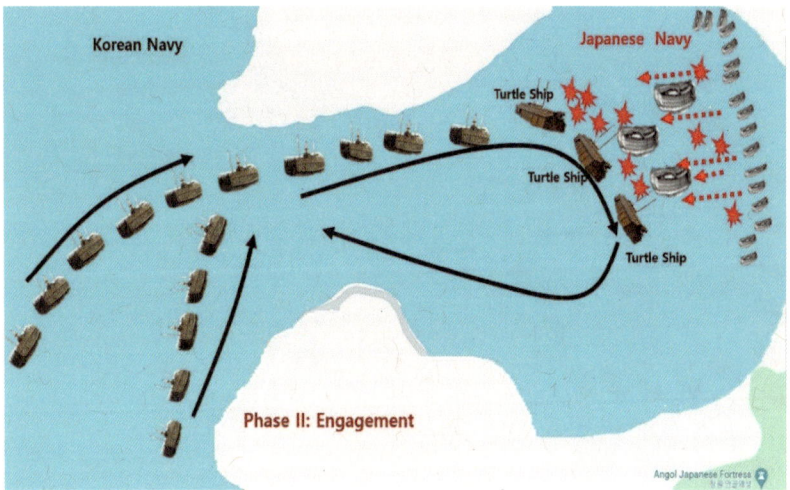

Figure 26: The Phase II (Engagement) Situation Map of the Battle of Angolpo

When the battle began, Admiral Yi Eok-gi's fleet joined in, and the Joint Fleet spent the entire day attacking the enemy vessels with various types of artillery fire. As a result, most of the enemy's vessels were burnt or destroyed.

Yi Sun-sin's attack method was as follows: First, the Turtle Ship was charged first and attacked the vessels at close range.

The Turtle Ship charged into the enemy fleet and mainly destroyed the hulls of enemy vessels. Next, the Panokseon captains took turns going in and out of the enemy vessels, killing the soldiers on them and mainly attacking the hulls of the enemy vessels with their weapons.

All day long, the Korean fleet approached the enemy fleet in column formation and fired large and small arrows from large vessels such as *Cheonja, Jija, and Hyeonja*, and the enemy's response was fierce. The enemy fleet's vessels were almost destroyed and most of the crew members were killed. During the battle, the Japanese soldiers moved the wounded to small boats, and when most of the vessels were destroyed, all surviving enemies fled to land. In the evening, Yi Sun-sin sailed to the open sea and spent the night without destroying several enemy vessels. He did not destroy all of the enemy vessels because he was concerned that the remaining enemies would harm the Korean people around Angolpo, so it was a strategic measure to open the enemy's retreat route. The next day, when Admiral Yi's fleet entered Angolpo and checked on the area, they found that the remnants of the defeated soldiers had fled at night on the remaining vessels.

There were signs that the enemy had gathered their dead in 12 locations on Angolpo land and burned them before fleeing from the area. Admiral Yi led the fleet at midnight, passed Hansan Island on the 12th, and reached Yeosu on the 13th. The combined fleet broke up there, and each group went back to its own base.

Regarding the Battle of Angolpo, the Japanese record *Goryeoseon Jeongi* states as follows:

*The fleets of Kuki and Kato went to Gadeok Island on the 7th of July, then anchored at Dangdo (Geoje Island) on the 8th. On the 9th, an enemy fleet (Korean fleet) of about 100 vessels attacked, and it seemed like it was raining arrows and cannon fire. Our side also fired cannons and there were casualties on both sides. The battle lasted from 8 AM to 6 PM, but we couldn't destroy the enemy vessels because they were all covered in iron. The enemy used iron-tipped rods for their fire attacks and shot them from close range, so our commanders on the deck were in grave danger.*

The vessels covered in iron refer to Turtle Ships, and the iron-tipped rods attached to long sticks refer to various types of bullets fired from cannons. *Goryeoseon Jeongi* records that Korea's Turtle Ship approached 5-9 meters away and fired its guns, destroying the Japanese battleship. In this battle, the Korean Navy destroyed 42 Japanese vessels.

## Outcomes and Significance of the 3rd Campaign

During the Battle of Hansan and Angolpo in the third campaign, the Korean Navy's combined fleet destroyed over 100 Japanese vessels. It inflicted heavy casualties on thousands of Japanese soldiers. While the Korean Navy didn't lose any of its vessels, they did suffer 19 fatalities and 124 injuries. This vital victory allowed the Korean Navy to control the southern coastal waters, except for the Busan area, hindering the Japanese Navy's ability to expand further west. Admiral Yi Sun-sin's brilliant *Hakikjin* tactic, used at the Battle of Hansan Island, played a vital role in this victory against the Japanese Navy. Following their crushing defeat at Hansan Island, the Japanese Navy altered its strategy. They began docking at ports and adopted a more defensive approach, the Fortress fleet strategy. In contrast, the Korean Navy gained confidence from their third naval campaign victory, believing they could win any battle they engaged in.

# The 4th Campaign: The Battle of Busanpo

### Background of the Battle

Unlike the Korean army, which had been losing one battle after another since the outbreak of the Japanese Invasion of Korea, the Korean Navy led by Admiral Yi Sun-sin won the naval battles of Okpo, Happo, and Jeokjinpo in its first campaign In addition, Yi Sun-sin's Jeolla Left Naval Force and Yi Eok-gi's Jeolla Right Naval Force won the second campaign (Battles of Sacheon, Dangpo, Danghangpo, and Yulpo).

When the Japanese fleet was defeated in the first and second campaigns, Toyotomi Hideyoshi reevaluated the capabilities of the Korean fleet and launched a strong counterattack in the Battle of Hansando, but he was defeated again. Because of this, the Japanese Navy limited the area of fleet activity to ports and sea areas and switched to defensive strategies to avoid naval battles. Meanwhile, the Korean Navy expanded its naval power to the vicinity of Gadeokdo in the Gyeongsang sea area through the first, second, and third campaigns and victories in naval battles. Still, there was a possibility that the main fleet of the Japanese Navy encamped in Busan appeared on the southern coast at any time and attempted to advance west.

Figure 27: The 4th Campaign Route of the Korean Navy (Battle of Busanpo)

Therefore, the Korean Navy attempted to attack and annihilate the enemy's heartland stationed in Busan. The expedition to Busan was a big adventure for the Korean Navy. This was a significant incident similar to the current Korean fleet combat vessel departing from the Republic of Korea Naval Operations Command sailing a long distance to the Philippine Strait and engaging in a naval battle with the enemy.

Let's look at this in terms of time and space. The sea route from Haenam, Jeolla Province, where the headquarters of Yi Eok-gi's navy, which participated in the war as the main unit of the Joint Fleet, is located, is approximately 320 km from Busan. This is a 60-hour cruise at an average speed of 3 knot (approximately 5.5 km per hour). If the average sailing speed of a modern destroyer class is 15 knots (about 27 km per hour), the 60-hour cruise is 1,620 km.

It is no different from the situation in which the Republic of Korea Navy, departing from the current Korean Naval Operations Command, engages in a fleet decisive battle with the enemy in the Philippine

Strait.

Assuming that a decisive battle must be fought against the enemy in Philippine waters, will it be possible to gather all the combat vessels currently in the Republic of Korea Navy and fight a naval battle? At the time, the great expedition to Busan was possible because of the great fighting spirit of the Korean naval commanders, including Yi Sun-sin.

## Processing and Engagement of the Battle

Admiral Yi Sun-sin requested Yi Eok-gi, commander of the Jeolla Right Naval Forces in Haenam, to allow the entire fleet to join the Jeolla Left Naval Base in Yeosu, by the end of July. Yi Eok-gi's fleet gathered in the seas off Yeosu on August 1st. Yi Sun-sin met with Yi Eok-gi and explained his strategic plan, requesting cooperation. Yi Eok-gi had complete trust in Yi Sun-sin's loyalty, leadership, judgment, tactics, and character, and readily agreed to cooperate. Seeing the strong friendship between the two commanders, the officers and soldiers of the two fleets also became united and worked in perfect harmony. After completing 23 days of combined fleet training, they set sail from Yeosu on August 24th at 4 pm and continued sailing at night. When they reached Mojarangpo, off the coast of Samcheonpo, on August 25th, a thick fog had set in, making it impossible to see. They anchored for a while, and when thefog lifted, they weighed anchor and headed for Saryang, where they met Admiral Won Gyun.

On the night of August 25th, the three commanders, Yi Sun-sin, Yi Eok-gi, and Won Gyun, held strategy meeting. At sunset on August 26th, the combined fleet of 173 vessels (81 Panokseon and 92 Hhyeopseon: small ship) passed Tongyeong Dunduk and crossed the Gyeonnaeryang secretly at midnight. On August 27th, they passed Geoje Chilcheonryang and anchored at Seowonpo at sunset. The combined fleet mainly used night maneuvers during this campaign to avoid detection by the enemy. Yi Sun-sin felt a heavy responsibility as a fleet commander as he approached the enemy's stationed waters. On this day, he recorded his troubled feelings in his diary as follows:

*I crossed Jepo at sunset and arrived at Seowonpo. It was already well past 11 p.m., the west wind was cold, and the waves were rough. A scout from the Gyeongsang navy came and reported, the enemies in Goseong, Changwon, and Jinhae retreated on the 24th and 25th of this month.*

On the morning of August 28th, the combined fleet set sail and conducted a search operation while sailing towards the Gimhae river. When they reached Gugokpo, Jeong Keut-dol came and said, *"I was captured by the Japanese but escaped. All the enemy war vessels anchored in the Gimhae river for the past three days have disappeared."* Yi Sun-sin ordered the main fleet to hide northwest of Gadeokdo. He also ordered Eo Young-dam to lie in wait outside Gadeokdo, while sending scouts to the Gimhae and Yangsan areas.

At around 4 pm, the scouts returned and reported, *"we could not find anything except 4 small enemy vessels sailing away from the mouth of the Gimhae river."* When the first rooster crowed on August 29, the Joint Fleet raised anchor and sailed into the Gimhae and Nakdong rivers.

When they reached the river mouth, about 30 Japanese soldiers boarded 4 large vessels and 2 small vessels and headed to Yangsan. On their way out, they saw the Korean fleet and abandoned the ship and fled to land. After burning six enemy vessels, Yi Sun-sin returned to Gadeokdo Island and spent the night.

That night, Yi Sun-sin called Yi Eok-gi, Won Gyun, and Jeong Geol and said as follows:

*The enemy navy' main fleet gathers in Busan. We can only win this war by destroying this enemy and stopping their base in Busan, which is the Japanese Navy's main point.*

He stressed how vital the mission to Busan was. When the rooster first crowed on September 1, the combined fleet raised anchor and sailed to Busan.

Figure 28: The Engagements of August 29, 1592, Prior to the Battle of Busanpo (Phase I)

When the Korean fleet passed Molundae and reached Hwajungumi Port around 8 a.m., there were five enemy vessels, and Admiral Jeong Geol destroyed them all. The Korean fleet destroyed 24 vessels, including 8 enemy vessels off Dadaepo, 9 enemy vessels off Seopyeongpo, and 2 enemy vessels off Jeolyeongdo. Yi Sun-sin dispatched an intelligence ship to Busan to find out the enemy situation, and this ship returned and reported,

*About 500 enemy vessels are lined up and anchored at the foot of the*

mountain east of the pier, and four of them are coming out from the far east of Choryang.

Upon hearing about the presence of the enemy's large fleet, several commanders and soldiers were surprised and excited. In response, Admiral Yi Sun-sin summoned Yi Eok-gi and Won Gyun, and with unwavering determination, he resolutely stated as follows:

*Though our forces are at a three-to-one numerical disadvantage regarding the number of vessels, if we do not engage the enemy now and retreat, they will undoubtedly underestimate our naval strength. Even if it means fighting to the last man, we cannot go back without a fight.*

Yi Sun-sin expected that his forces would be outnumbered and that the enemy fleet would not engage in open battle, but would rather attack from both land and sea, supported by their land fortifications.

Figure 29: The Situation Map of the Battle of Busanpo on September 1, 1592 (Phase II)

Chapter II. Glorious Naval Battles of Admiral Yi Sun-sin    133

He understood that his forces would be vulnerable at sea and that a fierce artillery battle would be crucial to determine the outcome. Yi Sun-sin gave the order to attack.by. raising his signal flag and sounding the war drum. The Korean fleet formed a long line and stayed out of the enemy's firing range while launching a powerful bombardment with their cannons. The vanguard of the formation was led by the brave and skilled commanders of the Jeolla Left Navy, including Jeong Yun, Yi Eon-ryang, Yi Sun-sin himself, Kwon Jun, and Shin Ho.

The enemy fleet was anchored in three locations along the coast under the eastern hill of Busanjin Fortress. They had 470 vessels of various sizes, including large, medium, and small vessels. As the Korean fleet approached, the enemy soldiers on board the vessels, inside the fortress, and on the hills joined forces. They set up six camps on the hill and fired muskets, cannons, and arrows like rain, without leaving the protection of their land fortifications. The Korean fleet continued to approach the enemy while firing all sorts of cannons and various

Figure 30: The Situation Map of the Battle of Busanpo on September 1, 1592 (Phase III)

weapons. Yi Sun-sin recognized the importance of prioritizing the destruction of the enemy vessels and ordered his commanders to focus their attacks on them before engaging the land forces. The smoke from the cannons fired by the 600 or so vessels and the enemy land forces covered the sky over Busan Bay, and the sound of the cannons shook the heavens and the earth. The fierce artillery battle between the two sides continued for the whole day.

In this battle, about 100 enemy vessels were destroyed, and a large number of enemy soldiers were killed or wounded. Yi Sun-sin led his fleet back to Gadeokdo Island as the sun set. The Korean fleet suffered damage to several vessels but did not lose a single one. There were 6 deaths and 25 injuries. The 25 injured include four injured crew members of the Turtle Ship. The significant loss in this battle was the loss of Admiral Jeong Un, the brave and skilled commander. Jeong Un was 50 years old at the time. Yi Sun-sin lamented, *"The country has lost its right arm."* Yi Sun-sin anchored near Gadeokdo Island for one night and disbanded the combined fleet. He then returned to his headquarters in Yeosu on September 2nd and conducted a comprehensive assessment of the battle results.

**Achievements and Significance of the Campaign**

The 4th campaign involved several battles, including the Battle of Busanpo, as well as engagements at Jangnimpo, Hwajungumi, Dadaepo, Seopyeongpo, Jeolyeongdo (Yeongdo), and Choryang while en route to Busanpo. Over 130 enemy vessels were destroyed during the 4th campaign, including over 100 at Busanpo. The Korean Navy participated in this battle with 82 vessels, and the Jeolla Left Navy suffered 6 deaths and 25 injuries, including the loss of Nokdo *Manho* Jeong Un. The Battle of Busanpo provides another glimpse of Yi Sun-sin's masterful use of combined Turtle Ship and Panokseon tactics. Upon receiving Yi's command, the Turtle Ships led by Captain Yi Eon-ryang charged at the enemy fleet, devastating bombardment from their cannons and disabling several large vessels.

Following this initial assault, the remaining Korean vessels formed a long line, resembling a giant snake, and bombarded the enemy with cannons and arrows. Employing a hit-and-run strategy, the Korean vessels evaded the artillery fire from the Japanese land forces and engaged in fierce close-quarters combat, destroying over 100 enemy vessels. However, this intense battle came at a cost. Admiral Jeong Un was killed instantly by enemy gunfire, and Turtle Ship and Panokseon crew members were wounded. As mentioned earlier, the 4th campaign was the first expeditionary naval battle experienced by the Korean Navy, including the Jeolla Right Navy, headquartered in Haenam, Jeolla Province. Nevertheless, the Korean Navy demonstrated its might by attacking the main force of the Japanese Navy, demoralizing the enemy and significantly hindering their westward advance strategy. The Japanese Navy also experienced the limitations of naval attacks by anchoring in ports to avoid naval battles and responding from land fortifications. Although the need for Joint operations with the army was crucial, such cooperation was not achieved.

## Chapter III

Yi Sun-sin's Battles and Preparations
for Future Naval Warfare:
During China-Japan Negotiations
in 1593-1596

# The 5th Campaign: The Battle of Ungpo

**King's Order and Preparations for the Naval Expedition**

In January 1593, they planned to retake Seoul after the Joint Korean-Chinese forces recaptured Pyongyang on January 9 and Kaeseong on January 19. At this time, Admiral Yi Sun-sin received an order from the royal court. The main points of the king's order were as follows:

*The military forces of China have recaptured Pyongyang and are pursuing the enemy, who are fleeing one after another. The vicious enemy will definitely retreat to Seoul. Admiral Yi is to lead the naval forces and combine their strength to crush and completely eliminate the enemy, ensuring that not even a single plank of their vessels remain.*

After he received this order, Admiral Yi Sun-sin prepared to destroy the enemy fleet stationed in Busan harbor. He formed a Joint Fleet by making a prior agreement with the Jeolla and Gyeongsang naval commanders, and set sail. On February 6, 1593, he departed from Yeosu port with the Jeolla naval fleet and anchored at Saryangdo, where he spent the night. The next day, on February 7, he joined forces with Gyeongsang naval commander Won Gyun at Gyeonnaeryang.

On February 8, they received information from Won Gyun that

Chapter III. Yi Sun-sin's Battles and Preparations for Future Naval Warfare

*"a powerful enemy naval force is stationed in Ungpo (Ungcheon),"* and decided to attack the enemy fleet there. Yi Sun-sin aimed to prioritize attacking the enemies in Ungpo (Ungcheon) because Ungpo was strategically located on the route to Busan, which was the main base of the Korean Navy's adversaries. Later that day, the Jeolla naval fleet led by Yi Eok-gi arrived with around 40 vessels at Gyeonnaeryang where Yi Sun-sin and Won Gyun were located. After forming a Joint Fleet, they moved to Oncheon Island (Chilcheon Island) and anchored there for the night. The next day, February 9, they planned to depart to attack the enemy, but heavy rain prevented them from doing so. Rain caused navigation problems and reduced the effectiveness of gunpowder due to humidity.

## Battles and Challenges at Ungpo (The naval battle and landing operations)

At that time, the Japanese Navy established a camp at Angolpo, Jepo, and Ungpo between the mouth of the Nakdong river and Jinhae, and stationed about 115 vessels and 10,000 navy soldiers on the coast below the camp to defend Busan and advance to the West Sea. As mentioned earlier, it was confirmed that the Japanese naval forces were re-encamping in the waters where they had retreated after being defeated in a naval battle by the Korean Joint Fleet. This situation has been repeated since the first deployment.

To attack the enemy at Ungpo, Yi Sun-sin led the Korean Joint Fleet on the morning of February 10th. He stationed the main force of the fleet at Songdo, which was about 2,700 m from the entrance of Ungpo Bay. The Korean Navy tried to lure the enemy fleet into the open sea by sending fast vessels into Ungpo Bay, but the enemy's war vessels didn't move. As night fell, the Korean Navy anchored the fleet

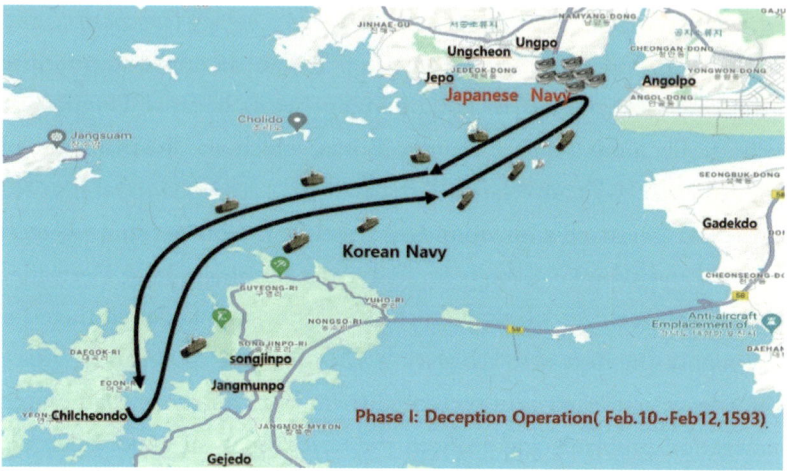

Figure 31: The Situation Map of the Lure and Deception of the Battle of Ungpo (Phase I)

at Songjinpo in the northern part of Geojedo. On February 11th, the weather was unfavorable, so Admiral Yi allowed the military to rest. Early in the morning of the 12th, Yi Sun-sin led the Korean Joint Fleet to the waters in front of Ungpo. He deployed several fast vessels to attack the enemy fleet and attempted to lure them out, but the enemy still remained within their coastal defenses.

That night, the Korean Joint Fleet moved to Chilcheondo. Due to unfavorable weather conditions, the Korean Navy couldn't engage in battle and focused on strategy meetings and military preparations at sea. On February 17th, Admiral Yi received an imperial command from King Seonjo with the message to annihilate every piece of the enemy's fleet without leaving a trace. On February 18th, at dawn, the Korean Navy departed from Chilcheondo, stationed the main fleet in the waters west of Gadeokdo, and appointed Kim Wan as the commander of a concealed fleet in front of Ungpo at Songdo.

When the Korean Navy deployed several fast vessels to attack the enemy at the entrance of Ungpo Bay, the Japanese, who had not seen

Chapter III. Yi Sun-sin's Battles and Preparations for Future Naval Warfare

Yi Sun-sin's leading fleet and Kim Wan's hidden traps, launched an attack on our fast vessels. Subsequently, Kim Wan's fleet concealed at Songdo, attacked and defeated the enemy. On that night, the Korean Joint Fleet anchored in Sahwarang (Changwon, Ungcheon) due to bade weather conditions, and they remained at sea until the 19th. On the following day, the 20th, the Korean Navy engaged in battle with the enemy. However, as the wind blew fiercely and it became difficult to control warvessels due to the collision between our own forces, Yi Sun-sin decided to halt the battle and return to Sojinpo. During this engagement, four of Korean Navy's war vessels collided and were damaged, possibly due to the inevitable sea conditions that affected the navigational capabilities of the vessels.

Figure 32: The Situation Map of the Landing Operation and Close Assault (Phase II)

Despite the four successive attacks by the Korean Joint naval fleet on February 10th, 12th, 18th, and 20th, the Japanese Navy adopted a strategy to avoid full-scale naval battles. The Joint Fleet headquarters thoroughly analyzed the repeated battles at Ungpo and devised a new plan. Since the Japanese Navy stationed itself securely in coastal fortress and avoided coming out to open waters, the Korean fleet decided that a combined land and sea operation was necessary to annihilate the enemy. After careful consideration, Admiral Yi Sun-sin carried out a solo naval landing operation. On the 22nd, the Korean fleet set out again and initiated the operation in the Ungpo area. Admiral Yi Sun-sin employed a deception strategy, deploying Korean landing forces on the coasts of Ungpo where enemy war vessels were stationed on both sides, making it appear as if they were planning to attack the enemy from both land and sea.

While the enemy was confused, the Korean main fleet advanced to Ungpo Harbor and defeated the enemy. During this battle, some of the Korean vessels inadvertently entered shallow waters and came under enemy fire but were rescued.

On the 22nd, Admiral Yi Sun-sin left strong criticism in his records for not rescuing his subordinates, specifically the underlings who were surrounded and attacked by the enemy at that time. While there is no specific record of how many enemy vessels were destroyed during this engagement, it can be inferred that many enemy vessels were annihilated, as noted in Admiral Yi Sun-sin's diary when he mentioned that the Joint Korean Fleet *nearly annihilated the enemy war vessels*. The Joint Korean Fleet returned to Songjinpo that night, stayed there until the 23rd, and then attempted to transfer to Yeongdeungpo on the morning of the 24th. However, due to unfavorable sea conditions, they returned to Chilcheondo.

The strong winds persisted until the 27th, so they remained at Chilcheondo. On the morning of the 29th, they moved to Gadeokdo to engage the enemy in Ungpo, but the enemy did not respond. They anchored at Sahwarang after nightfall but had to return to Chilcheondo due to unfavorable sea conditions.

Chapter III. Yi Sun-sin's Battles and Preparations for Future Naval Warfare 143

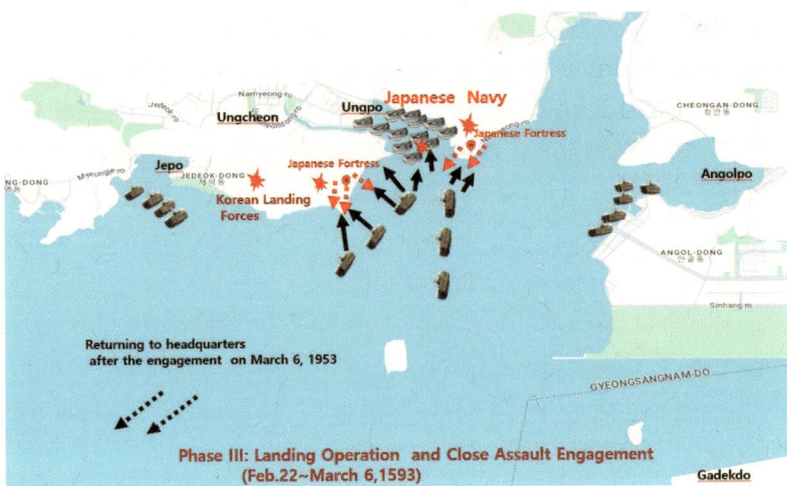

Figure 33: The Situation Map of the Landing Operation and Close Assault (Phase III)

Until March 5th, they stayed in Chilcheondo and devised a plan to attack the Japanese enemy in Uugpo. On March 6th, they set out and fired arrows and bows indiscriminately at the enemy troops on the ground, causing numerous casualties. In this operation, they used *Bigeokjincheonroe* to attack the enemy on the mountainsides. Unlike cannons loaded on war vessels and used to defeat enemy vessels, these *Bigeokjincheonroe* exploded on the ground. This was the first time Admiral Yi Sun-sin's fleet had employed such a weapon since the outbreak of the Imjinwaeran. The *Bigeokjincheonroe* is type of time bomb first created by Yi Jang-son during the reign of King Seonjo of Joseon . It was used in both land and naval battles during the Imjinwaeran. Records of its use against enemy war vessels in naval battles are difficult to find. Nevertheless, there is a record of it being fired at Japanese forces on land near the entrance of the harbor during the Battle of Ungpo. Even considering the low accuracy of naval guns in the battle at the time, it is presumed that if the target of the strike was not a ship at sea but on land, the projectile would have exploded and had a significant effect in killing people around it. For this reason, Yi Sun-sin fired *Bigeokjincheonroe* at the enemy camp midway up the mountain and killed many enemies. During this battle, they also rescued a Korean woman who was captured as a prisoner. After the engagement, the Joint Fleet returned to Chilcheondo, spent the night, and arrived at Hansando on March 8th.

They had departed from Yeosu Port on February 6th and formed a Joint Fleet at Geonnaeryang on February 7th. After a month of battling the Japanese, they returned to Hansando, where the naval headquarters is located.

## Surveillance Activities and Consideration on Farming

The Joint Korean Naval Fleet, since March 8th, primarily focused on maritime surveillance activities centered around Hansando while monitoring and scouting the Japanese naval forces remaining in Ungcheon. They were in a standoff with the enemy for approximately one month, but there were no actual engagements. As mentioned earlier, the Japanese naval forces avoided naval battles and established themselves on land. Admiral Yi Sun-sin requested the Korean army to attack the Japanese forces on land, but the army denied the request.

Meanwhile, the Korean naval forces, numbering around 40,000 people during their expedition, were mainly composed of people from coastal villages in Jeolla Province who were engaged in farming. Admiral Yi Sun-sin was aware of a labor shortage for agriculture in many villages because people from coastal villages were conscripted to fight. He understood that prolonging the conscription period could disrupt regular farming and cause critical issues securing provisions if the autumn harvest were affected. Under this situation, Admiral Yi

Sun-sin had to determine the timing of returning the troops. In his report on the results of the Battle of Ungpo to King Seonjo, Yi Sun-sin attached the following situation. The present is the farming season, and all the 40,000 naval troops in the left and right regions of Jeolla Province are farmers. If we completely abandon farming, we won't be able to hope for a good harvest in the fall again. Our country's provisions all come from this region alone. However, no one is left in the Jeolla Province due to the transportation of provisions, even the elderly and the weak. Spring has come, but no one is in the fields to do the farming.

After sending the above proposal, Yi Sun-sin disbanded the Joint Fleet on April 3, 1593, and returned to Yeosu, where the headquarters of the Jeolla Left Naval Forces were located, two months after dispatch.

## Characteristics and Significance of the Campaign

Admiral Yi Sun-sin's 5th Expedition (Ungpo Landing Operation) took place just five months after the Battle of Busanpo in 1592. In the previous year, the Korean Joint Fleet led by Yi Sun-sin had achieved significant victories over the Japanese at the battles of Hansan Island and Busanpo. However, the Japanese forces regrouped in Busan and expanded their presence to the nearby islands and even the waters near Hansan Island. Admiral Yi Sun-sin received orders for another expedition despite the challenging circumstances in this new situation. The Ungpo Battle differed from previous naval battles as the Japanese forces avoided direct naval confrontations and engaged in land-based warfare instead. The Japanese tactics remained unchanged despite repeated attacks by the Korean Joint Fleet. In an attempt to defeat a passive enemy, Admiral Yi Sun-sin proposed a joint operation with the Korean ground forces, but it was not realized. Therefore, he employed a deceptive strategy, making it seem like he would conduct a naval landing operation independently.

The Korean Navy used a pretended strategy to make it appear that they were preparing for a land and sea attack, causing the Japanese forces on both land and sea to panic. The Korean naval forces attacked the Japanese troops on the hills on both sides of the harbor with cannons and bows. In addition, for the first time in a naval battle since the Japanese Invasion of Korea outbreak, *Bigeokjincheonroes* were dropped to kill the enemy at the foot of the mountain.

During the 5th Expedition, in seven persistent battles, the Korean Navy adopted an offensive strategy against the Japanese forces, who mainly defended on land. The Japanese suffered significant losses, with dozens of their vessels destroyed and over 2,500 casualties. The Korean naval forces also sustained damage, with two of their vessels being affected and 380 casualties. This was the most significant loss suffered by the Korean Navy in their encounters with the Japanese. Unlike previous naval battles, the Korean Joint Fleet attempted to repeatedly defeat the Japanese ground forces during their extended two-month deployment in Ungcheon. Admiral Yi Sun-sin and the Korean naval forces faced significant pressure due to their mission on the orders of King Seonjo. Despite numerous attempts, the results were not as substantial as in previous naval battles, partly because of the passive defense strategy adopted by the Japanese forces on land and the failure to coordinate a joint operation with the Korean ground forces. Additionally, during the extended expedition covering a vast area from the waters off Jeolla Province to Gyeongsang Province, strategic weaknesses of the Korean Navy were exposed.

Most of the Korean naval forces were based in Jeolla Province, and given their geographic distance, they were forced to conduct expeditions to the waters off Gyeongsang Province. Admiral Yi Sun-sin recognized the need for centralized command and forward bases in the Gyeongsang waters, given the frequent enemy activities and the necessity to control enemy movements along the southern coast, preventing their westward expansion. The naval battle and landing operations in Ungpo marks a significant chapter in Admiral Yi Sun-sin's naval campaigns, where he faced new challenges and devised innovative strategies to adapt to changing enemy tactics and situations.

# The 6th and 7th Campaigns: The Battle of Danghangpo and the Jangmunpo Landing Operation

**Yi Sun-sin Becomes the Supreme Naval Commander**

As mentioned earlier, Admiral Yi Sun-sin, learning from the lessons of the Ungpo Naval Battle, aimed to improve the strategic challenges of long-term expeditionary warfare. On June 21, 1593, he established a forward base on Hansan Island and stationed his fleet there. When there were operations in the Gyeongsang waters, they would embark on expeditions from long distant locations like Haenam in Jeolla Right Navy and Yeosu in Jeolla Left Navy, engaging in combat with the enemy. After each operation, they had to sail a long way back to their main base.

The establishment of a forward base on Hansan Island was done to reduce the extended travel time of the warvessels and the fatigue accumulated by the soldiers, which significantly impacted their operational efficiency. Additionally, by moving the main forces' deployment area forward, they could not only take pressure on the main base of the Japanese naval forces in Busan but also aim to control the strategic effects of entering the Gyeongsang waters.

After relocating the forward base from Yeosu to Hansan Island, the Korean Navy secured the defense line along the Geonnaeryang route used by the Japanese naval forces. Previously, the Japanese naval forces freely invaded the coastal areas of Gyeongsang by passing through Geonnaeryang, causing suffering to the Korean people. On the day they moved to Hansan Island, Admiral Yi Sun-sin expressed his feelings in his diary as follows:

*As the autumn breeze enters the sea, the wanderer' feeling flutter. Moonlight shines on the vessels, and the minds clear, amidst the sleepless night, roosters crow.*

On August 15, 1593(Yi Sun-sin received his letter of appointment on October 1), the court established *Tongjesa* system to integrate command over the navy in the Chungcheong, Jeolla, and Gyeongsang Provinces. Admiral Yi Sun-sin was appointed as the first commander. Until then, there were many challenges in organizing Joint Fleets and commanding in war. This system continued for 303 years until King Gojong's reign in 1894, with 208 commanders serving during that time. At the end of 1593, Commander Yi Sun-sin began commanding a powerful Joint Fleet of about 250 vessels, including 90 vessels of Yi Sun-shin's fleet, 90 vessels of Yi Eok-gi's fleet, and 40 vessels of Won Gyun's.

In particular, even in difficult times after the Imjinwaeran, the Korean fleet quickly built war vessels. Notably, that the war vessels under the command of Won Gyun, the Commander of Gyeongsang Right Navy, who lost most of his vessels when the Imjinwaeran broke out, also came to possess around 40 war vessels.

## The 6th Campaign: The Battle of Danghangpo

In 1594, as the war entered its third year, there were frequent negotiations for a peace settlement between China and Japan due to changing circumstances. As a result, there were no large-scale battles. In this situation, Korea focused on retaliating against the Japanese and recovering their territory, but Korea did not have the strength to annihilate the enemy. Toyotomi Hideyoshi instructed the Japanese forces to defend critical strongholds along the southeastern coast of Korea, including 11 major fortresses and 7 smaller ones. They were positioned in locations such as Busan in the east, Soseongpo, Imrangpo, Gijang, Dongrae, Gimhae, Gadeokdo, Angolpo, Ungcheon, and Jangmunpo in the west. The Japanese carried out plundering acts on land and along the coast. During this time, Admiral Yi Sun-sin, *Tongjesa*, was on Hansan Island, strengthening his forces and military training, establishing an information network, and blocking the enemy's westward advance into the sea.

Then, on the 3rd of March in 1594 at 2:00 PM, information was received from a person named Je Han-guk, who had been observing the situation from Goseong, saying:

> *This morning, ten large enemy vessels, 14 medium-sized vessels, and seven small vessels left Yeongdeungpo. Among them, 21 large vessels headed towards Goseong, seven went towards Jinhae, and the remaining three moved towards Jeodo.*

Admiral Yi instructed Yi Eok-gi and Won Gyun to set out for battle, and at 8:00 PM that evening, the Joint Fleet set sail. Around 10:00 PM, the Joint Fleet reached its destination, and they formulated the following operational plan.

First, deploy 20 war vessels in Geonnaeryang to prevent the enemy's attack on Hansan Island headquarters. Second, select a few elite war vessels from the three provinces and, under the command of Jobangjang and Yeo Yeong-dam, engage in battles to defeat the Japanese

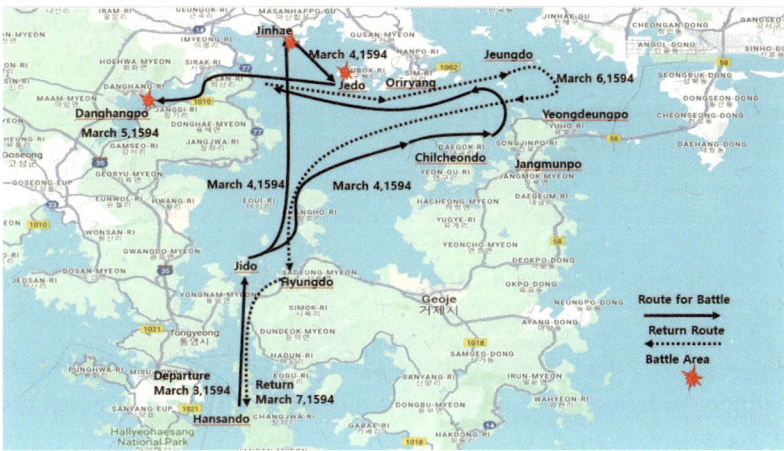

Figure 34: The 6th Campaign Route of the Korean Navy (2nd Battle of Danghangpo)

naval warvessels in Danghangpo and Oriryang. Third, the main force of the Joint Fleet will create a battle formation (Hakikjin) in the waters of Jangmunpo and Yeongdeungpo, in front of the enemy's positions. When the enemy's war vessels come out, encircle and annihilate them and block their escape route. Fourth, contact Sunbyeonsa (a special envoy who patrolled the borders on military duty by royal command during the Joseon dynasty) Yi Bin in Uiryeong and annihilate the enemy retreating to the land. Each commander followed these operational plans. Under the command of Yeo Yeong-dam, his fleet encountered and swiftly destroyed six warvessels from at Jinhae. His forces also set fire to two enemy vessels near Jeodo.

As Yeo Yeong-dam continued to lead his fleet towards Danghangpo, the Korean Navy found 21 enemy warvessels anchored there. Upon seeing the Korean naval war vessels, the enemy abandoned their vessels and retreated to the land. Yeo Yeong-dam reported the situation to *Tongjesa* Yi Sun-sin once again requested General Yi Bin to attack the enemy naval forces from the land. Yeo Yeong-dam attempted to attack the enemy, but the low tide prevented the ship from approaching the enemy. As night fell, the Korean Navy blocked the entrance to Danghangpo. On the following day, the 5th, Yeo Yeong-dam entered Danghangpo with the high tide and successfully defeated all 21 enemy vessels. Yeo Yeong-dam reported the operational progress to *Tongjesa* at 2:00 PM.

The Korean ground forces that Yi Sun-sin expected did not join the fight, and the retreating enemy forces on land could not be defeated. In this battle, the Joint Fleet destroyed 31 enemy vessels without suffering any damage or casualties. *Tongjesa* Yi Sun-sin led the Joint Fleet back to the base on Hansan Island on March 7.

## Geumtopaemun (Document Prohibiting the Conquest of Japan)

Admiral Yi Sun-sin received *Geumtopamun* sent by Chinese Seonyudosa Dam Chong-in on March 6 while returning to Hansan Island after winning the Battle of Danghangpo. The *Geumtopaemun* was a Chinese document stating that Korean troops should not attack the enemy because China and Japan were negotiating. On this day, Yi Sun-sin was so sick that it was difficult to even lie down. Yi Sun-sin was sick and had his staff write a reply, but the content was not appropriate. Yi Sun-sin, who was ill, barely woke up and wrote a reply to Dam jong-in and sent it by personal mail.

### A letter written by Yi Sun-sin to Dam Jong-in

*Korea's naval commander Yi Sun-sin took the time to write a reply to Seonyudosa Dam jong-in. It is a clear fact that the Japanese enemy started a war, led their soldiers across the sea, killed our innocent people, invaded Seoul and committed brutish acts. All public officials and citizens of Korea have anger built up in their bones and have pledged not to live under the same sky as these Japanese enemies.*

*- Omitted middle part -*

*Unexpectedly, I received the Geumtopaemun requested by Seonyudosa while returning to the base. After reading the text two or three times, I realized that your request was earnest. However, in the words of Geumtopaemun, 'Do not cause trouble in the Japanese forces unit.' However, the Japanese pirates are encamped in places such as Geoje, Ungcheon, Gimhae, and Dongrae in Gyeongsang Province. It's all our land, so what do you mean by telling us not to go near the Japanese army's camp?*

*You also told us to return to our hometown as soon as possible, but we had no way of knowing where our hometown was, and it was not we who raised the problem but the Japanese enemies. Also, the Japanese are so treacherous that I have never heard of them being faithful since ancient times. The vicious and cunning enemies have not ceased their cruel actions, have set up camp on the seashore, and are not retreating even as the years pass. They invade many places, murder, and plunder twice as much as the previous day, and have no intention of taking up their weapons and returning to Japan. Negotiating now is truly deception and lies. However, since it is difficult to go against your will, I will report this fact to the king and monitor Japan's movements for now. You should carefully examine the contents of this letter, and I hope you will help our enemies understand what it is to disobey Heaven's will and what it is to follow Heaven's will.*

After reading the letter, it is evident that Admiral Yi Sun-sin's sentiments reflect his strong determination and patriotism. He expresses a clear stance against Japan's brutal aggression and China's negotiations. Yi Sun-sin's words reveal his unwavering commitment to protect his homeland and its people. He firmly believes in fulfilling his duty to defend the nation. His letter underscores his unwavering sense of duty and faith in justice. Yi Sun-sin clearly understands his role and responsibility in the relationship between Korea and China, showing readiness to act devotedly to safeguard his country.

## Comparison of the 1st and 2nd Battles of Danghangpo

The 1st Battle of Danghangpo occurred during Admiral Yi Sun-sin's 2nd expedition on June 5, 1592. It was a decisive battle where the combined Korean fleet, led by Admiral Yi, attacked and surrounded the Japanese Navy at Danghangpo, effectively annihilating the Japanese forces. The tactics employed in the 1st Battle of Danghangpo were evaluated as similar to the *Hakikjin* formation.

The tactics in the 2nd Battle of Danghangpo differed from those in the 1st battle. In the 2nd battle, similar ambush tactics were used at the harbor entrance, but unlike the 1st battle, the Japanese Navy, while anchored, panicked and attempted to escape to the land. In response, the Korean Navy attacked and destroyed the Japanese vessels. Notably, some accounts and publications incorrectly claim that the *Hakikjin* formation was used to defeat the Japanese in the 2nd Battle of Danghangpo. According to Admiral Yi's records, the *Hakikjin* formation was actually used to threaten the enemy forces anchored at Yeongdeungpo and Jangmunpo to prevent Japanese rear support.

The 2nd Battle of Danghangpo was the first naval battle in which Yi Sun-sin commanded the Korean Navy with the authority of Joint commander. According to his diary records, he provided clear instructions, received reports, and effectively distributed the fleet, demonstrating a leadership style quite different from his previous Joint Fleet commander.

## The 7th Campaign: The Jangmunpo Landing Operation

### The Situation in Korea and King Seonjo's Hasty Dispatch Order

In 1594, the third year of the Japanese invasions of Korea, Korea was in a severe situation of securing food and military supplies due to poor harvests and epidemics since 1593. Moreover, the negotiations led by China and Japan have proceeded tediously and without conclusion.

As China's Lee Yeo-song returned to China and Yu Jeong was appointed as his successor, he even instructed the Korean military not to engage in combat with the Japanese army due to his popularity during the negotiations. At that time, Yu Jeong commanded about 5,000 Chinese soldiers in Korea but had no will to fight against the Japanese army.

Amidst all this, there was public opinion in the central government that General Kwon Yul should be replaced by Yi Won-ik, the Governor of Pyeongan Province, but this was not achieved. Even while fruitless negotiations between China and Japan were going on, the Japanese forces stationed in the castle in the coastal area of Gyeongsang Province were using defensive tactics. However, they were still plundering the surrounding people and frequently appearing around Geoje Island to provoke the Korean Navy.

In the situation where Admiral Yi Sun-sin had just concluded the Battle of Danghangpo and returned to the forward base in Hansan Island on March 7, 1594, he focused on monitoring the enemy's movements and emphasized training and education. To foster future military leaders, he established a special examination site on Hansan Island, conducting a two-day examination on April 7th and 8th to select 100 officers.

On the other hand, despite the Korean Joint Fleet in Hansando following their victory in the Battle of Danghangpo, the Japanese naval forces were actively stationed on Geojedo. They continued to make incursions into Ungcheon and Ungpo in the Jinhae area, gradually expanding their influence.

While the Korean naval forces were stationed at the forward base of Hansan Island, not far from Geojedo, and even after the 5th campaign, which attacked Ungcheon and Ungpo, the Japanese forces had established strongholds on land and continued their maritime expansions. Given these circumstances, the Korean naval forces realized that they had limitations in launching a counterattack with naval forces alone, necessitating Joint operations with the army.

The focus on strengthening defenses and fortifications at the forward base on Hansan Island after the 6th campaign was also driven by the realization that naval forces alone had their limitations in attacking the enemy. In early September 1594, King Seonjo sent a confidential directive to *Tongjesa* Yi Sun-sin, *Chechalsa* Yun Du-su, *Dowonsoo* Kwon Yul, expressing his dissatisfaction. The directive criticized that naval and land commanders were not to defeat the enemy but were instead merely looking at each other. In his diary, Admiral Yi Sun-sin expressed his frustration at the time. He mentioned that for the past three years, he had fought with other commanders at sea with the determination to die for their country.

*Now that the enemy is locked inside a strong castle, our troops cannot attack rashly. Moreover, if we know our enemy and know ourselves, we will not be in danger even if we fight a hundred times. I sit alone and think about the country's affairs, but there is no way to save the country. What should I do?*

This diary record reveals Admiral Yi Sun-sin's *deep devotion to his country and his profound frustration.*

As experienced in the Battle of Ungpo, the Japanese naval forces avoided direct naval confrontations, instead deciding on land warfare and taking refuge in fortifications. The Korean Navy faced difficulties in launching quick attacks due to this. Admiral Yi Sun-sin recognized that reckless naval attacks would be fruitless and put their own forces at risk. Consequently, he repeatedly requested Joint operations with the Korean army during battles like the one at Ungpo, but these pleas went unanswered. Unfortunately, King Seonjo, who did not grasp the realities on the ground, criticized the frontline commanders for their perceived inactivity and issued orders for ill-advised attacks. To command this operation, the government sent *Chechalsa* Yun Du-su to the field. At the time, *Chechalsa* could command *Tongjesa* Yi Sun-sin and General Kwon Yul. *Chechalsa* Yun Du-sul proposed a plan for a Joint landing operation to attack the enemy on Geoje Island. However, the king and his advisors opposed Yun Du-su's proposed Joint landing operation and, instead, ordered Admiral Yi Sun-sin to attack the Japanese forces stationed Yeongdeungpo in Geojedo.

### The Deployment Process of the Jangmunpo Landing Operation

The situation of the enemy in Geojedo was as follows. The distance between the enemy's strongholds, Yeongdeungpo and Jangmunpo, is approximately 6 km by land and about 8 km by sea, and they are adjacent to each other. About 1,600 enemy troops and 100 enemy vessels were stationed at Jangmunpo. The Japanese forces had placed obstacles made of rafts at the waterway entrance leading to Jangmunpo to obstruct the navigation of the Korean war vessels. They had also constructed fortifications on both sides of the waterway and installed cannons to fortify their defensive positions.

Yun Du-su moved to Suncheon, and Kwon Yul moved to Goseong in preparation for the operation, and they activated the frontline headquarters. On September 22, Admiral Yi Sun-sin received the operation plan from Kwon Yul. The operation commencement date was set for September 29. The Korean ground forces consisted of an irregular unit led by General Gwak Jae-woo and Kim Deok-ryeong, comprising 800 men, 140 men led by the commander of the Chungcheong army Commander, Seon Geo-i, and a reserve force of 2,000 men. On September 27, Yi Sun-sin sailed from Hansando, picked up army commanders on a ship off Hwado Island, passed through Gyeonnaeryang, and advanced all at once to the sea off Jangmunpo on the morning of September 29th. The enemy did not hide on the rugged mountain and guarded the castle. The Korean fleet defeated two enemy scout vessels and returned to Chilcheonryang. On October 1, Yi Sun-sin ordered Won Gyun and Yi Eok-gi to attack Jangmunpo with their fleets, while he, along with Yi Sun-sin, the commander of the Chungcheong naval forces (who shared the same name as *Tongjesa* Yi Sun-sin), attacked the enemy at Yeongdeungpo. However, the enemy anchored their vessels on the beach of the port and did not even make a single move and did not respond. Around 10 p.m., there was a lot of trouble. On October 2, the Korean fleet dispatched 30 war vessels to Jangmunpo to assess the enemy's situation and deploy decoy tactics, but the enemy still showed no response. On October 3, Yi Sun-sin also led his fleet to Jangmunpo and attempted battle, but the enemy's tactics did not change. *Tongjesa* Yi Sun-sin recognized the limitations of the current tactic in breaking the enemy's defense within the fortress and decided to launch an operation by landing ground troops on enemy territory. Admiral Yi Sun-sin's plan was as follows:

*First, send an advance force to Jangmunpo Bay to lure the enemy. Second, land troops at Jangmunpo Fortress. Third, the Joint Fleet waits outside Jangmunpo and begins Joint operations.*

## Significance and follow-up measures of the Jangmunpo Landing Operation

On October 4, the ground troops landed, but the enemy remained passive and only demonstrated from elevated positions. The ground troops observed the enemy's movements near the shore and returned. On October 6, the vanguard detachment was sent to Jangmoonpo, but the enemy had put up a sign saying, *Japan is in discussions with the Ming Dynasty, so there is no need for us to fight* and they did not engage. On October 8, the Joint Fleet conducted mobile demonstrations in the waters off Jangmunpo and Yeongdeungpo, and then returned to their main base in Hansando. The ground forces also withdrew to the land.

Although the Jangmunpo operation was the first Joint sea-land operation conducted by the Korean Navy, it ended without much success. While negotiations were in progress between China and Japan, Japan had no intention of engaging in combat and was using delaying

Figure 35: The 7th Campaign Route of the Korean Navy

operations within a castle in the coastal region of Gyeongsang Province.

Due to King Seonjo's unreasonable attack order, *Chechalsa* Yun Du-su, who could command the navy and army from the central government, came down to plan the landing operation and gave the operation order. Still he did not appear at the scene, he was directing the operation in Suncheon, Jeolla Province.

Also, General Kwon Yul, who could command the Korean naval forces according to the command system, was not at the scene of the operation. In fact, *Tongjesa* Yi Sun-sin oversaw the operation, cooperating with the commanders of the volunteer army, including Gwak Jae-woo and Kim Cheon-il, who were the landing force. The Korean fleet repeatedly approached the enemy's position and tried to fight, but the enemy did not want to fight. Yi Sun-sin's Joint Fleet could not fight a typical battle with the Japanese forces, which responded more defensively than the tedious Battle of Ungpo before the Battle of Jangmunpo.

Figure 36: The Situation Map of the Battle of Jangmunpo

In the end, the Korean fleet destroyed two enemy vessels, but four Korean vessels suffered damage. Although the Jangmunpo landing operation was the first Joint amphibious operation carried out during the Japanese invasions of Korea, it was not successful due to reasons such as King Seonjo's unreasonable order, the absence of *Chechalsa* Yun Du-su, the commander-in-chief of the landing operation, and *Dowonsoo* Kwon Yul, the chairman of the Joint Chiefs of Staff, from participating in the field, and the enemy's defensive operations. Yi Sun-sin's combat achievements were minimal compared to his great victory in the previous naval battle. After the Jangmunpo landing operation, which took place from September 29 to October 8, 1594, the evaluation of the central government, including King Seonjo, was cold. The central government defined the Jangmunpo landing Joint operation as a defeat. From November 1594 to February 1595, the central government continued to debate those responsible for the battle. Ultimately, King Seonjo dismissed Commander-in-Chief Yun Du-su and General Kwon Yul. Yi Sun-sin also received a light discipline. The dismissal of the highest-ranking members of the Korean military left a vacuum in the command system for a considerable time. King Seonjo appointed Yi Won-ik as the new *Chechalsa* on August 1, 1595, and sent him down to Gyeongsang Province to inspect the battlefield. At this time, as negotiations between China and Japan showed signs of breakdown, Toyotomi Hideyoshi was preparing to dispatch a large force from Japan to Korea. Yi Won-ik went down to the front lines, inspected the status of the army and navy and public sentiment, and reported the facts to King Seonjo on October 5, 1595. Yi Won-ik reported to King Seonjo that public sentiment was in disarray due to poor harvests, epidemics, and accumulated war fatigue, and many people were dying, leading to a severe shortage of naval forces. He also pointed out the inappropriate behavior of military commanders on the scene and that only Admiral Yi Sun-sin managed his troops well with a solid military spirit.

# Preparations for Future Warfare by Yi Sun-sin During Negotiations

## Negotiations and Yi Sun-sin's Response

In the early stages of the war in 1592, there were no formal negotiations between Korea and Japan. While the Korean army faced defeats on land in the first year of the war, under the leadership of Admiral Yi Sun-sin, the Korean Navy achieved perfect victories in all naval battles. This success blocked Japan's maritime supply lines, which extended from Busan through the South Sea to the West Sea. Blocking Japan's maritime supply lines was critical because it could cripple the Japanese army that had penetrated deep into Korean territory, especially with China's involvement in the conflict. As negotiations between China, which had come to support Korea, and Japan began, a noticeable change in Japan's formal attitude was observed. After the Japanese Navy suffered a significant defeat at the Battle of Busanpo in the autumn of 1592, there were no major sea battles between the Korean and Japanese navies until the end of that year. However, Japan continued establishing bases in the coastal areas of Gyeongsang Province, such as Angolpo, Ungpo, and Jeppo, avoiding confrontations with the Korean Navy. This was a strategic military move during the negotiations. Even during the negotiations, several naval battles occurred. Notable battles during the negotiation period from 1593 to 1594 included the Battle of Ungpo from February 6 to March 8, 1593, the Second Battle of Danghangpo from March 3 to 7, 1594, and the joint land and sea operation at Jangmungpo from September 27 to October 8, 1594. During the negotiations between China and Japan, Admiral Yi Sun-sin was appointed as *Tongjesa*, the commander of the Three Provinces Navy, on October 1, 1593. Negotiations during wartime are high-level political acts and reflect the nation's foreign policy. However, during the Imjinwaeran, negotiations were conducted primarily by China and Japan without involving the desires of Korea. This frustrated Admiral Yi Sun-sin, who hoped to conquer the enemy by force and suppress them on the battlefield. Let's explore Admiral Yi Sun-sin's perspective on the negotiations between China and Japan. On September 15, 1593, Admiral Yi Sun-sin wrote the following in his diary.

> *It has been two long years since the brutal invaders trampled our nation. Today is the time to restore what we've lost. I've been waiting daily, as if a day were a year, to hear the sound of Chinese military wagons and horses. However, the Chinese army focuses on the negotiations instead of defeating the enemy. The merciless enemy has momentarily retreated, but our country still carries the shame of being invaded for years. I feel massive anger and embarrassment. Although I may be foolish and timid, I am willing to pick up a bow and stones and offer myself first to repay our country's favor. If I miss this opportunity now, what use is there in regret?*

Throughout the Imjinwaeran, Admiral Yi Sun-sin was prepared to fight and win against the Japanese invaders in every naval battle from the Imjin year onwards. He was determined to chase the enemy out of Korean waters. This passage reveals the frustration and sincere sentiments of Admiral Yi Sun-sin while observing the negotiations between the enemy and China.

## Securing Stable Military Supplies and Establishing Military Discipline

During the long and fake talks between China and Japan, the central government closely watched on military matters. This was very different from what happened before the Imjinwaeran started in 1592. While China and Japan were discussing peace, Admiral Yi Sun-sin was ready to intercept enemy ships whenever necessary. He also focused on making sure there were enough military supplies. He couldn't just rely on the government for supplies during the war. Yi Sun-sin devised strategies and utilized various methods to secure supplies. He produced salt, went fishing to trade for food, and managed a farm called *Dunjeon*. Through *Dunjeon*, he assisted those in need and secured provisions for the navy.

As the talks continued, there weren't big naval battles in 1593. It was hard to keep the soldiers' spirits up and build military power. Admiral Yi Sun-sin had trouble managing the military because many were tired and didn't want to join the navy. Also, local leaders couldn't get people to join the navy effectively. Even though there weren't big battles, Admiral Yi Sun-sin, who had been winning battles since the Imjin War started, stayed in Jeolla Left Province.

He focused on preparing for future fights, ensuring the military and supplies were good to go. He worked hard to run *Dunjeon* well and informed the central government about how it was going. He cared about making *Dunjeon* work smoothly. When war broke out in 1592, Yi Sun-sin provided refuge and support during the harsh winter to refugees fleeing from the Gyeongsang region to the Jeolla region. At that time, Yi Sun-sin sent refugees to Dolsan Island in Yeosu to cultivate *Dunjeon* to make a living. Yi Sun-sin operated *Dunjeon* more systematically in 1593 during the *Tongjesa* mission. Yi Sun-sin created a policy to have refugees cultivate empty pastures and fields in the Jeolla region, collect half of the harvest from the refugees as a tax when they farmed the land, and use it as military food.

*Dunjeon* was a system where people were sent to farm strategically to make money for the government. It was often used for military reasons, such as getting soldiers to work on the land. In the Joseon dynasty, *Dunjeon* was used to help soldiers grow their food. Admiral Yi Sun-sin smartly managed *Dunjeon* during the war. He gave refugees farming jobs and collected taxes from them. This gave people work to do. His idea gave the people power and helped the navy get food by collecting taxes during wartime. Admiral Yi Sun-sin tried hard to get enough food, including running *Dunjeon*, but there wasn't enough. Things worsened, especially when the army took the navy's food without planning. On March 10, 1594, Yi Sun-sin asked the central government for help to avoid this crisis. At the time, thanks to Yi Sun-sin's wisdom, the Korean Navy secured its own food, but the army was absolutely short of food. Therefore, local armies frequently stole food secured by the navy. However, since Yi Sun-sin was stationed at the Hansando Naval Headquarters, he could do nothing. Therefore, Yi Sun-sin requested the central government to prevent the army from illegally seizing the food secured by the navy.

Let's look at how seriously Yi Sun-sin saw the problem. On March 10, 1594, there were 110 warships in Jeolla Left Navy and Jeolla Right Navy, with small boats and 17,000 people. They were the central part of the Korean Navy. The daily food per soldier is five hops (1 cup≈1 mug) for breakfast and dinner. In a month, they needed about 3,400 hops. Yi Sun-sin reported that the food left would only last until May 15. Yi Sun-sin urgently requested the central government to take measures to prevent the army from taking any more food from the navy, as the navy's food was insufficient. *Tongjesa* Yi Sun-sin demonstrated outstanding leadership during the tedious negotiations between China and Japan by ensuring military discipline, securing food, and providing relief to hungry residents.

## Admiral Yi Sun-sin's Command Challenges

Even after Admiral Yi Sun-sin was appointed as the commander-in-chief of the Korean Navy, commanding the three naval forces, there were no major naval engagements between Korea and Japan. Nevertheless, Japanese troops stationed in locations like Angolpo, Geoje Island, and Ungcheon occasionally attempted to enter Korean waters but were detected and repelled by the Korean Navy. Despite his new role, Yi Sun-sin faced challenges as the organization and structure of the navy remained unchanged. He managed the increased responsibilities personally, without additional resources or organizational adjustments. While no new staff or military advisors were appointed, the scope of Yi Sun-sin's responsibilities expanded significantly. Approximately one and a half months after his appointment, on November 17, Yi Sun-sin reported the changed circumstances to King Seonjo. He highlighted various difficulties arising from the expanded jurisdiction while controlling the areas around Hansando. Issues included unit inspections, supervision of subordinate units, and command authority disputes with local commanders. Yi Sun-sin emphasized the need for competent staff to manage distant units, overseeing logistics, and securing military resources. He mentioned occasional delays in communication due to relying on written correspondence and stressed the necessity of personally visiting remote units when required. Therefore, when needed, a staff officer capable of directly traveling to remote units to assist in logistics management, securing military resources, and supporting military operations was necessary. Yi Sun-sin demonstrated wisdom by requesting the appointment of a former administrator in Jangheung, Jeollado, as his chief of staff to oversee organizational management.

Even though Yi Sun-sin had been promoted from the regional commander of Jeolla Left Navy to the Commander-in-chief of the Korean Naval Forces(*Tongjesa*), challenges persisted in the hierarchical structure with superiors like regional commanders and Governors. Yi Sun-sin repeatedly requested central government intervention to resolve these conflicts.

## Efforts to Resolve Manpower Shortages and Secure Command Authority

Although he was initially appointed as Korea's top naval commander, he fell short of demonstrating strong leadership. Looking at the historical documents helps us understand what Yi Sun-sin did to tackle these problems. In a November 17, 1593 report, Yi Sun-sin highlighted the shortage of soldiers recruited in coastal areas. He pointed out that some individuals were exempted from conscription, and higher authorities ordered irregular enlistments. This inconsistency confused the coastal residents, who received conflicting directives from both land and sea commands. Consequently, many families found it difficult to cope, leading them to evacuate the area hastily. The widespread issues of famine and epidemics at that time compounded the difficulty of maintaining military morale and securing resources.

Yi Sun-sin appealed to the king, urging the central government to instruct regional commanders and Governors not to transfer personnel and resources recruited from coastal regions to the army but to keep them exclusively for the navy. As seen in the November report, Yi Sun-sin struggled to control the Three Provinces Navy entirely over four months into his role as the Commander-in-chief. Irrational decisions from national administrative agencies and higher-ranking military commanders posed significant obstacles to his mission. Therefore, he requested solid central government control over command authority, which he could not resolve alone. Yi Sun-sin continued efforts to secure his command authority. In a report dated February 25, 1594, he demonstrated outstanding leadership by directing subordinate commanders to assemble the Three Provinces Navy at the Hansando control camp for unified inspections and training, testing and strengthening the integrated capabilities of the navy.

Even though Yi Sun-sin tried hard, commanders Yi Eok-gi and Gu Sa-jik couldn't get their troops to Hansando on time because they couldn't find enough new soldiers. Also, local leaders didn't let the recruited people go, making it challenging to prepare the Navy. Yi Sun-sin scolded the commanders and leaders who didn't follow his orders. It's important to know that Korea had trouble getting enough soldiers and supplies at that time because of famine and epidemics. Yi Sun-sin knew about these issues. He tried to have more control and reported to the king what was happening with the navy in Hansando to help him understand the situation with the central government.

## Admiral Yi Sun-sin's Leadership amid Crisis: Struggles and Devotion in Command

On October 1, 1593, after receiving the appointment as *Tongjesa*, the inaugural Commander-in-chief of the Korean Naval Forces, Yi Sun-sin tirelessly strived to secure the command authority for efficient control of the Three Provinces Navy. However, even after a year in this role, he couldn't achieve satisfactory results. Anticipating another enemy invasion, Yi Sun-sin recognized the critical importance of unwavering leadership and robust military strength. Despite his personal efforts, he frequently reported to higher authorities seeking

Chapter III. Yi Sun-sin's Battles and Preparations for Future Naval Warfare

solutions but the reality was far from promising. During this period, Yi Sun-sin's frustrations and heartfelt devotion to the nation can be glimpsed in the following summary of his diary entry from November 28, 1594:

> *The coastal areas of Gyeongsang Province are overflowing with large enemy forces, an imminent threat that seems unstoppable. However, three years into the war, our resources are depleted, and a severe epidemic has spread, causing widespread death. Chinese General Yu Jeong has already withdrawn, leaving us with no viable defense strategies. The situation is dire, and a crisis looms with each passing moment. Relying on both land and sea, all forts and military resources are dependent on Jeolla Province, rendering it more desolate than a land struck by the calamity of war. I'm unsure how to proceed; there is no place to rely on for military provisions or support. The hastily gathered resources are dwindling rapidly.*
>
> *While the enemy fears our navy, there is not a single person willing to join the war efforts. Despite our naval strength, we are helpless against the wandering civilians, and the military, along with provisions, is dwindling due to the severe disease, leading to many deaths.*
>
> *Repeated pleas and reports detailing this dire situation were sent to Dowonsoo, Kwon Yul, and Governor, but there has been no response or solution. Urgent reports have been submitted to the king multiple times, yet there are no instructions on how to handle this. Despite contemplating every possible solution, there seems to be no way to defend and preserve. The naval forces are on the verge of collapse. I am willing to sacrifice myself, but how can we manage the affairs of the nation?*

When writing this, it was about a month after Admiral Yi Sun-sin's return from the 7th campaign on October 8, 1594. Although *Chechalsa* Yun Du-soo actively participated in the Joint amphibious operation, due to the enemy's fortress fleet operation and the lack of cooperation from the army, the overall outcome was not significant, and our side suffered considerable losses. It was a very distressing period for Admiral Yi Sun-sin. Finding records where Yi Sun-sin expressed his distress and desperation as explicitly as in the passage above is challenging. The content above reveals how desperate and dire the situation was for Yi Sun-sin as he commanded the Three Provinces Navy. Throughout the nation, diseases were spreading, leading to numerous deaths, and famine was rampant, causing people to starve even in remote military areas.

While stationed at the headquarters on Hansan Island, Admiral Yi Sun-sin faced a challenging situation in which the army continuously took supplies from the warehouses in the Jeolla Province granary areas, such as Suncheon and Heungyang. Due to severe shortages, this frequent removal of naval supplies made it difficult for the navy to carry out operations. Despite repeatedly reporting and suggesting solutions to address this critical and urgent situation, no measures were taken by the central command. At that time, the central command proposed no particular plans, leaving Admiral Yi Sun-sin alone to overcome this difficult situation.

## Resolute Leadership Despite Limited Resources and Internal Challenges

The actions of Yi Sun-sin and the Korean Navy between 1595 and 1596 have not been widely noted or well-known, and these years lacked battles due to peace talks between China and Japan. This chapter will examine how Yi Sun-sin managed his navy and prepared for war right before the Second Japanese Invasion started in 1597, highlighting his leadership skills. Under the leadership of Admiral Yi Sun-sin, the Korean Navy fortified its maritime defense and stationed on Hansan

Island to prepare for potential conflicts.

The Japanese Navy maintained strategic positions at critical locations such as Angolpo, Ungpo, and Geoje Island in Gyeongsang Province, using Busan as their naval base. While there were no major naval battles between the two navies during this period, the Korean Navy remained on high alert, stationed around Hansan Island, and engaged in a tense standoff with the Japanese forces. The navy conducted regular reconnaissance operations in the surrounding maritime areas to monitor enemy movements and implemented ambush operations, strengthening their defensive capabilities to deter provocations.

On January 1, 1595, Admiral Yi Sun-sin shed tears while thinking about his country and aging mother on the first day of the new year. He also threw a party and served alcohol to the officials who visited. The diary entries of *Nanjungilgi (the War Diary of Admiral Yi Sun-sin)* contain numerous mentions of Admiral Yi Sun-sin consuming alcohol. It may seem incomprehensible from today's perspective, but in the past, it was a cultural norm in Korea to offer alcohol to guests who visited one's home. Even in the 1960s, it was considered necessary for mothers to prepare a drink set when relatives or visitors came to their homes during holidays or special occasions. Admiral Yi Sun-sin often shared drinks with his subordinate officers when meeting them to provide comfort and encouragement. In January, Admiral Yi Sun-sin met with dozens of officials, including local leaders from Suncheon, Jangheung, Geoje, Heungyang, Goseong, Ungcheon, Yeongdeungpo, Yeongam, and Gangjin. On January 19, a fire broke out on four anchored warships, causing significant damage. Admiral Yi Sun-sin took disciplinary action against those responsible for managing the warships. Admiral Yi Sun-sin believed that strict military discipline was crucial for winning battles. In February, he questioned a corrupt county magistrate from Boseong and punished him for his wrongdoing. He also arrested a corrupt magistrate from Heungyang and disciplined soldiers who had damaged the battleship, showing that military laws were enforced strictly under his command. Meanwhile, he managed *Dunjeon* well and successfully secured military food by collecting taxes. Admiral Yi Sun-sin gathered around 300 seoks (around 20 kg of grain per seok) of *Dunjeon* tax. This was meant to be used for food for the soldiers, and he shared it among the different groups. Even though he punished the leaders of Hampyeong and Yeongam in Jeolla Province for not getting more soldiers and not making warships, he was kind to the local leaders who had come from far away, eating and drinking with them. He was good at keeping his job and his personal life separate.

Admiral Yi Sun-sin stayed on Hansando with the military leaders during the winter. They worked to keep ready and gathered food and other things they would need for the navy. He also told the leaders under him to prepare their soldiers and warships. He showed his leadership by rewarding or punishing them based on their actions. Even though there were no big battles during the peace talks, Yi Sun-sin worked hard to strengthen the navy. He was preparing for a big attack from the Japanese forces that might happen shortly.

It got warmer and drier in March, and a fire started on the warships. This caused much damage. A fire on Yi Kye-hoon's ship in the Chungcheong navy killed about 140 people, including the leader, officers, and sailors. Losing warships and sailors because of fires, not battles, was a big problem for the Navy. Admiral Yi Sun-sin looked into the accident and made plans to prevent it from happening again. The enemies, who had been quiet, started to get busy again in April. On April 25th, when Admiral Yi Sun-sin heard that about 50 enemy warships were moving from Ungcheon to Jinhae, he sent about 20 of his warships to that area and chased the enemy away.

As mentioned earlier, the enemies didn't fight because they were talking about peace. There was no fighting between the two sides on that day.

Securing military rations during a war was always a concern. Admiral Yi Sun-sin tried hard, catching fish and baking salt to provide rations, and supplemented military rations with *Dunjeon* taxes. However, the shortage of military rations was still a worry. On April 12th, he sent administrators to Suncheon, Gwangyang, Gwangju, Heungyang, Boseong, Gurye, and Gokseong because acquiring allocated military rations in each region was insufficient. The navy mainly received military rations from the granaries in Jeolla Province. Still, as the area continued to experience poor harvests, acquiring military rations there was also not smooth.

### Strengthening Naval Defenses Amid Negotiations

Negotiations between China and Japan were underway, but they didn't align with Korea's intentions as a country at war. Recognizing Japan's cunning plans, Korea strengthened its war readiness. The central government, unlike before the outbreak of the Imjin War, acknowledged the need for a maritime strategy to defend against enemy incursions by sea. Admiral Yi Sun-sin knew that the navy under his command would be the first to fight if Japan's major attack began. On July 27, a notice arrived that a secret envoy would visit the naval base on Hansan Island, where the maritime headquarters was located. The Secret Royal Emissary, Yi Sik, came to inspect Admiral Yi Sun-sin's fleet. Admiral Yi Sun-sin gathered his fleet around Hansan Island and demonstrated well-prepared naval combat capabilities. Like today's Joint Chiefs of Staff's combat readiness checks, this inspection required Admiral Yi Sun-sin's careful attention. Yi Sik inspected the Three Provinces Navy fleet for several days and returned on August 5.

After Yi Sik left, Admiral Yi Sun-sin and subordinate commanders and staff discussed the inspection evaluation. Anticipating the failure of negotiations between China and Japan, Admiral Yi Sun-sin focused on war preparations more than ever. On August 25, Admiral Yi Sun-sin inspected the naval units in the waters off Gyeongsang Province with Inspector Yi Won-ik to assess and check them. This on-site visit aimed to confirm conditions for unit consolidation, a unique strategy at the time to overcome military challenges and enhance combat capabilities. The military changed by combining coastal defense units such as Gokpo and Pyeongsanpo, Sangju and Mijo, Jeokryang and Samcheonjin, Sobipo and Saryang, Gabaeryang and Dangpo, Jiseypo and Joripo, Jepo and Ungcheon, Yulpo and Okpo, Angolpo and Gadeokjin.

Integrating two units into one unit was to improve combat efficiency and reduce budget. Yi Sun-sin organized meals and morale-boosting events for 5,480 military personnel after the *Chechalsa* inspection team left. The number of soldiers stationed on Hansan Island during this time significantly decreased, indicating the severe impact of widespread famine and infectious diseases on military readiness. The usual presence of over 10,000 soldiers from the Three Provinces Navy on Hansan Island had significantly reduced by the latter half of 1595, reflecting the challenging circumstances of that period. During the war, units without actual combat might experience a decline in morale, so Admiral Yi Sun-sin consistently emphasized military discipline. Simultaneously, to prepare for the potential future re-invasion by the enemy, Yi Sun-sin tirelessly collected *Dunjeon* usage fees to secure military provisions and had no rest for the construction of naval vessels.

*Chechalsa* Yi Won-ik came down to Samcheonpo in August and again in September 1595 to check combat readiness. Yi Sun-sin met with Yi Won-ik by ship from Hansan Island, reported on his preparations for battle, and discussed future measures. Yi Won-ik was a high-ranking official who recognized Yi Sun-sin's leadership and abilities. He later played a decisive role in rescuing Yi Sun-sin from a situation where he was almost executed. Even during this period, the enemy remained stationed in places like Angolpo and Ungcheon, periodically appearing in areas of Korean naval activity to provoke the Korean Navy. It was a form of psychological warfare. In response, Yi Sun-sin strengthened defenses, sent intelligence ships, and prepared for unforeseen circumstances. Securing provisions and firewood is just as crucial as military training during wartime. Before winter arrived, Admiral Yi Sun-sin secured various types of firewood from the islands near Hansan, gathering the '*Dunjeon*' tax to secure 820 seks (approximately 16 tons) of rice, beans, and other food supplies. He also mobilized soldiers to catch 20,000 bundles of herrings (approximately 400,000 fish) for food exchange.

As mentioned earlier, the provisions secured by Yi Sun-sin were regularly supplied to the army and to the military personnel directly under Yi Won-ik, who held higher command authority as *Chechalsa*. Despite the prolonged war destroying the land and the government's scarcity of military supplies, Yi Sun-sin independently cultivated crops, caught fish, and aimed at self-sufficiency. Furthermore, even though the provisions obtained by the navy were insufficient to feed the entire navy, Yi Sun-sin also supported the army with the provisions secured by the navy.

In 1595, even though there weren't big sea battles between the Korean and Japanese navies, Admiral Yi Sun-sin, who led the Korean Navy, strengthened his forces just in case Japan launched a major attack. He demonstrated leadership as a military leader by securing sufficient food in anticipation of a major enemy attack, building warships, and improving military equipment.

When 1596 started, not much changed in the military camps. Some Japanese soldiers who surrendered or ran away ended up at Korean Navy camps. This showed that the Japanese military was weakening as the war went on. Yi Sun-sin kept talking to central government officials like Yu Seong-ryong, Jeong Tak, Kim Myeon-gwon, and Nam I-gong, letting them know what was happening at the borders and getting replies. In May, Yi Sun-sin got the surprising news that a Chinese envoy staying with the Japanese in Busan had run away. This clearly showed that negotiations between China and Japan weren't going well. Even though Lee Jong-sung, the Chinese envoy, ran away, China later sent Yang Bang-hyeong and Sim Yu-gyeong as envoys to Japan. Also, during negotiations, Yi Sun-sin heard on May 13 that Japanese forces under Kato were leaving Korea, and the Chinese envoy in Busan would cross the sea with the Japanese.

As Yi Sun-sin got ready for possible future battles, he closely watched how China and Japan were talking. In case talks failed and the Japanese attacked again, Yi Sun-sin focused on training his officers, strengthening defenses, and preparing for war by shooting arrows and staying alert. Even though talks were happening between China and Japan at the central government level, the navy got orders to prepare for war in case the Japanese returned after hearing about them leaving.

Meanwhile, Admiral Yi Sun-sin, as a military commander, felt uneasy about the negotiations with Japan. Still, he had to accept cooperation with the central government while fulfilling his duties as the overall person responsible for the navy. He prepared three ships in July and sent them to Busan, the Japanese military base. Additionally, he arranged leopard skins and pottery, as requested by the Korean diplomatic delegation, leaving for Japan. In August, he constructed warships, discussed military operations with *Chechalsa* Yi Won-ik, stationed troops at coastal areas for border defense, and selected over a thousand soldiers to prepare wood for building warships. He also met with *Chechalsa* to gather military information.

Due to the wartime situation, there were no promotion exams under the central government's responsibility to boost military morale. Yi Sun-sin obtained permission from the central government to conduct independent promotion exams within his unit. This was a crucial military task for boosting the soldiers' morale while reinforcing preparations for war. Promotions significantly boost morale in the military. Promotions significantly boost morale in the military environment, whether it's wartime or peacetime. Therefore, even in modern navies, commanders pay great attention to the promotions of their subordinates. On August 10, 1596, Yi Sun-sin conducted exams within his unit, and many of his subordinates passed. Yi Sun-sin's nephew and son also passed the exam. As it reached the latter part of 1596, tension escalated in the border regions. Chaechalsa continued visiting Hansan Island this year for inspections, as he did last year. Since 1595, when Yi Won-ik was given the task of *Chechalsa* by King Seonjo, Admiral Yi Sun-sin maintained close contact with *Chechalsa* through letters or direct meetings.

They discussed preparing for enemy invasions, building ships, reinforcing troops, and overall strategic planning. On August 11, at Dangpo, Yi Sun-sin met with *Chechalsa* Yi Won-ik to report on military operations. Dangpo, where the Korean Navy achieved a decisive victory over the enemy in 1592, is under the maritime control zone of the Korean Navy. During the meeting, Yi Sun-sin likely stressed the importance of directly visiting naval forces under his command to assess war readiness and discuss plans for potential enemy attacks.

### Yi Sun-sin's Strategic Inspection and Leadership in War Readiness

After meeting with *Chechalsa*, Yi Sun-sin inspected the war preparations in remote areas of Jeolla Province for about 40 days. Yi Sun-sin thought it was imperative to directly check the discipline and morale of naval units geographically distant from the naval headquarters. Yi Sun-sin thought the Japanese might strike back hard, so he ensured the faraway troops stayed alert.

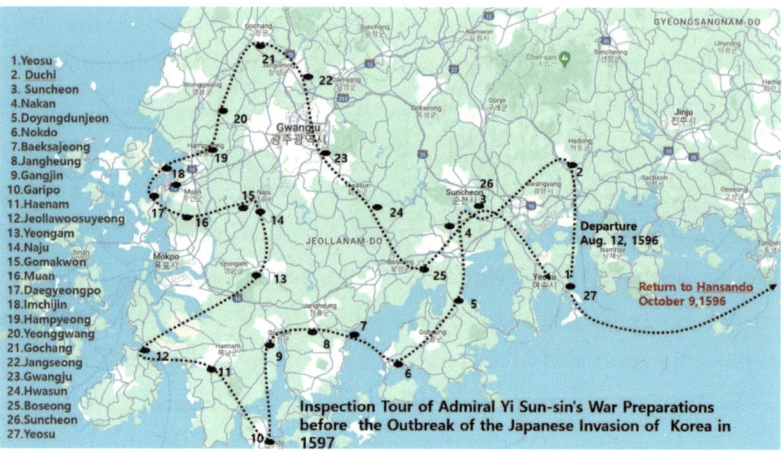

Figure 37: The Route of Admiral Yi Sun-sin's 40-Day War Readiness Inspection Before the 2nd Japanese Invasion

Three months after Yi Sun-sin completed his war preparation inspection of soldiers in remote areas, the Japanese forces attacked Korea in January 1598. Yi Sun-sin's prediction was correct. Admiral Yi Sun-sin began a 40-day inspection of his war preparations. He left for Yeosu on August 12 to visit his mother and inspected the naval forces in Jeolla Province on August 14. Yi Sun-sin's schedule overlapped with *Chechalsa* Yi Won-ik's for part of the journey, meaning some joint inspections and some separate ones. Starting his official inspection on August 14, Yi Sun-sin arrived at Doochi on the Seomjin River after treating his mother to breakfast on August 13. While moving to Gwangyang from Doochi, he saw a village devastated by Japanese invaders and noted the exemption of this region from specific tasks to ease the people's suffering. On August 15, he reached Suncheon and met with *Chechalsa* Yi Won-ik and his party. On the 17th, he visited Nakan, and on the 18th, he inspected various forts, ports, and islands in Nakan's terrain after climbing a mountain fortress.

On the 19th, while heading to Goheung Nokdo, Yi Sun-sin and

*Chechalsa* Yi Won-ik examined the fortress *Dunjeon*, praising Yi Sun-sin's self-sufficiency in military logistics. On the same day, Yi Sun-sin visited Goheung Nokdo with Yi Won-ik to secure military rations. On the 20th, along with *Chechalsa*, they arrived in Jangheung and inspected the site.

On the 21th, they reached Gangjin, where they met General Won Gyun, a naval ex-commander. Won Gyun faced conflicts with Yi Sun-sin during battles against the Japanese Invasion of Korea, leading to his reassignment as an army commander. On the 24th, Yi Sun-sin arrived at the naval base in Garipo, surveyed the islands from a hilltop observatory, and on the 25th, reached Haenam. They inspected the Jeolla Right Navy Headquarters the next day, marking Yi Sun-sin's first visit there. The day after returning from Jindo, *Chechalsa* and his party joined Yi Sun-sin in the Jeolla Right Navy Headquarters. *Tongjesa* and *Chechalsa* visited regional military units and local administrative agencies in Jeolla Province to inspect and seek cooperation from residents. This time, the central government thoroughly prepared for war, unlike the neglect before the Imjin War in 1592.

On August 29th, 1596, Admiral Yi Sun-sin and his group visited the Haenam County Office. They then traveled to Naju, arriving on September 1st and staying until September 2nd. They met with local officials during their stay to discuss important military matters. On September 6th, Yi Sun-sin said goodbye to a high-ranking official and continued his journey. He passed through Gomakwon in Naju before reaching Dakyeongpojin on the Muan coast. There, he met with the Yeonggwang County Magistrate to discuss how to be prepared for emergencies. The next day, September 7th, Yi Sun-sin inspected Imchijin, an island near Dakyeongpo. He also summoned Hong Gyeon, the manager of Imchijin, to talk about strategies against potential enemies. He climbed to Bongdaesan Fortress to assess the situation before moving to Hampyeong. It's important to note that

Dakyeongpo and Imchijin were located close to the naval routes used by Yi Sun-sin's fleet during their strategic withdrawal after the victory at the Battle of Myeongryang.

These locations served as vital points for communication between the fleet and inland administrators. Yi Sun-sin's decision might seem puzzling at first. Despite peace talks between China and Japan, the enemy controlled the waters from Busan to the western waters near Geojedo, close to the critical Hansando, where the main Korean Navy was stationed. When Yi Sun-sin left Hansando to inspect the naval units in remote areas, the possible outcomes were uncertain. However, he showed bold leadership by taking the risk and visiting the inland regions of Jeolla Province for the war readiness inspection. Yi Sun-sin was just unsure about the ongoing talks with China and Japan.

During this time, Japan had moved its main forces back to Japan, leaving only some troops in the southern part of the Korean Peninsula. However, Yi Sun-sin was aware of Japan's cunning plan. Like Japan's surprise attack in 1592 at the start of the Imjin War, he foresaw Japan deploying large forces for another invasion of Korea. Yi Sun-sin also recognized the active involvement of the Jeolla Province navy and the sacrifices of the local people and administrators during the intense battles since the start of the Imjin War in 1592. He knew their cooperation was crucial for naval victories. The Korean Navy had suffered setbacks in manpower and supplies since the intense battles in 1592 and the hardships in 1593.

The prolonged war had also led to worsening public sentiment and weakened cooperation from local officials. Yi Sun-sin believed that the most important thing was to ask the local people and administrators to cooperate in advance so that they could actively help the Korean military in the event of war. Moreover, effectively commanding was challenging due to the significant distance between Hansando and Jeolla Province.

To prepare for a possible new attack from Japan, Yi Sun-sin felt it was essential to visit the remote Jeolla Province in person. He wanted to check on the naval base there, ask the local people for help, and see how prepared they were for war.

### The Impact of Yi Sun-sin's 40-Day Inspection on Navy Rebuilding

Three months after Yi Sun-sin toured remote areas of Jeolla for 40 days, Japan launched its second invasion, known as Jeongyujaeran, just as he predicted. After the war broke out, Yi Sun-sin was dismissed, and Admiral Won Gyun took command of the Korean Navy but suffered a severe defeat at the Battle of Chilcheonryang. Following the devastating loss at Chilcheonryang, the Korean Navy couldn't control the seas off Gyeongsang and was pushed back to the southwestern sea near the Jeolla coast. When Admiral Won Gyun was defeated and killed in the Battle of Chilcheonryang, Yi Sun-sin, who was in the Baekuijongun, returned to the position of commander and miraculously won a significant victory in the Battle of Myeongryang. Despite being outnumbered 10 to 1, Yi Sun-sin's 13 ships defeated 133 Japanese ships in the miraculous Battle of Myeongryang just a month after his reinstatement. However, the Korean Navy had only 13 battleships left. Therefore, the most urgent task for *Tongjesa* Yi Sun-sin was to rebuild the power of the Korean Navy. After the Battle of Myeongryang, Yi Sun-sin's activities to reconstruct the Korean Navy began at the Gohado Wartime Command Base in Mokpo, and the decisive help of the people along the coast of Jeolla Province became the driving force in strengthening the naval power. With his reinstatement, the Korean Navy's strength rapidly increased, with 80 to 85 ships participating in the last naval battle, the Battle of Noryang, in November 1598. This increase was mainly due to the involvement of local administrative agencies and residents in Jeolla.

It is important to remember that Yi Sun-sin visited every naval base in remote Jeolla-do three months before the outbreak of the war and encouraged them to prepare for war. He also met with people near Jeolla-do to listen to their sentiments and ask them to cooperate in preparation for the coming war. The reconstruction of the Korean Navy, which began at Mokpo, continued until just before the Battle of Noryang, the final naval battle. The reconstruction of the Korean Navy was based on Yi Sun-sin's leadership, the efforts of the Korean Navy, and the cooperation of the people in the coastal areas who followed Yi Sun-sin.

# Chapter IV

## Yi Sun-sin's Dismissal, Won Gyun's Naval Defeat, and Yi Sun-sin's Return

# Dismissal and Rankless Service (Baekuijonggun)

Peace negotiations between China and Japan dragged on for a long time, but they ultimately broke down. Anticipating an enemy invasion, Admiral Yi Sun-sin and Yi Won-ik began reorganizing the Korean naval forces in preparation for war. Aware of the weakened naval forces in Hansando due to famine and epidemics, Yi Won-ik urgently dispatched Assistant Inspector Han Hyo-sun to Jeolla-do and Chungcheong-do to recruit military forces and dispatch warships to Hansando. Amid these preparations, the Japanese forces led by Kato launched a surprise invasion into the waters of Busan. King Seonjo held Admiral Yi responsible for failing to prevent the enemy's invasion in advance, dismissed him from his position as *Tongjesa*, and appointed Admiral Won Gyun as his successor.

On February 10, 1597, Yi Sun-sin sailed to the sea off Busan, the stronghold of the Japanese enemies, unaware that the central government was discussing his dismissal. While engaged in naval operations, Yi Sun-sin returned to Hansando immediately upon hearing of his arrest order. He handed over command to Won Gyun and was arrested on February 26. Subsequently, he was transported to Seoul, arriving on March 4. The supreme commander of the Korean Navy, who had ruled the seas and risked his life to defend Korea's territorial waters, suddenly became a criminal. Yi Sun-sin endured imprisonment, torture, and harsh conditions while King Seonjo, furious, attempted to execute him. In this dire situation, some ministers intervened to save Yi Sun-sin. Requests from Jeong Tak and others, including Yi Won-ik, who had discussed strategies against the enemy invasion with Yi Sun-sin, changed King Seonjo's mind. Ultimately, King Seonjo stripped Yi Sun-sin of all his public offices and ordered him to serve under *Dowonsoo* Kwon Yul as a rankless soldier in what is known as *Baekuijonggun*.

Yi Sun-sin was released from prison on April 1, 1597, 28 days after his imprisonment. After his release, he spent his first days outside Nammun (Namdaemun). On the first day after leaving prison, Yi Sun-sin met his family and even forced himself to drink alcohol given to him by acquaintances who came to console him. That evening, Jeong Tak, who had saved Yi Sun-sin's life by appealing just before his execution, and Younguijeong (equivalent to today's Prime Minister) Yu Seong-ryong, who sent people to comfort Yi Sun-sin, visited him.

On April 3, Yi Sun-sin departed for Hapcheon in Gyeongsang-do, where *Dowonsoo* Kwon Yul was stationed. He followed the instructions of the convoy official and set off for *Baekuijonggun* without having time to recover his strength, weakened by torture. A central government official accompanied him as a guide. On April 3, Yi Sun-sin crossed the Han River and arrived in Suwon at dusk. The next day, he headed south to Osan and Pyeongtaek. On April 5, Yi Sun-sin arrived in Asan and visited the tombs of his ancestors, shedding tears in endless sorrow.

While staying in Asan, Yi Sun-sin heard on April 13 (May 28 in the solar calendar) that his sick, elderly mother had died while traveling from Yeosu to Asan by sea. Yi Sun-sin was devastated. He ran to the beach in Asan, where his mother's body had arrived. Yi Sun-sin built a coffin on the beach and carried his mother's body back to his home in Asan on April 16. Yi Sun-sin began the funeral ceremony for his mother, enshrining her spirit tablet in his Asan home. At that time in

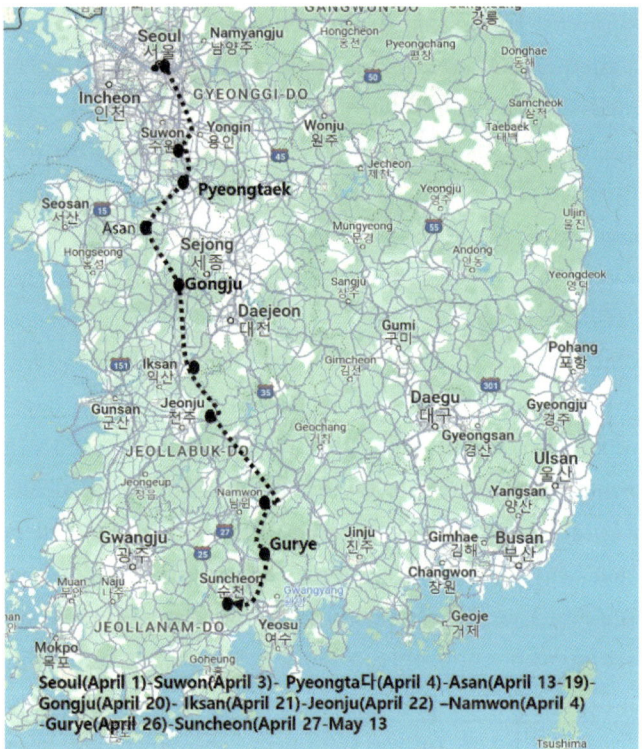

Figure 38: The Route of Yi Sun-sin's *Baeguijonggun* from Seoul to Suncheon

Korea, the mourning period for a parent's funeral lasted for about three years.

On April 19, during his mother's funeral, Yi Sun-sin, though now a rankless soldier of *Baekuijonggun*, had to leave for Kwon Yul's army in the south before the funeral was over. He wept bitterly, expressing his guilt for being an unfilial son, and took heavy steps forward as he moved south. In each town, officials and acquaintances comforted Yi Sun-sin, who had to fulfill his *Baekuijonggun* duties despite his mother's death. Yi Sun-sin arrived in Suncheon in the south of the Korean Peninsula on April 27, shedding bloody tears after passing through

Gongju, Nonsan, Iksan, Jeonju, Imsil, Namwon, and Gurye. *Dowonsoo* Kwon Yul, considerate of Yi Sun-sin's condition, advised him to rest briefly to recover his strength before resuming his duties at the camp.

While recovering in Suncheon from torture and fatigue, Yi Sun-sin recorded his situation in his diary as follows:

*May 4:* *It was my mother's birthday, so I couldn't bear the sadness and grief. When the rooster crowed, I sat up and cried.*

*May 5:* *Why am I being punished for going on a war mission a thousand miles away, leaving my mother's funeral far away, and not even being able to attend her funeral? There is probably no case like mine in the past or present. It hurts like my heart is being torn apart. I can only lament that the time was not right.*

*May 6:* *I met my two deceased brothers in a dream. They held each other and cried, "My younger brother left a thousand miles away before the funeral, so who will hold the funeral?" Even though I'm crying, there's nothing I can do. I miss my mother every morning and evening, and it's so sad. Even though my tears are like blood, why can't the distant sky take care of my situation? Why can't I just die?*

# The Tragic Battle of Chilcheonryang

## Leadership Confusion and Prelude to the Battle of Chilcheonryang

As the China-Japanese negotiations broke down, Toyotomi Hideyoshi's invasion of Korea proceeded relentlessly. Kato Kiyomasa left Tsushima Island with hundreds of warships and invaded the waters of Busan, including Seosaengpo and Dadaepo, from January 12 to 15, 1597. The government impeached Yi Sun-sin for failing to stop the invading enemy and appointed Won Gyun as the Commander of the Three Provinces' Naval Forces. Won Gyun, appointed as the new commander, could not control the Korean Navy due to his ineffective leadership. The morale and discipline of the soldiers were quite different from what they had been under Yi Sun-sin. In addition, the relationship between *Dowonsoo* Kwon Yul and Won Gyun was not smooth, exposing differences in strategies for attacking the enemy. The enemy's offensive continued after January 1597. The government ordered the navy to attack the enemy in the waters of Busan. Won Gyun proposed an amphibious operation against Angolpo and Geoje Island, but the government did not allow it. In particular, the opposition from *Dowonsoo* Kwon Yul was strong. Since Won Gyun became the Commander of Three Provinces, even before the Battle of Chilcheonryang, there were several battles between the Korean and

Japanese navies. The first engagement occurred on March 8, 1597, when the Korean Navy, having received information about Japanese warships, departed from Hansan Island and arrived at Gamunpo on Geoje Island, presumed to be on the northern coast of Okpo Port. In this encounter, the Korean Navy fought and captured three Japanese warships. The second engagement occurred on June 18, 1597, when the Korean Navy departed from Hansan Island and clashed with the Japanese forces stationed at Angolpo and Gadeok Island on June 19. Admiral Won Gyun had requested a joint land and sea operation against the enemy, but his proposal was not accepted. Essentially, Won Gyun conducted the naval operation independently under the pressure of General Kwon Yul.

## The Catastrophe of Chilcheonryang and Devastation: Collapse of the Korean Navy

On June 18, 1597, Won Gyun led a fleet of around 90 warships, spending a night at Jangmunpo before encountering Japanese warships near Angolpo and Gadeok Island. Engaging in battle against the fleet led by Japanese commanders, the Korean Navy fought bravely but eventually retreated to Hansan Island. In this battle, An Heung-guk lost his life, and Admiral Kim Chuk of Pyeongsan *Manho* suffered injuries from enemy gunfire. The third battle occurred during the advance toward Busan in response to a powerful request from the royal court. Won Gyun refused the royal command, and in reality, the forces of Won Gyun and Jeolla Left Province did not participate. The troops under the command of Gyeongsang Province, Admiral Choi Ho of Chungcheong Province, and Admiral Yi Eok-gi of Jeolla Province were engaged in the battle. The Korean Navy set sail from Hansan Island on July 4, anchoring at Chilcheondo on July 5, spending the night, and then anchoring at Okpo on July 6. Departing Okpo Harbor on the morning of July 7, the Korean fleet defeated eight enemy ships at Dadaepo and moved to Jeollyeongdo on July 8. The Korean Navy encountered a Japanese fleet from Tsushima Island outside Jeollyeongdo (Yeongdo in Busan). To make matters worse, the waters outside Jeollyeongdo were turbulent with solid waves, causing the Korean naval vessels to lose their maneuverability and drift aimlessly. According to records in the *Nanjungilgi*, it is estimated that the Korean naval fleet lost around 20 ships outside Jeollyeongdo.

On July 11, General Kwon Yul summoned Admiral Won Gyun to the headquarters and strongly reprimanded him for not participating in the battle on July 4. When Won Gyun returned to Hansan Island, he was frustrated and issued orders to his subordinate commanders without proper preparation. The Korean fleet set sail on the 12th, spending a night at Chilcheonryang, and arrived at Okpo on the 13th before heading to Busan on the 14th. As the Korean fleet reached the waters in front of Busan near Jeollyeongdo, strong winds and high waves prevented the ships from advancing despite vigorous rowing. Unable to find a safe anchorage as the night darkened, the Korean Navy struggled when the enemy fleet from Busan approached. Won Gyun ordered an attack to all his commanders. The soldiers, exhausted from rowing through rough seas for over 10 hours without proper rest or food, were already worn out. The storm intensified, further draining their energy. The Korean fleet, unable to maintain an organized attack formation, was wavering while the enemy ships maneuvered more feely, taking advantage of the calmer waters near the coast. Instead of engaging directly, the enemy fleet approached, attacked with cannons, and retreated.

The Korean Navy couldn't respond effectively, and morale plummeted. As the night deepened and the storm worsened, the Korean fleet, scattered in disarray, lost around 20 ships amidst the chaotic situation. Won Gyun ordered a retreat. The enemy, anticipating that Won Gyun's retreating joint Korean fleet would land on Gadeok Island to seek water and wood, placed a unit led by Takahashi Naotsugu on the island to lie in wait. Assuming the enemy would not pursue, Won Gyun dropped anchor upon reaching Gadeok Island, and the troops hastily disembarked. Suddenly, the enemy ambushed from all directions, launching a coordinated attack. Won Gyun suffered significant losses. He quickly raised the anchor and headed to Yeongdeungpo, located north of Geoje Island. However, he faced enemy attacks there as well. He was forced to retreat to Chilcheonryang Outer Harbor.

In this hasty move, Won Gyun ventured into the waters before Busan, losing 20 ships and around 400 soldiers in battles near Gadeok Island and Yeongdeungpo. Returning to Chilcheonryang on the night of the 15th, Won Gyun gathered several commanders to discuss the next steps. He emphasized as follows:

*Although the enemy's military strength is formidable, won't heaven assist our righteous navy? Let's fight with one heart until death and confront the enemy naval forces again tomorrow.*

Gyeongsang Right Naval Commander Bae Seol suggested as follows: *The commander must know how to fight bravely and when to retreat in war. We lost 20 ships and 400 soldiers in this engagement. Courage alone will not suffice. Our combat strength is weakened, and the soldiers are exhausted. We should return to Hansan Island for reorganization before venturing out again. We cannot drag the troops into the sea of death.*

However, Won Gyun strongly rejected the proposal and determined to proceed with the next battle. On the morning of the 16th, the

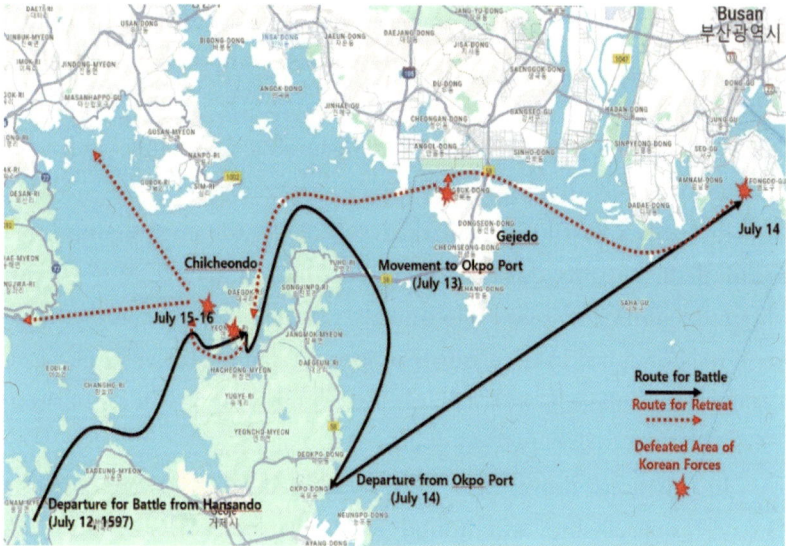

Figure 39: The Route of the Battle of Chilcheonryang

weather was cloudy and drizzling. At around 6:00 AM, the Japanese fleet surrounded Won Gyun's fleet. The vanguard fleet attacked and burned Korean ships on the outskirts, then narrowed the encirclement and fired muskets and cannons fiercely. Won Gyun was surprised by the Japanese surprise attack and sounded the drums and trumpets to announce the enemy's assault.

The Japanese simultaneously attacked the Korean fleet, firing guns, cannons, and flaming arrows. Won Gyun's fleet fought without even having time to raise their anchors or sails. The sky over Chilcheonryang was filled with thunderous cannon fire and smoke as if the earth had been turned upside down. At this time, Gyeongsan Right Naval Commander Bae Seol fled to Hansando with ten or so ships. The Japanese fleet formed a double encirclement, leaving only the open sea in front of Goseong open and narrowed in to attack. Won Gyun's fleet fought while trying to escape through the path left open by the enemy. When Won Gyun's fleet went out to the open sea, the Japanese encircled them again and attacked fiercely. The Korean fleet was caught by surprise while anchored and at anchor and fought to the death without even having time to form their ranks, but the tide of battle turned. In the Battle of Chilcheonryang, many Generals were killed, including Won Gyun, Jeolla Right Naval Commander Yi Eok-gi, Chungcheong Naval Commander Choi Ho, and Bae Heung-rip. Approximately 256 Korean naval ships and thousands of soldiers were lost. As a result, the Korean Navy was nearly annihilated.

## Evaluation and Lessons of the Battle of Chilcheonryang

In Korea, research and interest in the naval battles of the Imjin War have focused primarily on the victories of Yi Sun-sin. As a result, the Battle of Chilcheonryang has not received as much attention regarding research and assessment of the causes of its defeat. Here is a brief overview of the causes and lessons of the Battle of Chilcheonryang.

*First, problems with the command structure and ignoring the proposals of the field commanders.*

Even in battles where communications are well-developed today, the decisions of the commanders on the field of battle are critical to the outcome of the fight. However, the war command, the government, and the supreme commander, Kwon Yul, ignored the request of the field commander, Won Gyun, for a joint operation with the army to attack the Japanese forces in Angolpo and Gadeokdo before the advance on Busan. Ultimately, Won Gyun led his forces to Busan under Kwon Yul's coercion, leaving the Japanese forces in Angolpo and Gadeokdo behind.

*Second, the war command failed to consider the sea conditions.* Even today, the waters off Busan, where the Busan Port is located, are known for their rough waves and strong currents. The sea conditions can change rapidly. If the sea conditions are not good, the maneuverability of the ships is reduced, which can hinder the battle. The war command's obsession with advancing on Busan and the supreme commander Kwon Yul's forced mobilization of the Korean Navy, ignoring the sea conditions, were excessive.

**Third,** *the limitations of the leadership of Won Gyun, the naval commander.*

In addition to the reasons mentioned above, the leadership of Won Gyun, the battle commander, was also problematic regarding strategy and tactics. Commanders cannot win every battle. Battles are not always fought under favorable conditions for the friendly forces. Even in unfavorable conditions on the battlefield, commanders must demonstrate the best leadership. Won Gyun, the naval commander, failed to control his troops. This is well illustrated in the diary of Yi Sun-sin, who met with Kwon Yul in June 1597. The record states as follows:

*In the general's (Kwon Yul's) order, the naval commander Won Gyun does not move forward and only says that the enemy in Angolpo must be attacked first. He has many differences of opinion with the other naval commanders, and Won Gyun will not come out and will never agree with them, so he will ruin things.*

This means that there are significant problems with the control of the troops due to the differences of opinion between the naval commander Won Gyun and the generals who were trained under the command of Yi Sun-sin in the past, such as strategy and tactics. As mentioned above, on July 4, 1597, when Won Gyun was dissatisfied with the order of the war command and did not participate in the first advance on Busan, his subordinate commanders went to sea with their subordinate naval forces and retreated from the battle. It is rare in the history of any naval battle. In addition, during the Battle of Chilcheonryang, led by Won Gyun, Gyeongsang Right Naval Commander Bae Seol also led his subordinate generals out of the field. It can only be seen as a complete lack of leadership; such is not happening in the nature of the military. The Battle of Chilcheonryang is a representative example of how the failure of a commander to control his troops can lead to a fatal defeat in actual combat.

## King's Regret and Yi Sun-sin's Return to Tongjesa

When Yi Sun-sin arrived at Kwon Yul's camp, the Korean Navy faced challenges from the Japanese forces controlling the waters from Busan to the area around Hansan Island. The Korean Navy was contemplating how to counterattack, specifically considering attacking locations like Jinhae and Angolpo on the southern coast. Conflicts arose between Admiral Won Gyun and General Kwon Yul during this process. Yi Sun-sin began hearing about the defeats of the Korean Navy on July 14. The naval defeats peaked in the destructive Battle of Chilcheonryang on July 18. In this battle, Admiral Won Gyun and other vital leaders died, and the Korean Navy was almost destroyed. When Yi Sun-sin heard this news, he felt sad and hopeless. After the Korean Navy suffered a devastating defeat in the Battle of Chilcheonryang, General Kwon Yul suggested that Admiral Yi Sun-sin should inspect the navy, even though Yi Sun-sin wasn't in charge. Yi Sun-sin agreed to the suggestion. On July 18, when Yi Sun-sin heard about the Battle of Chilcheonryang, he and his team immediately assessed the situation. They traveled through Hadong and Gonyang, reaching Noryang, where they sent a letter to Kwon Yul informing him of the confirmed situation. On August 3, while staying at Son Gyeong-rae's house in Jinju, Yi Sun-sin learned he had been reappointed as the Naval Commander of the Three Provinces. During these difficult times, Yi Sun-sin took on the role of Naval Commander for the Three Provinces. He was deeply concerned about how to defeat the enemy with the weakened navy and how to lead the remaining soldiers after the defeat, but there was no time to waste. The content of the message that King Seonjo sent to Yi Sun-sin when he reappointed Yi Sun-sin as the Naval Commander for the Three Provinces is as follows:

> *Our country relies heavily on the navy for defense, but heaven's anger still hangs over us. With the Three Provinces' navy wiped out in one battle, who will safeguard our coastal forts, especially with Hansando already lost? I remember when you first took charge of the navy, your name became well-known. Your achievements have been outstanding since the victorious Imjin year, earning trust as solid as the Great Wall among our frontier forces. My past decision to remove you was because of my own mistakes. Now, with the shameful defeat of our navy, what more can be said? Given your crucial role, I choose to bring you back. I cancel your dismissal and appoint you again as the Naval Commander for Jeolla Province, overseeing Chungcheong, Jeolla, and Gyeongsang Provinces. On assuming your duties, gather your team, reassure them, bring together those scattered in fear, and establish a solid naval base. Safeguard key military points to ease concerns and restore public confidence. Knowing our prepared defense deters the enemy, do your best. Strengthen your loyalty, aiming to save our nation. I issue these orders, hoping my wishes are fulfilled.*

## Immediate Actions for Reorganization and Battle Preparations

On August 3, reappointed as the Naval Commander of the Three Provinces, Yi Sun-sin promptly visited Hadong, Gurye, Gokseong (on August 4), Suncheon, and Boseong (on August 9), gaining a more detailed understanding of the actual state of the defeat. Local administrative officials were fleeing, warehouses were set on fire, and many villages were deserted. During this process, he met with commanders who had fought in the Battle of Chilcheonryang and assessed the situation of the navy. From August 4 to August 17, while exercising his command as the Naval Commander of the Three Provinces, Yi Sun-sin received orders from the king on August 7 and August 15. Although not recorded in his diary, it is clear that Yi Sun-sin received instructions from the king on August 7 or August 15 to

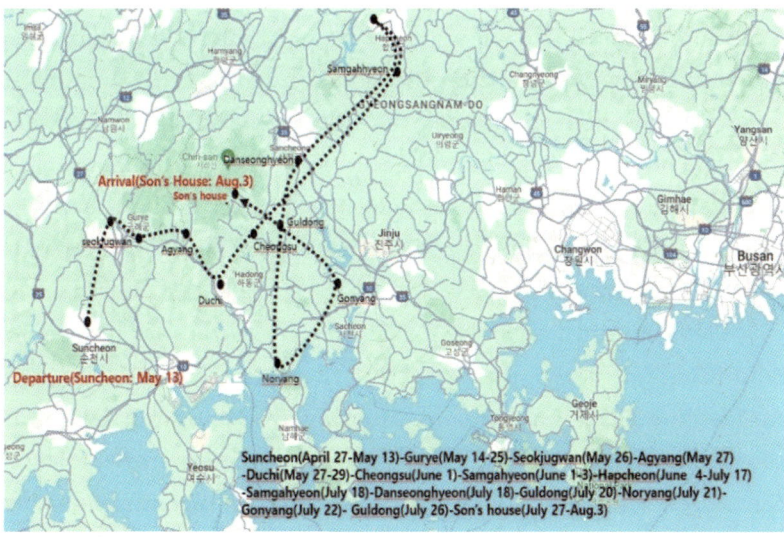

Figure 40: The Route of Yi Sun-sin's *Baekuijonggun* from Suncheon to Son's House

abolish the navy and incorporate it into the army. He submitted reports on August 14 and August 16.

The excerpt from the Records of Admiral Yi Sun-sin, written by Yi Sun-sin's nephew Yi Bun, reveals Yi Sun-sin's stance on the king's order to disband the navy as follows:

*For five to six years since the Imjin year (1592), the enemy dared not directly attack Jeolla Province and Chungcheong Province because the navy guarded those routes. Now, there are still twelve warships. If we exert all our efforts, we can fight. If we eliminate the navy now, the enemy will consider it a stroke of luck. In that case, they will advance through Jeolla and Chungcheong to the Han River. I will only fear this. Even though there are few warships, the enemy will not dare to look down on us as long as I am alive. Who protects the sea against the enemy except the navy?*

After the devastating defeat of the Korean Navy in the Battle of Chilcheonryang, the central government and the king, in their confusion, reinstated Yi Sun-sin as the Naval Commander of the Three Provinces. However, realizing the situation of the remaining naval forces, they no longer expected the navy to play a significant role. Consequently, after appointing Yi Sun-sin as the Naval Commander of the Three Provinces, the king immediately ordered him to serve in the army. Yi Sun-sin told King Seonjo that keeping the navy strong for maritime security was crucial.

The king did not disband the navy and dedicated himself to rebuilding and strengthening it for the country's military goal. Amidst the chaotic command situation involving the king and the central government, Yi Sun-sin's firm handling of the crisis continued. On August 18, 1597, 15 days after his appointment as the Naval Commander, Yi Sun-sin gathered 12 warships at Jangheung Hoeryeongpo and declared the commencement of his command.

# Chapter IV. Yi Sun-sin's Dismissal, Won Gyun's Naval Defeat, and Yi Sun-sin's Return

Figure 41: The Route of Naval Reorganzaation acd Arrival at the Myeong Battle Site after Reappointment as *Tongjesa*

After being taken from Hansando Headquarters to Seoul just six months before, on February 26, 1597, Yi Sun-sin again took command of the Korean Navy. However, the reality of the Korean Navy was vastly different from the past. Almost the entire Korean fleet had been annihilated, leaving only 12 ships. The fear of war had left both soldiers and commanders psychologically shaken. Yi Sun-sin faced the task of overcoming a difficult situation with only 12 ships. Announcing his appointment by the king as Naval Commander of the Jeolla, Chungcheong, and Gyeongsang provinces, Yi Sun-sin held a ceremonial event in front of commanders and soldiers to declare his command. Admiral Bae-seol protested Yi Sun-sin's appointment as Naval Commander-in-Chief by refusing to participate. Consequently, Yi Sun-sin punished the admiral's subordinate and maintained strict military discipline. After their victory at the Battle of Chilcheonryang, the Japanese Navy was determined to seize control of the southwestern waters, particularly the Jeolla Province region. Their ultimate goal was to advance through the West Sea and reach the Han River in Seoul. However, Yi Sun-sin, with his limited forces, was unable to either remain in one location or engage the enemy head-on. Combining defense and meticulous planning, the Korean Navy prepared for a final, decisive battle.

## Movement to the Myeongryang Strait for Decisive Fight

As Yi Sun-sin led the Korean Navy, they set sail from Hyeoryeongpo towards the designated battle site, the Myeongryang Strait. Even during the voyage, the enemy's relentless pursuit continued. Following a significant defeat at the hands of the Japanese under Admiral Won Gyun, the newly appointed naval commander, Yi Sun-sin, found himself facing the enemy's pursuit, unlike before. Yi Sun-sin wasn't a high-ranking admiral who previously commanded hundreds of warships and tens of thousands of soldiers. Instead, he was a humble Korean naval commander with only 12 warships and a few hundred soldiers. The Korean Navy was retreating, trying to avoid pursuit by the Japanese Navy, heading towards the final decisive battle site. While sailing toward the decisive battle, Yi Sun-sin's fleet was joined by one ship, increasing the number to 13 ships.

To avoid the Japanese Navy, Yi Sun-sin's fleet sailed through Hyeoryeongpo, Ijin, Eolanpo, and Jangdo before dropping anchor at the entrance of the Myeongryang Strait, known as Byeogpajin. On August 29 (October 9), Yi Sun-sin arrived at Byeogpajin, a vital spot in the southwestern seas since the Goryeo era. He knew that the Japanese Navy, in relentless pursuit, would soon launch a major attack. Yi Sun-sin heightened maritime alertness and kept a close eye on the enemy's movements at the entrance of the Myeongryang Strait. He adjusted formations, gearing up for the final battle. Signs of a major attack by the Japanese Navy began to appear. Several ships that seemed to be the enemy's advance team pursued them to Byeogpajin, but were chased away by the Korean fleet. Unfortunately, Admiral Bae Seol deserted as the enemy's advance was imminent. In a miserable situation, Yi Sun-sin made every effort to raise the combat morale of his soldiers. Yi Sun-sin moved his fleet to the Myeongryang Strait (the sea in front of Jeolla Right Navy Headquarters, also called *Uldolmo*k), which he designated as the final battle site.

The following is the content of Yi Sun-sin's diary, which recorded the situation in the few days before moving to the Myeongryang Strait:

***September 2:*** *Early in the morning, Admiral Bae Seol fled.*

***September 7:*** *Around 10 p.m., when enemy ships fired cannons, it seemed like many ships were frightened by the nighttime attack. I issued strict orders, and as my boat immediately sailed toward the enemy ship and fired cannons, the enemy couldn't withstand it and fled by midnight.*

***September 14:*** *Information came that 55 enemy ships had already entered the Aoran Sea. I sent a messenger ship to Usuyeong (Jeolla Right Navy Headquarters) to instruct refugees to evacuate to the inland.*

***September 15:*** *The tide came in. I commanded the fleet, moved to the sea off Usuyeong, and spent the night. Many strange signs appeared in my dreams.*

# The Truth about Yi Sun-sin's Claimed Disobedience

## The Outbreak of the Jeongyu War and the Impeachment of Yi Sun-sin

Japan illegally invaded Korea in 1592, and in a short time, the Japanese army captured Seoul, causing the king to flee to the Chinese border. As the war dragged on, China, which entered Korea to help, began peace talks. During the prolonged peace talks, Japan withdrew some troops but left some camped in Gyeongsang Province, Korea. By setting up camp in the south and responding to the Korean military with a long-term war strategy, they continued to inflict damage on the Korean people. Despite the active offensive of the Korean naval forces, the enemy responded passively. The peace talks between China and Japan, led by Konishi and Shim Yu-gyeong, from 1593 to 1596 had failed. Toyotomi Hideyoshi ordered an attack on Korea in early 1597, launching a second major attack after the breakdown of peace talks. Between January 12 and 15, 1597, Japanese forces led by General Kato invaded the waters of Busan, leading to a full-scale re-invasion. This second invasion, the Jeongyujaeran (Jeongyu War), was part of the Imjin War, including Japan's first invasion in 1592 and the second in 1597.

The Korean government impeached Yi Sun-sin for failing to

prevent the Japanese invasion in advance and appointed Won Gyun as *Tongjesa*. Yi Sun-sin was arrested at the Hansan Island headquarters and transported to Seoul. King Seonjo, following the persistent suggestions of conscientious subjects like Jeong Tak and Yi Won-ik, spared Yi Sun-sin from execution. Instead, he was stripped of his rank and ordered to serve as a rankless soldier under *Dowonsoo* Kwon Yul. When Yi Sun-sin was a young officer at the border of Hamgyeong Province, he had already experienced the first *Baekuijonggun* service (rankless military service) due to a superior conspiracy.

## Misunderstandings about Admiral Yi Sun-sin's Disobedience

For over 420 years after Yi Sun-sin's death, it was widely believed in Korean society that the fundamental reason for his *Baekuijonggun* service was his refusal of King Seonjo's order to go to war just before the Jeongyujaeran. However, recent research by Kwangsoob Ko has revealed that 'Yi Sun-sin's refusal of King Seonjo's order' is, in fact, groundless. This research result was shocking to Korean Yi Sun-sin researchers but was reconfirmed as fact by Korea's top Yi Sun-sin researchers. This chapter presents a brief overview of the so-called Admiral Yi Sun-sin's disobedience, which asserts that he refused King Seonjo's dispatch order at the beginning of the Imjin War. For detailed information, refer to the author's paper published in the academic journal. Admiral Yi Sun-sin is still respected as a hero of Korea today, not only for his naval battle victories that shine in the world's history of naval warfare but also for the spirit of sacrifice he showed during his lifetime. His actions to save the country during the unjust times of *Baekuijonggun*'s suffering are recorded in his diary and are still well known today. The sacrificial spirit he showed for his country in humiliating and miserable situations such as *Baekuijonggun* is only a small example.

## Reassessment of Historical Evidence and Misconceptions

Until recently, nothing was revealed about the so-called 'Yi Sun-sin's refusal of King Seonjo's order to dispatch,' which was recognized as the fundamental factor in Yi Sun-sin's impeachment. Therefore, most Yi Sun-sin researchers and the public believed that Yi Sun-sin refused King Seonjo's order to participate in the war for a long time. The fundamental background of Yi Sun-sin's refusal is found in the Annals of King Seonjo Sujeong, dated February 1, 1597. This record claims that Yi Sun-sin did not follow King Seonjo's wishes despite receiving an order to dispatch troops just before the Jeongyujaeran. However, the author's research papers revealed an error in the February 1, 1597 record of the Seonjo Sujeong Annals. Subsequently, the author unearthed a document by *Chechalsa* Yi Won-ik, Yi Sun-sin's superior, confirming Yi Sun-sin's operational plans just before the Jeongyujaeran, proving that the claim was fiction. The document drafted by *Chechalsa* Yi Won-ik on the eve of the enemy invasion clearly records *Tongjesa* Yi Sun-sin's operational plan to lead his troops and engage the enemy in the seas of Busan in the event of an invasion.

## Discovery and Analysis of Yi Won-ik's Reports

The historical materials unearthed by the author are contained in Ori Teacher's Collection of Works, a record written by *Chechalsa* Yi Won-ik. As mentioned, Yi Won-ik was Yi Sun-sin's superior and directly commanded him. As Japan's major attack became clear, Yi Won-ik went to the southern part of the Korean peninsula under a special order from King Seonjo and frequently met with Admiral Yi Sun-sin to discuss strategies for an enemy invasion. He then reported Yi Sun-sin's naval operation plan to King Seonjo in writing. Unfortunately, much of Yi Won-ik's report is not conveyed in the Annals of King Seonjo.

Fortunately, Yi Won-ik's report has been passed down in his collection of works but was ignored for a long time by researchers and historians. Luckily, these records were discovered during the author's research and made public. The records of *Chechalsa* Yi Won-ik included in Volume 2 of Ori Teacher's Collection are 29: 15 in 1596 and 14 in 1597. Among these were 13 cases from January to April 1596, with signs of a Japanese invasion, and 2 cases in December. Among the 14 cases in 1597, 8 are related to Admiral Yi Sun-sin before and after the Japanese invasion, reported between January and February, and 6 in other periods. Based on Yi Won-ik's report to the king, we will examine how Yi Sun-sin prepared for the Japanese invasion just before the Jeongyujaeran.

## Correction on Yi Sun-sin's Historical Errors

Yi Won-ik went south, established a command center in Seongju, and worked hard to report the inspection results of the army and navy's war preparations to the government. In the case of the navy, *Tongjesa* Yi Sun-sin's command ability allowed him to do his work well, but it was pointed out that there was a problem in securing military forces in each coastal area. This clearly shows the political atmosphere at the time due to distracted public sentiment and the passive cooperation of each local leader. Despite Yi Sun-sin's excellent leadership, there were limits to the military power of his subordinate naval forces. In December 1596, the Joseon dynasty government accepted the Japanese invasion again as an accomplished fact. Yi Won-ik was assigned a mission to *Chechalsa* and went south to resolve military problems between the army and navy actively. In the case of the navy, he tried to strengthen its military power from the beginning of his term. However, it was still weak, so he made an effort to resolve the issue of support from the civilian sector by securing military personnel by directly sending deputy inspectors to Jeolla-do and Chungcheong-do. Meanwhile, on December 7, 1596, about 35 days before the Jeongyujaeran outbreak, Yi Won-ik reported in *Janggye*, a document sent to the king, that Admiral Yi Sun-sin would reorganize his naval forces and dispatch troops to Busan to attack the enemy. In addition, on December 26, 1596, 17 days before the Jeongyujaeran outbreak, Yi Won-ik reported that he met *Tongjesa* Yi Sun-sin in Sacheon, Gyeongsang-do, and instructed him to block Kato when he crossed the sea with troops immediately. In the new year of 1597, as signs of a major Japanese attack became stronger, the plans of Yi Won-ik and Yi Sun-sin became more concrete. On January 4, 8 days before the Jeongyujaeran outbreak, Yi Won-ik reported the strategy of the Korean Navy, saying,

> Since the navy of the three provinces is now in a hurry to requisition, it is right to wait for the navy to gather, occupy Geoje Island first, and immediately block the sea route to kill the enemy.

Even more shocking details are confirmed in the report on January 12, 1597, the day of the Jeongyujaeran outbreak. On January 12th, Kato troops first appeared in Busan waters, but when Yi Won-ik wrote the report, the news of Kato troops entering Korean waters had not been reported to Yi Won-ik. This time difference is due to the different locations of Yi Won-ik and the official who witnessed and reported Kato's entry into Busan waters, making real-time reporting impossible as it is today. Several notable points in Yi Won-ik's operational status report on January 12th reveal that he had deep discussions with naval commander Yi Sun-sin about response plans in preparation for an enemy invasion. In particular, Yi Won-ik's January 12, 1597 report contains Yi Sun-sin's operational plan reported directly to Yi Won-ik. Yi Sun-sin's operational plan, confirmed in Yi Won-ik's report, was shocking and served as historical proof that could correct the distorted history of Yi Sun-sin that has been passed down for over 400 years after his death. The main contents of Yi Sun-sin's operational plan before the Jeongyujaeran included in Yi Won-ik's report are as follows: Yi Sun-sin, commanding the Three Provinces Navy at the Hansan Island Naval Headquarters, was well aware that Japanese troops consistently sailed with the east wind when moving from the mainland to Korea. According to the report, Admiral Yi Sun-sin mentioned that preparations should be made in case Kato's troops unexpectedly change their invasion route from the anticipated landing site due to the influence of the wind, directing toward the former stronghold of the enemy (Seosaengpo, Gyeongsang-do). Admiral Yi Sun-sin further stated that if the Korean Navy adopts a passive stance by merely observing the enemy's movements near Hansan Island, east of Geoje Island, they would be unable to monitor the enemy's maneuvers.

Therefore, Admiral Yi Sun-sin argued that it would be preferable for the Korean Navy to advance beyond Hansan Island, closer to Geoje Island, all the way to Dadaepo, Busan, and wait for the enemy before actively defeating them. Furthermore, according to this report, Yi Won-ik expressed concerns that Yi Sun-sin's aggressive operational plan might be exposed to the enemies stationed in Gadeokdo or Angolpo when the Hansando naval forces move to Busan waters. However, Yi Sun-sin acknowledged that it was unavoidable, so if the enemies around the route were to attack, he would defeat them and proceed to Dadaepo. Yi Sun-sin expressed his strong will to Yi Won-ik to break through the enemy along the route and advance to Dadaepo to attack

Kato's troops. He stated as follows:

*Considering the current situation, we cannot go out secretly or remain hidden. If the enemy on the hill takes a boat to go out to sea, we can attack them first. If the enemy is on the hill, there is no possibility of attacking us, so there is no need to hesitate to go out to avoid the enemy.*

This record shows Yi Sun-sin's strong will to fight, actively fighting and defeating enemies even if they were in the coastal waters of the route. The content of Yi Won-ik's report to the king on January 12, 1597, directly contradicts the record of February 1, 1597, in the Annals of King Seonjo's Sujeong, which states that even after receiving the king's order to go to war, Yi Sun-sin did not send his troops out because there were enemy soldiers on the route. It is decisive historical evidence that turns it upside down. Why is the material, such as the Annals of King Seonjo's Sujeong, entirely opposite of the Yi Won-ik report? First of all, since the Annals of King Seonjo's Sujeong were completed about 60 years after Yi Sun-sin's death, it can be assumed that collecting accurate historical information about Yi Sun-sin was difficult. Nowhere in the Annals of King Seonjo, which was written earlier than the Annals of King Seonjo's Sujeong and is recognized as highly reliable, is there any record that Yi Sun-sin refused King Seonjo's order to go to war before the outbreak of the Jeongyujaeran. Also, during the impeachment process of Yi Sun-sin, who was held responsible for failing to stop the enemy when the Jeongyu War broke out, there was no mention of Yi Sun-sin refusing the order to go to war. Before the outbreak of the Jeongyujaeran, Yi Sun-sin was planning to deploy to the Busan area, including Gadeok Island and Dadaepo. Yi Sun-sin never refused King Seonjo's order to participate before the outbreak of the Jeongyujaeran. The reason why it is said that Yi Sun-sin refused the orders of King Seonjo until recently, 420 years after his death, is simple. That is because incorrect historical records were cited repeatedly without factual verification. As explained earlier, Yi Sun-sin never refused King Seonjo's order to participate before the outbreak of the Jeongyujaeran. The author's research results have already been made known to Yi Sun-sin researchers in Korea, and there are no objections or refutations to the research results. As a result of this author's research, it is hoped that Yi Sun-sin's bad reputation will be restored and historical errors will be corrected.

# Chapter V

## The Miraculous Battle of Myeongryang and Rebuilding Navy

# The Battle of Myeongryang: Miraculous Victory

As mentioned earlier, the Japanese troops arrived at Busan with hundreds of ships in January 1597. On July 8, they arrived again with 600 ships carrying landing forces. After winning the Battle of Chilcheonryang, the Japanese Navy controlled the south coast sea and participated in the Battle of Namwon Castle through Duchijin in the Seomjin River Valley, using a combined water-land strategy. They successively captured Namwon Castle on August 16 and Jeonju Castle on August 25.

Meanwhile, the Japanese Navy, which had won the Battle of Chilcheonryang, transformed their tactics completely from previous battles. They began to pursue the modest Korean Navy under Yi Sun-sin, who was re-appointed as the Commander of the Three Provinces Navy. The Japanese Navy pursued Yi Sun-sin's fleet, which had set sail from Hyeoryeongpo on the coast of Jangheung, Jeolla Province, with 12 ships. The Japanese Navy chased the Korean Navy while following them to Byeokpajin, the entrance to the Battle of Myeongryang. Yi Sun-sin's fleet also drove away the enemy's reconnaissance ships on the way from Hyeoryeongpo to Byeokpajin. While staying in Byeokpajin, the Korean Navy received information that the Japanese Navy was pursuing the Korean Navy with a large fleet. Yi Sun-sin's fleet left Byeokpajin and moved to the decisive battlefield of Myeongryang. The

Korean fleet anchored in front of the Jeolla Right Naval Headquarters on the morning of September 15 and stayed up all night. Yi Sun-sin judged Myeongryang (also known as *Uldolmok*) the final battlefield and moved the fleet there. *Uldolmok* is a narrow strait with many rocks on the coast and a current speed of 7 to 12 knots (about 3 meters per second). Yi Sun-sin applied geographical factors and the military tactics he had learned to choose this place as the final battlefield. *Uldolmok* is a narrow channel suitable for a smaller fleet. Therefore, *Uldolmok* was the optimal place to deal with hundreds of enemy ships with a small number of ships.

Comparing just the military power, retreating in a typical military situation would be rational. However, Yi Sun-sin and the Korean Navy could no longer retreat. If *Uldolmok* was breached, the Japanese Navy could control the last remaining south coast sea and advance to the West Sea via the waters in front of Mokpo. The Japanese troops had been trying to advance to the west coast of the Korean Peninsula and secure a maritime supply line to secure the supply line for the Japanese forces operating in the interior since 1592.

However, the Japanese Navy was defeated by Yi Sun-sin's fleet, which was guarding the southwest coast of the Korean Peninsula, and failed to achieve its goal. However, they secured the opportunity to advance to the West Sea by defeating the Korean fleet led by Commander Won Gyun. Knowing this situation well, Yi Sun-sin was destined to block the enemy's large fleet with a decisive battle. Yi Sun-sin and the Korean Navy had no choice but to fight to the death at *Uldolmok*. Therefore, Yi Sun-sin showed leadership to strengthen the morale of the terrified soldiers after losing the Battle of Chilcheonryang and to make them ready to fight to the death. Yi Sun-sin gathered the soldiers to reaffirm his determination to win before the battle. He said to the soldiers who were trembling with anxiety and fear in front of the fight with enemies,

*It is said in the military law that if you want to live, you will die, and if you fight with the determination to die, you will open the way to live.*

He also emphasized the responsibility and duty of a soldier by saying, even a thousand enemies will tremble with fear if one soldier guards the gate. He spent the evening thinking about the tactical formation to strengthen the defense against the invading Japanese Navy.

## Battle Progress and Results

Yi Sun-sin commanded a Korean fleet of 13 ships and moved to the Myeongryang Strait to avoid the pursuit of the Japanese Navy, set up a defensive line, and prepared to fight a desperate battle against the sizeable Japanese Navy. On the morning of September 16, a reported to Yi Sun-sin that about 200 Japanese ships would soon arrive at the Myeongryang Strait, where the Korean fleet was stationed. Yi Sun-sin immediately raised anchor and set sail. The Korean fleet, under Yi Sun-sin's orders, headed for the Myeongryang Strait in the direction of the current. The battle occurred in the waters off Yangdo, north of the bridge connecting Jindo and Haenam. The initial battle formation, a straight line, was disrupted due to the battle's intensification and the current's influence. About 133 Japanese ships swarmed and surrounded the Korean fleet. The soldiers were afraid and did not advance. Yi Sun-sin led his flagship into the enemy lines and ordered the crew to fire cannons and arrows.

Even the soldiers on Yi Sun-sin's ship showed signs of fear. During the battle, Yi Sun-sin reassured his crew that even if the enemy had a thousand ships, they would not be able to attack immediately. He urged his crew not to be afraid and to shoot the enemy with all their

Chapter V. The Miraculous Battle of Myeongryang and Rebuilding Navy

Figure 42: The Phase I Situation Map of the Battle of Myeongryang

might. The crew fired cannons and arrows toward the enemy. Amid the battle, Yi Sun-sin called for the admirals' ships that participated, as they were still behind. The vessels of Kim Eung-ham and An Wi also began to join the attack. Yi Sun-sin called An Wi and shouted at him,

*"Do you want to die under military law? Do you think you can live if you run away?"*

When An Wi heard this and tried to attack the enemy, the enemy commander's ship and two other enemy ships came close to An Wi's warship and attacked An Wi's ship. Seven or eight of An Wi's rowers jumped into the sea.

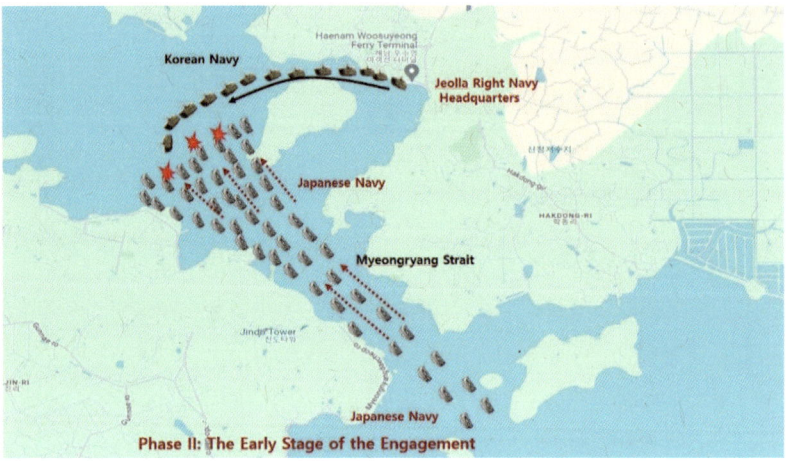

Figure 43: The Phase II Situation Map of the Battle of Myeongryang
*(Admiral Yi Sun-sin's fleet of 13 vessels made an emergency departure to engage in a desperate battle against the 133 Japanese warship)*

Because Japanese naval ships had lower hulls than Korean warships, they tried to weaken the mobility of Korean warships by staying close to the Korean warship Panokseon and attacking the soldiers inside the hull with rifles. To rescue An Wi's warship that was under attack, Yi Sun-sin approached and fired at the enemy ship with cannons and bows. The battle continued and was in a state of chaos. The Korean Navy destroyed 20 enemy ships with cannon fire. Under the command of a Japanese flagship, Japanese naval ships surrounded the Korean Navy. Nokdo *Manho* Song Yeo-jong and Yeongdeungpo *Manho* Jeong Yeong-du joined and destroyed 11 enemy ships.

Yi Sun-sin's ships were surrounded during the fierce fighting, and the generals were afraid. Nevertheless, in the end, Yi Sun-sin and the generals fought bravely, as they had vowed to do before setting sail.

Chapter V. The Miraculous Battle of Myeongryang and Rebuilding Navy

Figure 44: The Phase III Situation Map of the Battle of Myeongryang
*(Admiral Yi Sun-sin's fleet destroyed 31 Japanese vessels)*

Around 2:00 p.m the direction of the current changed to a favorable south-southeasterly current for the Korean Navy. As the Korean Navy's attacks intensified, the Japanese Navy lost its will to fight and began to retreat. If you look closely at the battle record of Myeongryang, the ships on both sides mostly fought in close proximity from the beginning to the end of the battle. The Korean fleet destroyed 31 Japanese ships surrounding the Korean ships with naval cannons. The record of a Japanese general who fought in the Battle of Chilcheonryang states that the Japanese warship was lower than the Korean ship, so it came close to the Korean ship and attacked the rowers with rifles. It is worth noting that, taking advantage of the experience of the Battle of Chilcheonryang, the Japanese Navy approached Korean ships and attacked them. Referring to the author's published paper, the author has already described in detail the effective range and blind spot of the Turtle Ship's cannons when explaining the Turtle Ship. Since the effective range of Korean ships' cannons is approximately 10-15 meters, close combat proved effective for directly targeting enemy ships with Korean vessels, enhancing accuracy.

The Japanese Navy had about 200 ships tracking the Korean Navy, but only 133 participated in the Battle of Myeongryang. The remaining vessels were waiting outside the Myeongryang Waterway. Because the currents in the Myeongryang Waterway are fast and the waterway is narrow, more than 200 ships could not be deployed at once. Most of the Japanese Navy's warships in the war were small ships called *Sekibune*, while the large battle ship *Adakebune* served as the flagship of enemy commanders, and only a small number participated. Yi Sun-sin achieved the miracle of Myeongryang, destroying 31 enemy ships without losing a single ship of his own in a battle against an enemy fleet of 133 ships against 13 ships. The Japanese commanders who participated in this battle were Kuroshima Michifusa, Madaishi, and Badashinshi, one of whom, Madaishi, was killed in action. The Korean casualties were Kim Tak and Gye Seong, crew members of Yi Sun-sin's flagship, who were killed by enemy fire, and Park Young-nam, Bonghak, and Yi Guk-shin, who were wounded. In particular, the people's cooperation in the battle significantly contributed to the victory. The refugee ships, which did not go far until just before the battle, disguised their ships as warships and cheered on Yi Sun-sin's fleet from behind the battle site. The refugees who watched the battle situation sighed and felt sorry when the Korean fleet was cornered and cheered with tears when they finally won. After a fierce battle, the Battle of Myeongryang ended in a miraculous victory for the Korean Navy. Yi Sun-sin wrote in his diary that this victory resulted from heaven's help.

## Evaluation and Significance of the Battle of Myeongryang

The Battle of Myeongryang was an unprecedented and immortal great naval battle in which a group of Korean naval officers and soldiers, led by the outstanding commander Admiral Yi Sun-sin, fought against 133 Japanese naval ships with only 13 ships — a force far from adequate. After the Japanese occupation, many films about Admiral Yi Sun-sin were produced in Korea. Among them, the 2014 film *"The Admiral: Roaring Currents"*, based on the Battle of Myeongryang, exceeded 17 million viewers, demonstrating immense popularity. This underscores why the Battle of Myeongryang is hailed as a brilliant battle in Korean naval history and world history.

First, the driving force behind Admiral Yi Sun-sin and the Korean Navy's miraculous victory in the Battle of Myeongryang is revealed in Yi Sun-sin's quote below. Even when the king ordered Yi Sun-sin to disband the Korean Navy and fight on land, Yi Sun-sin replied, *"I still have 12 ships"*. He firmly believed that the enemy who invaded by sea should be stopped at sea. Before the Battle of Myeongryang, Yi Sun-sin encouraged his men by saying,

*"Those who are determined to die will live; those who seek to live will die."*

He led the charge in the actual battle, showing a posture of fighting to the death. Yi Sun-sin also declared,

*"If one soldier guards the pass, even a thousand enemies will tremble in fear."*

He lured the enemy into the narrow Myeongryang Strait and defeated a large navy with forces far inferior to the enemy. The Battle of Myeongryang impressed the Japanese Navy with the realization that the Korean Navy, although outnumbered, could consistently deliver a decisive blow to the enemy. The victory of the Battle of Myeongryang by Admiral Yi Sun-sin is significant in that it broke the will of Japan, which had been persistently trying to advance to the West since the outbreak of the Imjin War, to dominate the Joseon Kingdom.

The Japanese Navy, defeated in the Battle of Myeongryang, joined forces with the navy in the waters off Jindo the next day to pursue the Korean Navy. However, the Korean Navy moved its naval base to the small island of Dangsado off Amtaedo through the waters off Mokpo on the night of the victory of the Battle of Myeongryang. The reason for moving the fleet north instead of staying at the battle site after the great victory at the Battle of Myeongryang was Yi Sun-sin's strategic action to avoid the enemy's retaliatory attack and plan for the future. The Battle of Myeongryang was an immortal great naval battle in which a group of Korean naval officers and soldiers led by the outstanding commander Admiral Yi Sun-sin fought against 133 Japanese naval ships, with only 13 ships being far from enough.

# Rebuilding the Devastated Korean Navy

### Yi Sun-sin's Suffering after the Victory in the Battle of Myeongryang

The fact that Yi Sun-sin retreated for a significant period after the great victory of the Battle of Myeongryang, shedding tears of pain, is rarely known or emphasized by the general public and even those who claim to know him. There are various reasons for this, but it is generally due to the great emphasis on Yi Sun-sin's heroic battle results. He is perceived solely as a god or hero of war, but there are also reasons for the lack of research and illumination on his military strategy and naval operations.

Yi Sun-sin and the Korean Navy had no time to enjoy the joy of victory after the great win at Myeongryang. The battle was not truly over when it ended. Although the Japanese Navy was defeated in the battle at Myeongryang, Yi Sun-sin judged that the main force of several hundred ships would still be stationed outside the Myeongryang Strait. As mentioned, only 133 out of more than 200 Japanese ships that pursued the Korean Navy fought near the Myeongryang Strait. Any naval commander would have judged that the remaining 150 ships would be waiting outside the Myeongryang Strait or near Jindo.

Predicting a retaliatory attack by the Japanese after regrouping the next day, Yi Sun-sin's Korean Navy could not stay with the naval

Figure 45: The Routes of Admiral Yi Sun-sin and the Korean fleet before and after the Battle of Myeongryang

forces at Jeolla Right Navy Command in their victorious area even after winning the battle. Eventually, Yi Sun-sin and the Korean Navy traveled north along the sea road bathed in full moonlight, dropped anchor around an island called Dangsado in Sinan County, which was deemed safe, and spent their first night after winning the battle. Being pursued by the Japanese and without any specific immediate plans, Yi Sun-sin's state of mind, leading the last remaining 13 ships of the Korean Navy, was truly indescribable. Yi Sun-sin and the Korean Navy's strategic retreat was an inevitable choice.

After winning a decisive victory at the Battle of Myeongryang, Admiral Yi Sun-sin left the Battle of Myeongryang area on the evening of September 16 and sailed north to the island of Dangsado, about 20 miles (about 37 kilometers) away. Dangsado is a small island in Muangun, on the right side of the Angel Bridge that opened in April 2019. Currently, about 60 households live on the island. Admiral

Yi Sun-sin spent his first night after the victory on Dangsado. After that, until he landed on Gohado, Mokpo, the sacred land of the reconstruction of the Korean Navy, on October 29, 1597, he spent about 40 days on the remote islands in the southwestern sea of the Korean Peninsula.

The Korean fleet won a decisive victory at the Battle of Myeongryang. Still, the victory factors were primarily due to Admiral Yi Sun-sin's leadership and the Korean Navy's fighting spirit. However, it can also be seen as a matter of luck, as Admiral Yi Sun-sin said, *"It was a stroke of luck"* immediately after the battle. Admiral Yi Sun-sin thanked Heaven for winning when the Japanese Navy far outnumbered him.

He felt the need to rebuild the navy and prepare for the future while conducting defensive operations with his outnumbered fleet. On the evening of the day the battle ended, Admiral Yi Sun-sin moved to Dangsado while maintaining a safe distance from the enemy. Many refugee fishing boats from various provinces had already anchored there. Admiral Yi Sun-sin found refugees on the islands and anchorages the Korean fleet visited on September 17, Uido, and September 20, Wido. He comforted them, and the refugees donated food and clothing to the Korean Navy. On September 17, he moved to Uido (located in Jidomyeon, Muangun) and stayed there until he left for Beopseongpo in Yeonggwang on September 18. On September 18, he visited Beopseongpo, returned to Hongnunggot, and slept on the sea. September 20, he sailed to Wido, and on the morning of September 21, he moved to Gogunsando.

While leading the Korean fleet through the southwest sea, Admiral Yi Sun-sin was also in constant contact with officials on land. On September 18, the military leader of Imchijin came to the sea fleet of Admiral Yi Sun-shin and cooperated by providing information on the war situation on land. The Imchijin was a naval unit located in a port near the sea of Dangsado, and it was afraid to shoot the enemy with all its might. Admiral Yi Sun-sin met the governor of Jeolla Province, who was responsible for the total administrative area of Jeolla Province, who came by boat on the sea of Gogunsando. He heard about the war situation and information on land. On September 27, he sent a report on the results of the Battle of Myeongryang to the king on the sea of Gogunsando. It was not until ten days after the victory at the Battle of Myeongryang that the report to the king confirmed that 13 ships had participated.

Immediately after the fierce battle, *Tongjesa* Yi Sun-sin was extremely exhausted. In his diary on September 27, the day he sent a letter to the king, he wrote that his whole body was tired and in pain all night. On October 2, he wrote that he felt as if his heart was being torn into a thousand pieces as he sat alone on his ship. That is understandable. Although he had inflicted a terrific blow on the enemy at Myeongryang with the help of heaven, the Japanese Navy had a much more extensive fleet than the Korean Navy. It still wholly controlled the sea in the southern region. In this situation, the only thing *Tongjesa* Yi Sun-sin could do immediately was to feed and shelter the hungry and tired Korean Navy and ensure their safe passage through the winter. In addition, *Tongjesa* Yi Sun-sin's urgent task was to reinforce the Korean Navy to drive the enemy out of the sea.

However, he could not see a single inch ahead. The central government, which was in charge of the war, could not provide any assistance to the Korean Navy, so *Tongjesa* Yi Sun-sin had to solve everything on his own. Yi Sun-sin was heartbroken to see the refugees moored at the port to avoid the enemy's troubles, but the fishing boats that were supposed to be fishing did not catch any fish.

Yi Sun-sin continued his lonely winter voyage while encouraging refugees and devising a strategic plan for rebuilding the Korean Navy. While sailing in search of the navy's residence in the west sea of Jeolla-

Chapter V. The Miraculous Battle of Myeongryang and Rebuilding Navy

do, the seasons changed rapidly, and snow fell, cold winds and bad weather continued. The worries of Yi Sun-sin and the Korean Navy also grew. In the end the end, after the Battle of Myeongryang, Yi Sun-sin, and the Korean Navy, unable to find a safe place despite moving north and sailing to Gogunsando, changed their course back to the south and came down to the sea near the Jeolla Right Navy Headquarters in Haenam, where the Battle of Myeongryang took place. The day Yi Sun-sin and the Korean Navy returned to the place was October 9th. Yi Sun-sin confirmed that the Japanese Navy's retaliation had ruined the Jeolla Usuyeong, the Jeolla Right Navy Base.

## Plans for Strengthening Forces at an Unknown Island

Yi Sun-sin decided that the Jeolla Usuyeong could not be used as a military base. Yi Sun-sin was forced to find a place where his navy could stay. He moved his navy to the unknown island of *Anpyeondo* and landed on the island. After landing on the island, Yi Sun-sin went up the mountain with his staff to find a place to hide the ships and discussed military affairs such as security of the stay until the afternoon. The next day, he began to stay on the island in earnest, but his heart was filled with anxiety and sadness about what to do in the future to drive out the enemy from the sea and save the country from crisis. The island of *Anpyeondo* did not exist in Korea, so it was not revealed until recently, and it was only estimated to be a few islands. In this way, the unknown island of *Anpyeondo*, which had not been confirmed for an extended time, was revealed in 2019 when Professor Kwangsoob Ko announced it in a research paper to the relevant academic society after persistent exploration of Yi Sun-sin's route and on-site survey. The unknown island of *Anpyeondo*, where Yi Sun-sin landed and stayed on October 11, 1597, was confirmed to be *Anjwado*, located in

Anjwamyeon, Sinangun, Jeollanam-do.

The mountain Admiral Yi climbed after landing was confirmed to be *Maebong Mountain* in *Anjwado*. It was confirmed that *Anpyeondo* was real after 422 years. Yi Sun-sin's temporary headquarters on Anjwa Island began, but there was no way to block the Japanese Navy's offensive then.

Yi Sun-sin, who was forced to retreat to the rear in the face of the Japanese Navy's offensive and was staying on an island in the remote countryside, was only thinking about strengthening his navy and defeating the enemy in the future.

While staying at the temporary headquarters on Anjwa Island, he exchanged information with local governors in the coastal areas of Jeollanam-do, such as Jangheung, Mokpo, Muan, Naju, and Haenam. In particular, if an incident occurred that violated the rules of war during the war by local governors, he summoned them to the island and severely punished them. He also brought food left by the enemy from Haenam by boat. He managed salt production on 13 islands, etc., doing his best in military affairs while considering the search for a new navy headquarters. Yi Sun-sin recorded his frustrations about being on the run on the remote island of Anjwa Island in his diary. Let's take a look at some of the records.

*October 11:* *In the evening, the weather was warm, like spring, and there were many signs of rain. In the early evening, the moonlight was as fine as silk, and I sat alone at the ship's window, so my regrets were endless. At 10 o'clock, my whole body was hot and sweaty.*

*October 13:* *On this night, the moonlight was as fine as silk, and no wind, but I couldn't soothe my heart sitting alone on the boat. I tossed, turned, sat, lay down, and couldn't sleep all night, just sighing at the sky.*

Chapter V. The Miraculous Battle of Myeongryang and Rebuilding Navy

On the fourth day after Yi Sun-sin landed on Anjwa Island, he heard that his third son Myeon, who was at his home in Asan, Chungcheong Province, had been killed while fighting against the Japanese army. Yi Sun-sin, who heard the news of his son's death on an island in the remote countryside during the war, wept.

*October 14: Before I even opened the envelope, my bones and flesh trembled first, and my mind was confused. I roughly opened the outer envelope and saw the word "Weeping" written on the back of the letter written by my son Yeol. I knew that Myeon had died, and my liver fell, and I cried out. How can the sky be so unkind? It feels like my liver is burning and tearing. The sky is dark, and even the sea has changed its color. Sad, my son, where have you gone leaving me? My brother, sister, and mother have nowhere to rely on, so I still have to endure and live, but my heart is dead, and only my form remains, so I can only cry out. A day feels like a year.*

*October 19: I had a dream in which I wept bitterly for my dead son. I had a nosebleed (more than 1 liter) when it got dark. I sat at night thinking and crying. How can I tell everything? I feel so sad and heartbroken that I can't bear it.*

Admiral Yi Sun-sin was heartbroken to hear the news of his son's death on an isolated island. However, he had no time to grieve. On September 24, he learned that the Chinese navy had arrived in Ganghwado. China, which had only provided ground forces support since the outbreak of the war in 1592, had finally decided to send naval forces after realizing the seriousness of the situation. The Chinese government had rushed to send its navy after concluding that if the Korean Navy lost control of the South Sea after the Battle of Chilcheonyang, it could threaten the border of China.

The king ordered Yi Sun-sin to secure a new naval base in preparation for the Chinese intervention. The Chinese navy's participation was a golden opportunity to turn the tide of the war, but Admiral Yi, who was in a strategic retreat, had several tasks to accomplish. The priority was to secure a base for the combined fleet and strengthen the Korean Navy. Yi Sun-sin could no longer remain on Anjwa Island, far from the mainland. His top priority was moving his fleet to a location closer to the mainland so that he could work with the central government and local governments to strengthen the navy and prepare to establish a combined fleet with the Chinese navy. Yi Sun-sin chose Gohado, located in front of Mokpo, as the site for the reconstruction of the navy. On October 29, he led his fleet to Gohado. Finally, after his desperate wandering life, immediately after the Battle of Myeongryang, he settled in Gohado and began to rebuild the Korean Navy. He also began accelerating the acquisition of naval bases for the combined fleet. After Yi Sun-sin led his fleet and made a strategic retreat after his victory in the Battle of Myeongryang, we will examine the movements of the Japanese forces. Kang Hang's *Gangyangrok* confirms the record of the Japanese Navy pursuing the Korean Navy for revenge after the great defeat in the Battle of Myeongryang. According to Kang Hang's record, after the Battle of Myeongryang, the Japanese Navy arrived at Usuyeong with a large force to attack the Korean Navy. However, they did not find the Korean fleet because it immediately left the battlefield after the naval battle. Therefore, the Japanese Navy chased after the Korean Navy that had passed through Muan, Hampyeong, and Yeonggwang. Still, they did not find the Korean fleet, which only caused trouble for the Korean people before returning to the Japanese castle in Suncheon.

Also, let's compare the visit dates of the Japanese Navy recorded by Kang Hang and the places of transit, such as Muan and Yeonggwang, that the Korean fleet passed through while moving from the

Myeongryang area to Gogunsando on September 16. We can find a very interesting fact. In other words, the Japanese Navy's activities appear a few days after the Korean Navy stays and leaves the area. Also, if we look at the dates when the Korean Navy moved south from Gogunsando, we can see that the Japanese Navy's activities hav already appeared several days ago.

The Korean Navy arrived at the sea before Jeolla Usuyeong, passing through the places the Japanese Navy had visited. Yi Sun-sin gave up the ruined Jeolla Usuyeong and moved to Anjwa Island. As mentioned earlier, Yi Sun-sin's retreat from the Battle of Myeongryang was a very strategic move.

## Efforts to Rebuild the Destroyed Navy at Gohado

During the Seven Years' War of Imjin, Admiral Yi Sun-sin served as the Navy Commander of the Three Provinces' Navy at four naval headquarters *(Tongjeyeong)*: the naval base in Tongyeong in Gyeongsang, the naval base on Anjwa Island *(Anpyeon* Island) in Sinangun, the naval base on Gohado in Mokpo, and the naval base on Gogeumdo in Wando. Except for Anjwa Island in Sinangun, which the author identified, the remaining naval bases are well-known historical sites managed by the government and local governments in various ways since the death of Admiral Yi Sun-sin. Among them, Gohado is a place of great historical significance as it was the site of the reconstruction of the Korean Navy, which was annihilated in the Chilcheonryang Naval Battle.

After landing on Gohado, Admiral Yi Sun-sin prioritized rebuilding the navy. With only 13 ships participating in the Battle of Myeongryang, no suitable naval operation could be taken against the Japanese Navy. It was important for Admiral Yi Sun-sin to choose the time and place to reconstruct the Korean Navy. After considering various factors, including the acquisition of manpower resources, shipbuilding, the acquisition of military provisions, the procurement of raw materials, and the cooperation of local governments and the people, Admiral Yi Sun-sin chose Gohado as the temporary headquarters of the navy reconstruction command.

The Gohado Naval Base was a temporary naval base that was not included in the organization of the Korean Navy. However, it was the site of the temporary wartime headquarters. In other words, it can be seen as having a similar character to the wartime temporary Kyungmudae in Busan during the Korean War in 1950. Given that it was wartime, the purpose of Yi Sun-sin's establishment of the Gohado Naval Base and his decision to reside there was also apparent. Before landing on Gohado, Yi Sun-sin had maintained continuous communication with local officials and the government in the southwestern sea area while staying at the *Anjwado* Naval Base. He planned to rebuild the Korean Navy as soon as possible and defeat the enemy in the future. While staying in *Anjwado*, Yi Sun-sin learned of the news of the Chinese Navy's participation, and he received an order from King Seonjo to secure the Chinese Navy's naval base. In his diary from December 1 to 27, 1597, the period of his stay in Gohado, there is a record of the Provincial Inspector visiting and discussing military measures, and he also took military measures to strengthen his forces, such as assigning 19 coastal counties in Jeolla Province to the navy. For the Korean Navy to act as the leading force after establishing the Korean-China Allied Forces, it was urgent to strengthen its forces. The news that the Chinese Navy would join was great for the Korean Navy, which was struggling during the war. But it also meant that the commander of the allied forces needed to make new plans. This is because things would change greatly if the Korean and Chinese navies worked together, compared to when the Korean Navy was fighting alone under Admiral Yi Sun-sin.

On this matter, Yi Sun-sin was thinking about acquiring a new integrated naval base following the establishment of the Korean-China Allied Forces, the urgent need to strengthen the Korean Navy, and the acquisition of the wartime operational command of the allied forces. In the above situation, the top priority task after landing on Gohado was settling and stabilizing the unit quickly. As soon as the Korean Navy landed on Gohado, they began to secure a landing place and install a command post. They then proceeded with the construction of warships, the search for a location for the allied naval base following the establishment of the allied forces, the understanding of the enemy's situation in the front, and cooperation with local officials and the government. At that time, they sent out scouting ships to the vicinity of Wando and Suncheon in the front to understand the enemy's situation and strengthen maritime surveillance while they were rebuilding the navy.

Admiral Yi Sun-sin's goal of strengthening the Korean Navy was to build ships, manufacture weapons, secure troops, and procure provisions. The warships were constructed in Gohado and many other provinces, mainly in Jeolla Province. Yi Sun-sin sent people to supervise shipyards in different regions. The 13 existing warships needed to be repaired to the level of construction after being exhausted by long-term sailing after the Battle of Myeongryang. Salt was baked in salt pans on islands around Mokpo to secure provisions, and a sea pass was issued. He also devoted himself to constructing weapons and securing troops mounted on new warships. In particular, including 19 counties in the Jeolla Sea area as naval management areas on Anjwa Island before landing in Gohado was a great help in strengthening the forces.

### Strategic Movements: From Gohado to Gogeumdo

While Admiral Yi Sun-sin was focusing on the reconstruction of the Korean Navy on Gohado, news of the arrival of the Chinese navy in Korea was announced. In addition, it was also learned that the Konishi forces were strengthening the fortress in Suncheon Castle in Suncheon and that the enemy commander Shimazu was fortifying and increasing his forces in Sachon. It was also learned that Toyotomi Hideyoshi was dispatching reinforcements to Korea. Admiral Yi Sun-sin's strategy also faced a new phase. Although he was staying on Gohado to rebuild the navy and strengthen his forces, Gohado was too far from the main bases of the Japanese Navy in Busan and the Gyeongsang Sea. Once the reconstruction was somewhat accomplished, it was necessary to move the naval base to a place where it coul check and threaten the enemy as soon as possible and be stationed with the allied navy. Admiral Yi Sun-sin reviewed the results of the reconstruction of the navy and drew up a plan to move to Gogeumdo in Wando.

Yi Sun-sin moved the naval headquarters from Gohado in Mokpo to Gogeumdo in Wando on February 17, 1598. According to different records, the number of warships at the time of departure from Gohado was estimated to be 53, and the number of troops was about 8,000. This number alone suggests how much Yi Sun-sin had accelerated the reinforcement of his forces during his 106-day stay. Forty warships were newly built during his stay in Gohado. By the end of June, four months after moving to Gogeumdo, the fleet had grown to 85 warships and 85 auxiliary ships, and the number of troops had increased to about 17,000. This resulted from continued reinforcement of the fleet after the move to Gogeumdo. Given the military situation at the time, Gohado was unsuitable as a long-term naval base. The enemy had controlled the southern coast, centered on Busan and Geojedo. Before the arrival of the Chinese fleet, Yi Sun-sin chose Gohado, which was in the rear, as a suitable location for the reconstruction of the navy. Gohado was a good place to strengthen its forces relatively stably outside the enemy's maritime control zone. Therefore, Yi Sun-sin moved to Gogeumdo, which was suitable for the allied fleet, after completing the reconstruction of the navy and narrowing the operational distance between the enemy fleet.

**Gogeumdo: Key to Naval Reconstruction and Final Victory**

Gogeumdo was located at the mouth of Gangjin Bay, about 100 kilometers from Suncheon Castle, where Konishi Yukinaga was stationed, and was surrounded by Wando Cheonghaejin to the west, Joakdo to the east, and Sinjido to the south, making it very difficult to attack from the outside. Yi Sun-sin's move to Gogeumdo had been to block the retreat of the enemy's main force, the Konishi forces, which were gathering in Suncheon, and to destroy the enemy with a combined sea and land attack. Yi Sun-sin had reported to King Seonjo after settling in Gogeumdo. The following is a summary of the article's contents in the Annals of King Seonjo on March 18, 1598. In the report, Yi Sun-sin stated that the enemy had been acting arbitrarily in the southern seas of Nankan and Heungyang, and that it had been challenging to patrol the enemy from Gohado in Mokpo, which was geographically far away. He mentioned that he had moved the naval headquarters before spring because he was concerned that the enemy's military activities would increase in the spring. In particular, Admiral Yi Sun-sin also reported that Gogeumdo was strategically superior to Hansando Naval Base. He noted that the surrounding area had many farms and planned to have about 1,500 households farm there. He also mentioned that he had been farming since he was the commander of the Jeolla Left Naval Commander in 1593 and that he planned to continue doing so in the future. The operation of Dunjeon, military farming, was an essential means of securing military rations.

In another March 18, 1598 report, Yi Sun-sin reported that the Japanese forces had strengthened and built fortifications at the Suncheon Castle (Waeseong) fort after learning that the Korean

Navy had moved to Gogeumdo. Yi Sun-sin's move to Gogeumdo also threatened the Japanese forces stationed at the Suncheon Waeseong fort.

After hearing that the Korean Navy had moved, the Japanese forces strengthened the fort.

At the time of the great victory at the Battle of Myeongryang, the Korean Navy had only 13 warships. Even though Admiral Yi Sun-sin achieved a miraculous victory, he faced the urgent challenge of quickly rebuilding the small Korean fleet to stand against the mighty Japanese Navy.

Therefore, during the 40-day retreat after the battle, he focused on increasing the number of Korean ships and planning a combined fleet with the Chinese navy. Admiral Yi set up a temporary naval base at Goha Island and worked hard to rebuild the fleet. Over 106 days, he added more than 40 ships, raising the total to 53 warships and about 8,000 soldiers.

In February 1598, four months after moving the naval base from Goha Island to Gogeum Island, the Korean fleet grew to 85 warships and 85 support vessels, with the number of soldiers increasing to around 17,000. This remarkable recovery happened just over a year after the Korean Navy was nearly wiped out at the Battle of Chilcheonyang in July 1597 under Admiral Won Gyun's command. On July 16, 1598, around 5,000 Chinese naval troops joined the Korean fleet at the Gogeum Island base. The Korean and Chinese navies formed a united fleet to fight against the Japanese Navy. The Gogeum Island base (Tongjeoyeong) was the last naval headquarters where Admiral Yi served. It played a key role in leading the Korean-Chinese Allied Fleet to victories in the Battle of Jeolido Island and the final battle of the Imjin War, the Battle of Noryang.

# Chapter VI

## The Last Victory of Yi Sun-sin and the End of the Imjinwaeran

# The Truth about the Battle of Jeolido

The major victories achieved by the Korean Navy during the Japanese Invasion of Korea can be ranked by the number of Japanese ships destroyed as follows:

**Battle of Noryang (1598):** In this final war clash, Admiral Yi Sun-sin decimated the Japanese fleet with a daring attack, destroying over 200 ships and ending the threat of Japanese invasion.

**Battle of Busanpo (1592):** A bold offensive strike against the Japanese base in Busan, destroying over 100 ships. This victory dealt a heavy blow to enemy morale and symbolized Korean determination to resist.

**Battle of Hansando and Battle of Angolpo (1592):** Yi Sun-sin's ingenious use of the "Crane Wing Formation" surrounded and annihilated a Japanese fleet of over 100 ships, cementing his reputation as a brilliant naval tactician.

**Battle of Jeolido (1598):** Though often overlooked by other victories, this battle saw the Korean Navy, led by Admiral Yi, decisively defeat a Japanese fleet of over 50 ships, further securing the southern coastline and paving the way for the ultimate victory.

**Battle of Myeongryang (1597):** In this battle, 13 Korean ships defeated the Japanese Navy's 133 ships, destroying over 30 enemy ships and blocking the enemy's advance to the west. This naval battle

Chapter VI. The Last Victory of Yi Sun-sin and the End of the Imjinwaeran

is renowned for achieving great victory despite insufficient ships. The Battle of Jeolido (currently called Geogeumdo), which took place during the Imjin War, is an important naval battle not well known to the general public, except for those who study Admiral Yi Sun-sin. The main reason is that only a few historical records provide information about the battle situation. Today, 420 years after the battle, there are only records of the outcome but no specific records, making it difficult to depict the situation of the battle at that time. Previous explanations or research on the Battle of Jeolido have been based on inconsistent historical records, making it difficult to understand the battle comprehensively and concretely. This chapter summarizes the research conducted by the author and published in a thesis to clarify the reality of the Battle of Jeolido by comprehensively reviewing and analyzing some historical records of the battle, as well as the situation of the battle, the battlefield environment, and Admiral Yi's maritime strategy and tactics.

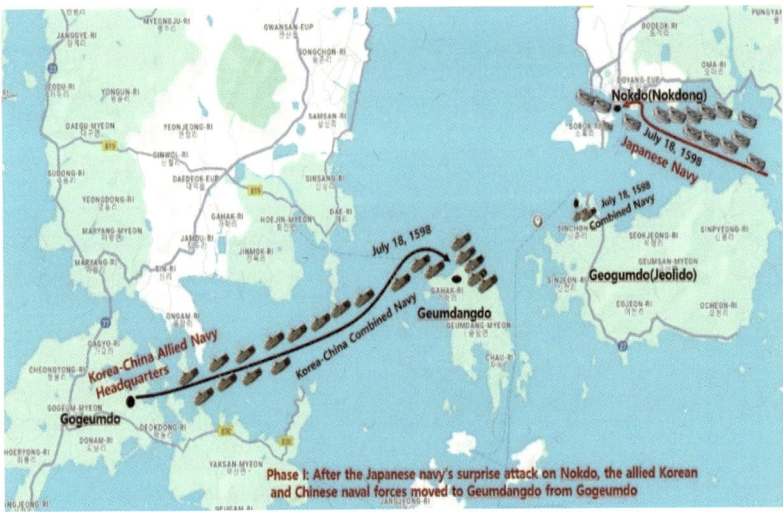

Figure 46: Phase I Situation Map of the Battle of Jeolido

In July 1598, Admiral Chen Lin of the Ming Dynasty of China and around 5,000 Chinese naval forces joined the Korean Navy at Gogeumdo Island in Wando on July 16. On July 18, during a welcoming banquet hosted by Admiral Yi Sun-sin for Chen Lin and the Chinese naval forces, a report was received that about 100 enemy ships were approaching Nokdo. When Yi Sun-sin's navy and Chen Lin's forces mobilized and reached Geumdangdo Island, they discovered two enemy ships. Upon seeing the allied naval forces, the two enemy ships fled to the main camp.

Yi Sun-sin and Chen Lin waited at Geumdangdo after positioning their border units across Nokdo. Later, they received intelligence that an enemy fleet of over 100 ships had set sail from Nokdo, passing through the waterways of Sorokdo and Jeolido, heading for an attack. Yi Sun-sin's Korean fleet swiftly advanced from Geumdangdo, engaging the enemy fleet at full speed. The naval battleground, encompassing Sorokdo, Jeolido, and Geumdangdo, was the most expansive space

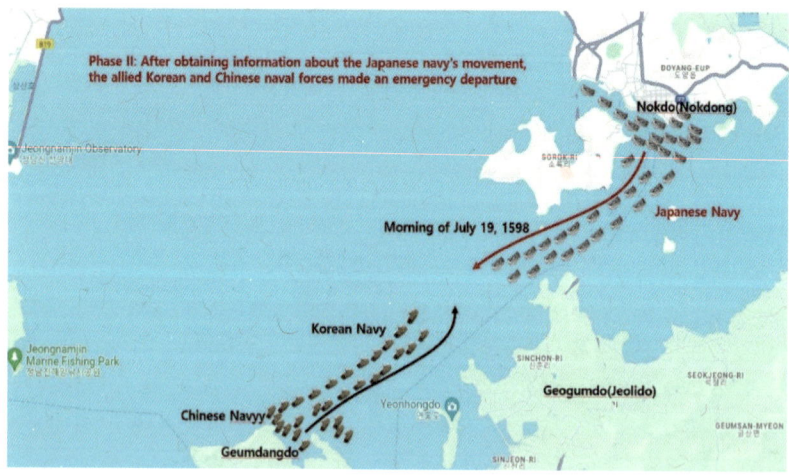

Figure 47: Phase II Situation Map of the Battle of Jeolido
*(After obtaining information about the Japanese Navy's attack on Nokdo, the allied Korean and Chinese naval forces made an emergency departure)*

where both sides could freely maneuver. The figures in the chapter simulated scenarios of the combat situation on July 18 and July 19, respectively.

The simulations considered the battlefield environment in the Jeolido area, Yi Sun-sin's strategic tactics, the maneuver characteristics of the Korean and enemy forces, and historical records. On July 19, around 5:00 AM, the border units, aware of the enemy's mobilization, reported urgently to the main base in Geumdangdo. The Korean Navy swiftly responded, encountering the enemy near Udo, northwest of Gorageum Beach, around 6:00 AM on July 19.

Because the sea area involved was sufficiently wide, it is assumed that Yi Sun-sin's naval battle tactics were not much different from his previous tactics. Yi Sun-sin's fleet usually maintained a crane-wing formation or used siege operations while approaching the enemy fleet. The northwestern sea area of Jeolido Island, which is presumed to be the sea area where the Battle of Jeolido took place, satisfies favorable conditions for the use of the crane-wing tactics in terms of engagement space and fleet movement direction. Analyzing Yi Sun-sin's representative tactical formations used in the Imjin War, it was evident that the *Hakikjin* tactics were the most suitable for the Jeolido naval battle.

Yi Sun-sin's fleet approached the enemy fleet by firing threatening shots with the guns mounted on their ships while simultaneously killing people with bows from around 100 meters away. There were no Turtle Ships in the Battle of Jeolido. Attacking the hull with the Panokseon's cannons without receiving the tactical benefits of the Turtle Ship was riskier than in other naval battles. To hit the hull of the enemy fleet with Panokseon's cannons, Panokseons had to approach the enemy ship at least 15-20 meters away. Even under these circumstances, the Korean fleet destroyed over 50 enemy ships with minor damage.

The victory at the Battle of Jeolido is significant in that it was the first naval battle in which the Korean Navy began to regain control of the southern coast after the Korean Navy, commanded by Admiral Won Gyun, was nearly annihilated in the Battle of Chilcheonryang. It is also significant as it was the first naval battle in which the Chinese navy joined the Allied navy during the Japanese invasions of Korea.

Figure 48: Phase III Situation Map of the Battle of Jeolido
*(Advance and Engagement in Hakikjin(Crane Wing Formation) By Korean Navy, Observation instead of engagement by the Chinese Navy)*

# Korean-Chinese Allied Naval and Ground Operations

## The 4 Routes for Simultaneous Land-Sea Campaign

In June 1598, Chinese troops entered Korea to support the country, and the Simultaneous Land-Sea Campaign along 4 Routes began in September. This campaign was a joint operation between Korea and China that used land and sea forces to attack along four different routes. It was a major offensive plan proposed by Xingge, the highest-ranking Chinese general in the late Imjin War.

**East Route:** Chinese Admiral Ma Gui led troops from Seoul to Chungju, Andong, and Gyeongju. He joined forces with Korean General Seon Geo-i and attacked Kato Kiyomasa in Ulsan.

**Central Route:** Chinese Admiral Dong Yil-won, with Korean forces led by Jeong Gi-ryong, attacked Sacheon Castle.

**West Route:** Chinese Admiral Yu Jeong marched from Seoul to Gongju and Jeonju, joining Korean General Gwon Yul to attack Konishi Yukinaga in Suncheon Castle.

**Sea Route:** Chinese Admiral Chen Lin teamed up with the Korean Navy under Yi Sun-sin to attack Suncheon Castle, working alongside Admiral Yu Jeong. Despite their efforts, the Korean-Chinese forces faced defeats in both the Battle of Ulsan and the Battle of Sacheon. The attack on Suncheon Castle, led by Admiral Yu Jeong, also failed.

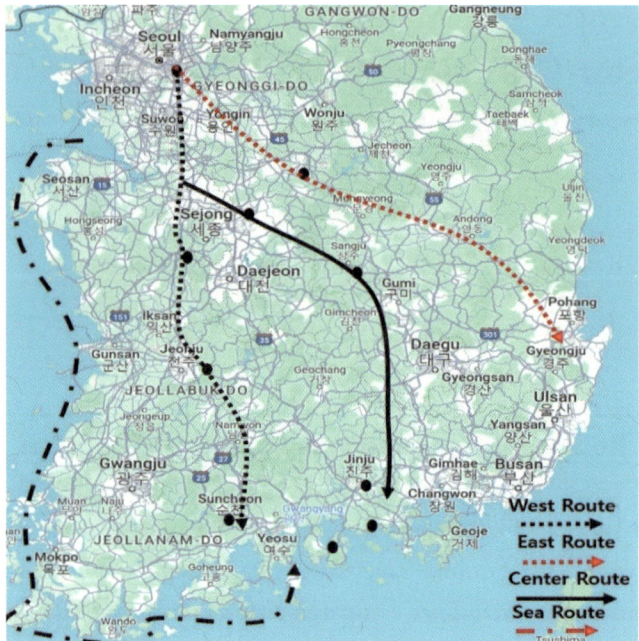

Figure 49: The 4 Routes Simultaneous Land-Sea Campaign

## Blockade Operations by the Korean-Chinese Allied Fleet

While the Korean and Chinese forces were coordinating their operations along Korea's southern coast, Toyotomi Hideyoshi died on August 18, 1598. Before his death, he had ordered the withdrawal of Japanese troops from Korea. The withdrawal plan was as follows:

*Troops in Sacheon and Goseong were to retreat to Geoje Island. Konishi's forces in Suncheon Castle were to retreat by sea and gather in Busan.*

Naval commanders like Kuki Yoshitaka, Wakisaka Yasuharu, and

Todo Takatora withdrew and transported these troops. Kato burned down Seosaengpo, Yangsan, and Jukdo Castles before withdrawing to Busan. The Korean-Chinese allied fleet stationed in Gogeumdo on the east coast participated in the joint operation to attack Konishi's forces in Suncheon Castle, in line with the Simultaneous Land-Sea Campaign along 4 Routes. The Konishi forces in Suncheon Castle planned to withdraw by sea. The Korean-Chinese allied fleet knew about this plan and aimed to block the sea lanes near Suncheon Castle. According to a report in the Sejong Sillok on August 24, 1598, Right Prime Minister Yi Deok-hyung informed King Seonjo that the enemy in Suncheon Castle did not seem to be withdrawing as they were strengthening the castle and cutting down trees. On the same day, it was reported that the Korean-Chinese Allied Fleet had set sail to intercept the enemy. They aimed to guard the sea based on intelligence about the enemy's withdrawal plans.

Yi Sun-sin reported to the king that Chen Lin, the admiral of the Korean-Chinese Allied Fleet, was obstructing their efforts to eliminate the Japanese before their joint land and sea attack on Suncheon Castle. According to a report in the Sejong Sillok on September 10, 1598, Yi Sun-sin said that Chen Lin forcibly stopped his plan to attack the enemy when an opportunity arose. He reported that it was difficult for the Korean Navy to operate independently under the Korean-Chinese command structure.

After the Chinese navy joined the Korean Navy in Gogeumdo in July 1598, forming the Korean-Chinese Allied Fleet, Chen Lin's arrogance became a significant obstacle for Yi Sun-sin. This attitude started immediately after the Jeolido sea battle. It became evident that Chen Lin began to restrain Yi Sun-sin when the Korean-Chinese Allied Fleet was formed.

A letter Yi Sun-sin wrote to his nephew on August 6, 1598, illustrates how he struggled with the Chinese navy. Here is an excerpt from that letter *(Source from Park Jong-pyung's Yi Sun-sin's Diary):*

*I am always sad and longing, being far away in the southwest. I am even more sad and sorrowful now that I have met my nephew Won and read your letter. Didn't your brother and others want to go home? Although I am barely breathing, the Chinese general (Chen Lin) comes to me one after another and urges and demands so much that it is too annoying to respond one by one, so I can't do anything. I have no way to do anything. What are you doing in your hometown? It would be best to come down quickly. Show this letter to Hoe (Yi Sun-sin's eldest son).*

On September 15, the Chinese army led by Yu Jeong and the Korean-Chinese Allied Fleet, set sail from their Gogeumdo headquarters to attack the Konishi forces in Suncheon Castle. Yi Sun-sin's diary records the details of the operation starting September 15. The fleet left Gogeumdo, anchored in Narodo on September 15, stayed for two days, and arrived at Bangdap in Dolsando around 2 pm. During their stay in Narodo, Chen Lin and Yi Sun-sin discussed the operation plan while drinking. The next day, on September 19, the fleet moved to the waters of the Jeolla Province and anchored at the Left Navy Base. That day, Yi Sun-sin saw the Jeolla Province Left Navy Base from the sea for the first time since his arrest on Hansando on February 26, 1597, and transferred to Seoul. Yi Sun-sin recorded his sorrowful impressions of seeing the Left Navy Base in Yeosu in his diary.

He learned that the Japanese, who had taken control of the southern coast waters after the Chilcheonryang Naval Battle, had already destroyed the Jeolla Province Left Navy Base. Yi Sun-sin, who had been the commander of the Jeolla Province Left Navy Base, prepared for the war by building Turtle Ships and leading many successful naval battles, including the first battle in 1592, the Battle of Okpo. Even while serving as the Commander of the Three Provinces

Navy on Hansando, Yi Sun-sin also commanded the Jeolla Province Left Navy, frequently visiting Yeosu and leading the navy. Yeosu was also where his mother and family stayed, making it a place of personal attachment. Seeing the ruins of the Left Navy Base, Yi Sun-sin felt profound anger and resentment towards the enemy.

On September 20, around 8 am, the fleet arrived at Udo (Songdo, Gokyang-myeon, Gwangyanggun) and, in a joint operation with Chinese ground forces led by General Yu Jeong, attacked the Japanese fortress at Suncheon Castle. The allied navy engaged in a series of battles, launching artillery attacks on the enemy. Fierce fighting continued on the 21st and 22nd. On the 21st, they attacked the enemy with bows and cannons all day. During the operation, they were unable to advance further at low tide. On the 22nd, there were also casualties in the Korean Navy. Eleven Chinese soldiers were killed. The enemy shot Jisepo *Manho* and Okpo *Manho* of the Korean Navy.

During the Korean-Chinese Joint Land-Sea Operation, the passive attack by Chinese ground forces under General Yu Jeong allowed the Konishi forces to focus on countering the Allied navy's attacks. On the evening of September 30, the Chinese navy, led by Wang Yu-geuk and Bok Yu-geuk, joined the main force with over 100 ships, significantly strengthening the allied navy.

It is estimated that the morale of the Korean Navy was high; as Yi Sun-sin wrote in his diary, "the light was bright, and the enemy's hearts must have been beating." The battle on October 2 was intense, starting at 6 am and lasting until noon. The enemy suffered many casualties, but the Korean Navy also incurred significant losses. Sado Chemsa was killed, and Yi Cheong-il also died. Jisepo *Manho*, Saryang *Manho*, Haenam County Governor, Jindo County Governor, and Gangjin County Governor were also shot but survived. The Chinese ground forces also suffered serious damage that day. On October 3, the battle began in the early evening and lasted until midnight. Forty-two ships of the Chinese fleet led by Admiral Chen Lin ran aground on a sandy beach. Most of these ships were burned or destroyed due to reckless operations by Chen Lin's forces, who failed to coordinate the tide schedules and nearly got trapped and killed. The Korean Navy, including Yi Sun-sin, rescued Chen Lin and the Chinese navy.

After heavy losses on October 3, the combined navy pushed forward to the coast near Suncheon early on October 4 and fought all day. They returned to Udo and anchored, spending the day at sea. On October 5 and 6, there was no fighting due to strong winds, but news came from General Yu Jeong, the Chinese army commander, that he was withdrawing. On October 6, upon hearing this news, Yi Sun-sin wrote in his diary,

*"How sad, how sad. What will happen to the country in the future?"*

Reluctant to participate in the joint operation, General Yu Jeong ordered a withdrawal after learning of the Allied army's defeat at Sacheon Castle. He did not want to fight actively, fearing significant bloodshed. Yu Jeong thought it was best to open the way for the retreating Konishi forces, reflecting the basic strategy of the Chinese troops. Yi Sun-sin's report on the Battle of Suncheon is recorded in the Annals of King Seonjo on October 13, 1598. In this report, Yi Sun-sin noted that the Chinese army did not fight and only watched during the battle on October 2. He reported that 29 Korean naval personnel were killed, and 5 Chinese soldiers were also killed.

# The Battle of Noryang and the Death of Yi Sun-sin

## The Naval Battle Process and Engagement

The Simultaneous Land-Sea Operation along 4 Routes, which had been ambitiously launched, mostly ended in defeat for the Allied forces. After the defeats of the Eastern and Western route armies, General Yu Jeong of the Western army also retreated, ending joint operations. Eventually, the enemy focused on safely withdrawing from Korea according to Hideyoshi's will. Most enemy forces could quickly gather in Busan, but Konishi's forces in Suncheon had to withdraw to Busan by sea. The Korean government was aware of this plan. The allied fleet, which had returned to Gogeumdo after a month of operations near Suncheon Castle, closely monitored the enemy's withdrawal. On November 8, they received information about the enemy's withdrawal. On this day, Yi Sun-sin attended a banquet hosted by Chen Lin, the Chinese navy commander, and heard the news from him. Chen Lin, who had received the information from the Chinese army, proposed urgently advancing to block and defeat the retreating enemy.

For Yi Sun-sin, this was a golden opportunity for revenge. After returning to the Korean naval camp, Yi Sun-sin ordered battle preparations, and on November 9, he set sail with the Chen Lin fleet and stationed at Baekseoliang (Nammyeon, Yeosu City). On the 10th,

Figure 50: The Battle of Blocking the Enemy's Withdrawal by Korea-China Allied Navy

they passed the sea in front of the Jeolla Province Left Navy Base and arrived at Udo in Gwangyang Bay on the 11th, taking a guard position, effectively entering a naval blockade operation. On November 13, enemy ships appeared at Jangdo. Yi Sun-sin's fleet blocked the enemy ships that tried to escape from the coast. On the 14th, two enemy ships appeared, and the negotiator from Konishi's forces met with Chen Lin, offering bribes, including a sword. That evening, the Japanese commander came to Chen Lin's camp by boat, offering two pigs and two large bottles of wine as bribes. On the 15th, Yi Sun-sin met Chen Lin, urging him not to be deceived by the enemy's tricks, but the enemy continued visiting Chen Lin's camp that day, begging for the naval blockade to be lifted. Chen Lin's indecisiveness became evident.

On November 16, shortly after Chen Lin sent someone to the enemy camp, the enemy came to the Chinese navy's camp with three ships loaded with horses, spears, swords, and other bribes. Yi Sun-sin argued with Chen Lin that he should not open the way for the enemy's retreat. The enemy continued to persuade Chen Lin, but he refused, saying he could not open the way because of Yi Sun-sin's opposition.

As a result, Konishi sent someone to Yi Sun-sin to try to bribe him, but he failed. Instead, Yi Sun-sin scolded the envoys, saying, *"How dare the Korean enemy come to the Korean naval camp?"* and sent them back.

On November 17, Sogyenam, the commander of Balpo (*Manho*), and Johyo-yeol, the commander of Dangjinpo (*Manho*), who went out as scouts, returned and reported that they chased an enemy ship to the sea near Hansando, seized the enemy ship and provisions, but these were taken by the Chinese navy. The enemy in Suncheon Castle continued to bribe Chen Lin, but they failed to secure a sea escape route due to Yi Sun-sin's strong opposition. Eventually, Konishi requested reinforcements. Intelligence indicated that enemies from Gonyang and Sacheon would gather in the Noryang Sea area. The

Figure 51: The Korea- China Allied Forces Moved to the Noryang Battle Area

Korean fleet also prepared thoroughly for the decisive battle.

On November 18, enemy ships gathered in the Noryang Sea area in large numbers. Around 10 p.m., Yi Sun-sin and Chen Lin set out together for Noryang. They aimed to attack the enemy fleet in Noryang rather than blocking the sea area around Suncheon Castle.

Yi Sun-sin gave one Panokseon to Chinese commanders Chen Lin and Deputy Commander Deng Zilong to use as a command ship.

After arriving in the Noryang Sea, Yi Sun-sin washed his hands and prayed on his command ship at midnight. The *Yi Chungmugong Yusa* records that he prayed,

**Oh, Heaven! Please help me defeat these enemies quickly! On the day I defeat the enemy, I will repay the country with my death.**

The Korean-Chinese Allied Fleet moved to the Noryang Sea area, with the Chinese Navy waiting at Jukdo in the northwest and the Korean Navy waiting above Gwaneumpo in the eastern part of Noryang. This was to surround the enemy from both sides. Admiral Yi Sun-sin, Gyeongsang's Right Naval Commander, sent a spy ship to report the enemy situation to *Tongjesa*, Admiral Yi Sun-sin. The report said that hundreds of enemy ships were sailing through the Noryang Sea area past Gugsabong, the northeastern tip of Namhae Island, towards Gwangyang Bay. The allied fleet set out for Noryang and arrived around 2 a.m.

The Noryang Sea area, like Myeongryang Strait, is narrow, making it difficult to engage in a horizontal battle formation. Due to the narrow strait, the enemy fleet had to sail in a small column. At the strait's entrance, the allied fleet fiercely attacked the enemy fleet from both sides. The Japanese, whose momentum was broken by the Allied fleet's attack, scattered and fought back desperately. The allied fleet launched a fire attack using cannons, bows, and flaming arrows. The

Chapter VI. The Last Victory of Yi Sun-sin and the End of the Imjinwaeran

Figure 52: The Situation Map of the Battle of Noryang
*(Yi Sun-sin's death and the end of the war)*

damage to the Japanese Navy increased due to the Allied forces' shelling and fire attacks, which took advantage of the northwest wind at night. Finally, they began to look for a way out. The Japanese Navy retreated to Gwaneumpo, but the way was blocked, and fierce fighting continued between the Allied and Japanese navies.

The Japanese fleet was scattered, boosting the Korean Navy's morale. Garipo Cheomsa Yi Young-nam, Nakan County Governor Park Deok-ryong, and Heungyang Hyeongam Ko Deuk-jang used the Japanese Navy's boarding tactics to board enemy ships and engage in close combat, killing many enemy soldiers. The Chinese navy also fought bravely, with Chen Lin's fleet surrounded by the Japanese Navy and rescued by Yi Sun-sin. Similarly, Chen Lin's navy rescued Yi Sun-sin's fleet when it was in danger. Deputy Commander Admiral Deng Zilong was killed in battle. Deng Zilong, the highest-ranking Chinese naval officer at the time, was 70 years old and killed many Japanese soldiers before dying gloriously. The waters of Gwaneumpo were visible with the allied navy and the enemy engaged in battle. The battle between the combined navy, trying to block the enemy's retreat, and the enemy, trying to escape with all its might, was incredibly fierce. As dawn broke, the defeated Japanese Navy began to flee, entering Gwaneumpo in the wrong direction and becoming trapped. Some enemies abandoned their ships and fled to Namhaedo, while others turned their bows 180 degrees and launched a desperate counterattack. It was a final effort. Yi Sun-sin led the fleet, commanding the battle and pursuing the enemy. Haenam Hyeongam Yu Hyeong, Dangjin *Manho* Jo Hyo-yeol, Jindo Governor Seon Ui-gyeong, and Sarang *Manho* Kim Seong-ok also joined. Hyeongyang Hyeongam Ko Deok-jang and Yi Eon-yang jumped on enemy ships and killed the enemy in close combat and died in battle. Yi Sun-sin was shot during close combat around 10 am.

A bullet from somewhere pierced his left armpit. *Tongjesa* Yi Sun-sin died from the gunshot but left a will saying,

**The battle is urgent! Do not announce my death!**

On November 19, 1598 (December 16 in the Gregorian calendar), Admiral Yi Sun-sin, the Commander of the Three Naval Provinces, passed away at 54 years of age. After Yi Sun-sin's death, the battle continued until noon and then ended. The Japanese retreated, and Konishi's forces in Suncheon Castle took advantage of the battle to flee along the sea route. They went down to Yeosu Bay and retreated to Geoje Island, circling Namhae. The Japanese forces gathered in Busan before the end of November 1598, and all withdrew to Japan. They had invaded Korea on April 13, 1592, devastating the country, but they had now fled. Thus, the seven-year war came to an end. Gwangneumpo, where General Jeong Ji of the Goryeo Dynasty defeated Japanese pirates before the Joseon dynasty, has a victory tower to commemorate the victory.

## Achievements and Significance

As Yi Sun-sin arrived at the Noryang Strait before the Battle of Noryang., he washed his hands on his command ship at midnight and prayed,

*Oh, Heaven! Please help me defeat these enemies quickly! On the day I defeat the enemy, I will repay the country with my death.*

As he prayed, Yi Sun-sin died while saving the country.

In addition to Yi Sun-sin, more than ten generals were killed. Deputy Commander of the Chinese Navy, Deng Zilong, was also killed. The combined fleet in the Battle of Noryang. included 80 Korean and 200 Chinese ships, facing 500 Japanese ships. The 200 enemy ships were destroyed.

The Battle of Noryang is significant because it was the last battle of the Imjin War. Yi Sun-sin led the final battle to victory, ending the war. It is also significant that Chen Lin, initially difficult and arrogant, was impressed by Yi Sun-sin's leadership, eventually strengthening the combat power of the combined fleet and leading to the last battle's victory. Yi Sun-sin died in battle, but his death was not announced during the fight. Afterward, when his death was announced, the waters of Gwaneumpo became a sea of tears. Chen Lin, who had previously clashed with Yi Sun-sin and even tried to open a retreat for Konishi's forces, also wept bitterly. When news of Yi Sun-sin's death reached the Korean government, King Seonjo and government officials were deeply saddened. Officials were sent to hold a memorial service on December 4, promoting him to Right Prime Minister. Yi Sun-sin's body was temporarily buried on Gogeumdo, where the allied fleet was stationed, and then sent to Asan. His remains were moved to Asan on February 11, 1599, and 16 years later, to the foot of Mount Orasan (mountain).

In 1604, six years after Yi Sun-sin's death, he was posthumously appointed as the first-class meritorious subject of the first rank and *Jwauijeong* (Left Prime Minister). Later, in 1793, King Jeongjo promoted him to Prime Minister, and in 1643, he was given the posthumous title of *Chungmugong*.

To this day, shrines, monuments, and commemorative facilities are erected at Yi Sun-sin's historical sites and battlefields throughout Korea to honor *Chungmugong*.

Major organizations and institutions hold commemorative events on April 28 (Yi Sun-sin's birthday) and December 16 (the day of his death). Many scholars continue to research Yi Sun-sin's legacy.

## Descendants of Chinese Admiral Chen Lin in Korea

Chen Lin, a Chinese Admiral, led 5,000 Chinese sailors to join Admiral Yi Sun-sin's Korean Navy in Gogeumdo, Jeollado, Korea, during the Imjinwaeran. Chen Lin and Yi Sun-sin initially disagreed over credit and operations. Still, Chen Lin was eventually impressed by Yi Sun-sin's leadership and fought bravely in the final Battle of Noryang, risking his life. After the war, Chen Lin returned to China, gaining the trust of the Chinese government. When the Ming Dynasty fell, Admiral Chen Lin's grandson Chen Yeong-so led his family to Korea. From this time on, the Guangdong Chen clan lived in Korea. Chen Lin's descendants first settled in Jangseungpo, Gyeongsang Province, and later moved to Gogeumdo, Wando County, where Chen

Lin was stationed. Chen Lin's descendants then moved to Hwangjo-ri, Haenam and settled there. Korea built the *Hwangjo Byeolmyo Shrine* to house Chen Lin's counterfeit money in 1871, and it is managed as Haenam County Local Cultural Heritage No. 10. The following is from a speech given by Chinese President Xi Jinping at Seoul National University on July 4, 2014.

*"When the Imjin War broke out on the Korean Peninsula about 400 years ago, the soldiers of the two countries fought side by side with hostility. Ming Admiral Deng Zilong and Korean Admiral Yi Sun-sin died together in the Battle of Noryang., and the descendants of Ming Admiral Chen Lin still live in Korea."*

The following is from a speech given by South Korean President Moon Jae-in at Peking University on December 15, 2017.

*"In Wando County, South Korea, a project is underway to commemorate Korean Admiral Yi Sun-sin and Chinese Admiral Chen Lin, who defeated the Japanese during the Imjinwaeran. Currently, about 2,000 descendants of Chen Lin live in Korea."*

Chinese dignitaries, including ambassadors, often visit it. Haenam County maintains exchanges with Chen Lin's descendants in China. Chen Lin and his descendants' story highlights the shared history and friendship between Korea and China, with both countries working together for a better future.

## Yi Sun-sin's Fleet Operation Concepts and Naval Operational Principles in Imjin War

Alfred Mahan said that the fleet battle is a concept pursued by the British Navy in the past, meaning a decisive struggle between two main fleets in hostile relationships, such as the Battle of Salamis, the Battle of Lepanto, and the Battle of Tsushima. The fleet-in-being is a concept of naval power management where its mere existence checks the enemy fleet and restricts freedom of action by avoiding battle and preserving the fleet's power. The Beach Head Battle in 1609 is an example. On the other hand, the fortress fleet is a concept that avoids maritime battles, protects coastal bases, and defeats the enemy with the cooperation of coastal ships when the fleet approaches favorably. This was the case with the Russian Navy, which failed to use Japanese military maritime traffic routes and disruptions and cruiser fortresses during the Russo-Japanese War in 1905 *(Source: Naval Combat Development Group, Marine Strategy Glossary, p. 162)*.

The principles of naval operations are fundamental principles necessary for conducting naval operations. They can be considered the basic doctrine of the Navy, derived from common conclusions accumulated through numerous wars in both the East and the West. While somewhat supplemented over time, the basic doctrine of the Navy includes goals such as offense, concentration, maneuver, integration, and surprise. In this chapter, we will examine Yi Sun-sin's major naval battles in terms of fleet operations and the principles of naval operations.

## Admiral Yi Sun-sin's Main Battle Fleet Operation

In the early days of the Japanese invasion during the Imjin

War, Yi Sun-sin's first campaign (the Battles of Okpo, Happo, and Jeokjinpo) and the second campaign (the Battles of Sacheon, Dangpo, Danghangpo, and Yulpo) canot be broadly classified as fleet battles or fortress fleet battles. The Korean Navy unilaterally defeated enemy fleets docked at ports or retreating to ports. However, in the Battle of Hansan Island, Yi Sun-sin's strategy changed from his first and second campaigns. In July 1592, Toyotomi Hideyoshi strongly demanded that naval commanders Wakizaka, Kato, and Kuki defeat the Korean Navy, leading the Japanese Navy to mobilize a powerful naval force for an aggressive fight.

The South Korean Navy faced an aggressive and powerful Japanese Navy to prevent the Japanese from advancing into the West Sea and Jeolla Province, marking a shift from previous engagement methods. The Battle of Hansando was the first mutually aggressive naval skirmish since the Imjin War outbreak in 1592. However, after the Battle of Hansan, the Japanese Navy adopted the fortress fleet strategy in subsequent engagements, such as the Battle of Pusan in September 1592, and avoided fleet battles, as seen in the Battles of Ungpo (February to March 1593) and Jangmunpo (March 1594). After Won Kyun's defeat in the Battle of Chilcheonryang, Yi Sun-sin reappointed as the Korean Navy Commander-in-Chief (*Tongjesa*) and had to lead the Korean fleet.

Following their victory in the Battle of Chilcheonryang, the Japanese Navy controlled the southern seas of Korea, except for the southwestern part of the peninsula. Yi Sun-sin had to conduct defensive operations with only 12 vessels (13 at the Battle of Myeongryang). The Japanese Navy sought to annihilate Yi Sun-sin's fleet, leading to the decisive Battle of Myeongryang (*Uldolmok*), where Yi Sun-sin chose fleet battle tactics, diverging from conventional maritime strategy. Yi Sun-sin won a miraculous victory in the world's naval history. Until the Korean fleet was rebuilt after the Battle of Myeongryang, Yi Sun-sin employed typical fleet-in-being operations. However, in later battles like Jeolido and Noryang, after the fleet's rebuilding at Gohado and Gogeumdo, decisive fleet battles led to victories against the Japanese Navy.

## Review of Yi Sun-sin's Naval Battles Applying Naval Operation Principles

Examining Yi Sun-sin's naval battles from today's perspective of naval operation principles, Kang Young-ho, a Korean maritime strategist, made noteworthy analyses by applying elements of Korean naval war principles to them. Referring to Kang Young-ho's research, the author selectively applied elements of today's basic naval doctrine to Yi Sun-sin's battles, focusing on those not heavily influenced by the times.

### The Principle of the Offensive

In war, the principle of the offensive involves taking the initiative and attacking the enemy, allowing the commander to control the battle. Yi Sun-sin's naval battles were primarily offensive. His aggressive fighting style was particularly evident in battles involving the Turtle Ship. The Turtle Ship led his fleet, focusing on close combat and destroying enemy hulls with artillery fire. Panok ships following the Turtle Ship maintained a safe distance, providing cover and using bows to kill enemy naval forces on board. When necessary, they fired threatening shots with naval guns, breaking enemy morale with the tremendous cannon sounds. After the Turtle Ship damaged the enemy hulls, Panok ships approached and destroyed the enemy ships with cannons, boarding or setting them on fire.

### The Principle of Vigilance

In war principles, vigilance means preventing enemy surprise attacks or intelligence-gathering activities. It involves maintaining a state of alert to preserve combat power and ensure freedom of action. Yi Sun-sin consistently sent scout ships to monitor enemy movements. When enemy ships were detected, they notified the fleet of the invasion. Even when anchored, Yi Sun-sin dispatched scout ships to monitor enemy movements, thoroughly preventing surprise attacks. During the rebuilding of naval forces at Gohado before moving to Gogeumdo after the Battle of Myeongryang, Yi Sun-sin continued maritime surveillance by sending scout ships as far as Haenam and Wando.

### The Principle of Maneuver and Concentration

Maneuvering involves moving combat power to advantageous positions to influence the enemy's center and create favorable situations. Concentration involves focusing superior combat power at decisive times and places to secure relative superiority. Yi Sun-sin often used attack tactics on enemy ships anchored on the coast, employing formations like sieges or the *Hakikjin* in spacious battlefield environments. In the Battle of Hansando, he utilized maneuver and concentration principles by luring the enemy into the wide Hansando sea area, favorable for battle, and destroying the enemy navy by concentrating firepower. Similarly, in the Battle of Myeongryang, he led the outnumbered Korean Navy to Myeongryang Strait at a critical moment, blocking the waterways and destroying the enemy by concentrating firepower. This was a remarkable application of maneuver and concentration principles, aligning with today's naval operational principles.

# Chapter VII

## Lessons from
## Yi Sun-sin and His Deep Love for
## Mother

# The Five Spirits of Chungmugong Yi Sun-sin

It is not easy to express the spirit of Yi Sun-sin in just one word or sentence. Nevertheless, in Korean society, the five core spirits related to his legacy are known as *the Five Spirits of Chungmugong*. The Korean Navy established *the Five Spirits of Chungmugong* in the 1970s based on Yi Sun-sin's lifetime achievements, his life philosophy, views on the nation, naval strategy, tactics, and leadership. *The Five Spirits of Chungmugong*, established by the Republic of Korea navy, are summarized as follows:

- The spirit of loving the country
- The spirit of prioritizing justice
- The spirit of fulfilling responsibilities
- The spirit of pioneering with creativity
- The spirit of enduring sacrifice.

Although *the Five Spirits of Chungmugong* comprehensively express the spirit of Yi Sun-sin, some experts say that the lessons from Yi Sun-sin are too vague and sound like catchy slogans. The author, who spent more than 40 years as a naval officer and professor at the Naval Academy and University in Korea, also shares this view. In other words, the author felt that in the educational field, *the Five Spirits of Chungmugong* are difficult for modern young people and future generations to truly empathize with because standardized phrases can feel too conceptual or slogan-like. These thoughts gave rise to the author's desire to express Yi Sun-sin's lessons more concretely. The author discovered *The 12 lessons left by Yi Sun-sin* introduced in this book through discussions with students during lectures and research on the spirit and leadership of *Chungmugong* at the university for several years. *The 12 lessons* are based on the existing *Five Spirits of Yi Sun-sin* but focused on expressing them in more practical terms. These lessons were proposed by students who had taken Yi Sun-sin's spirit and leadership course. After an open discussion, several candidate lessons were selected to select the most appropriate ones. This process was repeated for three years, and *the 12 lessons* were finally chosen from about 20 candidate lessons. In limiting the number of lessons to 12, it was considered that 12 is the number that most symbolically represents the spirit of Yi Sun-sin. At the Battle of Myeongryang, Yi Sun-sin defeated a Japanese naval force that was more than ten times larger, based on the 12 ships left behind after Won Gyun's crushing defeat at the Battle of Chilcheonryang. The author encourages readers to think about the cases that apply to *the 12 lessons* introduced below as they read this book.

# The Lessons of Chungmugong Yi Sun-sin

- Repay the benevolence of the nation.
- Act with fairness.
- Lead by example in righteous acts.
- Respond wisely to dangers.
- Cherish time and respect parents.
- Continuously learn and refine knowledge and skills.
- Think prudently and act decisively.
- Do things with such sincerity that it moves the heavens.
- Anticipate and prepare for potential crises.
- Never retreat in everything you start, see it through to the end.
- Prioritize the place where events occur.
- Boldly give up the small to attain the greater.

## One Example of Lessons of Yi Sun-sin

### Cherish time and Respect the Parents

Admiral Yi Sun-sin was appointed commander of the Jeolla Left Navy in Yeosu, Jeolla Province, Korea, on February 13, 1591, two months before the outbreak of the Imjin War. At that time, his mother and family lived in Asan, Chungcheong Province, Korea, the mother's hometown, where Yi Sun-sin had lived in his youth. The mother and family moved to Yeosu in the spring of 1593. About a month after the family moved to Yeosu, on June 21, 1593, Admiral Yi Sun-sin deployed the Jeolla Left Navy forces to Hansando, a strategic location in Gyeongsang Province. This was necessary to position the forces closer to the enemy strongholds controlling the Gyeongsang Province sea area. Although the family had moved to Yeosu, where the Jeolla Left Navy Base was located, they couldn't reside with Admiral Yi Sun-sin. Because it was wartime, he couldn't travel to work and had to remain within the base. Furthermore, just a month after the family relocated to Yeosu, Admiral Yi Sun-sin transferred the Jeolla Left Navy forces to Hansando, Gyeongsang Province. Therefore, Admiral Yi Sun-sin and his family had little opportunity to meet in person. Admiral Yi Sun-sin, who had spent his entire life living in remote military bases and island seas, was used to living apart from his family. However, he always had a feeling of longing and sadness for his elderly mother in his heart.

Admiral Yi Sun-sin's extreme filial piety to his mother is fully reflected in his diary, which is still handed down today. The diary of Admiral Yi Sun-sin, which has been handed down to this day, records 1,594 days from January 1, 1592, to November 17, 1598, two days before his death. During this period, there are over 200 records about his mother. These include impressions of the days when he missed his mother in Hansando, when he wrote letters, when he sent gifts, and the days when he visited her. In particular, the impressions of his mother's sadness during his stay in Hansando, a remote place far from Yeosu, are very impressive.

The following are excerpts from his diary that were introduced:

***1593.6.12. (Age 49):*** *I pulled out about 10 gray hairs this morning. Although getting gray hair as one ages is natural, I pulled them out because I worried my aging mother would be saddened by seeing them.*

***1594.1.12. (Age 50):*** *On the day of my departure to war, my mother gave me these parting words: "Go forth and do your best to cleanse the shame of our country."*

***1595.7.21. (Age 51):*** *Today is my father's birthday. I was filled with sadness, and I couldn't stop myself from crying.*

***1596.1. (Age 52):*** *I couldn't sleep all night because I was so sad while thinking about my mother.*

***1596.8.12. (Age 53):*** *I was surprised when I saw my mom in bed. She looked weak and had gray hair. I was scared she might not be around much longer.*
*I hugged her tight and stayed with her all night, trying my best to make her feel better and calm her down.*

During May 1593, even after his mother came down to Yeosu, Admiral Yi Sun-sin, during his prolonged naval expeditions in the waters of Gyeongsang Province or his stays on Hansando, communicated news of his mother's well-being through ships for Yeosu. As 1596 approached, distressing new reached Hansando that his mother's illness had worsened, and there was uncertainty about when she might be dead. Yi Sun-sin, who hadn't even witnessed his father's death while stationed at the distant borders in the past, became increasingly anxious about not being able to see his mother's final moments.

## The Last Party for His Mother

In August 1596, Yi Sun-sin tearfully requested a leave of absence from *Chechalsa* Yi Won-ik through a letter. *Chechalsa* Yi Won-ik then sent the reply to Admiral Yi. The following contents are extracted from his diary, as recorded in Park Jong-pyeong's *Nanjungilgi* (War Diary of Admiral Yi Sun-sin).

### To *Chechalsa* Yi Won-ik

*I prostrate myself and submit a letter. There are situations in life, and there can be situations in human feelings that are too urgent. Because a matter had to be done urgently as a human being, I have inevitably committed a sin against the country. It is because I have bent my loyalty to the country for my actions for my mother.*

*I have an old mother. She is 81 years old this year. At the beginning of the Imjin War, my family feared being harmed. Fortunately, my family finally decided to preserve our lives and went south by boat. My family temporarily stayed in Yeosu of Suncheon. At that time, I was only honored to be able to meet my mother and had no time to plan for anything else. Even though I am a poor and inadequate person, I have a heavy responsibility to carry out the important tasks of the country, so I am not free to act because I cannot neglect my duties. I can only think of my longing for my mother, but I cannot comfort my mother's heart, which is worried about her child. It is said that parents always stand outside the door, looking to see if their child returns if they go out in the morning and do not return. Even though I have not seen my mother for three years, how sad would my mother's heart be? Recently, a messenger from the household came. My mother asked someone else to write a letter and send it. In the letter, she said, "My old illness is getting worse, so I don't know how much longer I can live. My wish is to see your face again before I die." Oh! Even if someone else hears it, they will cry their eyes out, but what about the heart of the person who is the child of that mother? Since I read those words, my mind has been in turmoil, and I have not been interested in what I should do. Today, it also seems like the sun has set. If I suddenly suffer the tragedy of my mother's sudden death in the morning, it means that I am becoming a child of unfilial piety again. My mother will also not be able to close her eyes even in heaven. If I can't go and see her this winter, I will never be able to leave the headquarters because the preparation for the war in the spring is also urgent. I would be grateful if you would take a look at my very small sincerity to repay my mother's grace. If you give me a few days off, I can go by boat and see my mother once. If I can do that, it seems that my mother's heart will be a little comforted.*

**To Admiral Yi Sun-sin**

*The human affection for one's mother is the same for you and me. Your letter moves my heart. However, because this is a matter of distinguishing between work and personal issues, I dare not report it to the king lightly and obtain his approval.*

Yi Sun-sin wrote a letter to *Chechalsa*, requesting a leave of absence to visit his mother, who was ill in Yeosu. However, *Chechalsa* replied that it would be difficult to grant his request. This letter alone gives us a glimpse of Yi Sun-sin's filial piety. We can also see *Chechalsa*'s sense of duty as a public official. Even in the *Nanjungilgi*, we can read about Yi Sun-sin's filial piety. However, I think the content of this letter is the most crucial material for understanding Yi Sun-sin's filial piety. We can also see *Chechalsa* Yi Won-ik's attitude as a public official. Yi Sun-sin's letter and other official documents were sent to *Chechalsa* on August 11, 1596. *Chechalsa* then sent a letter stating that the request for leave was not possible. However, about a month after sending the letter, Yi Sun-sin went to Yeosu to meet his mother from Hansando. This was the day after he met *Chechalsa* Yi Won-ik, who had come down to Dangpo base. A miracle had happened. *Chechalsa* had said it would be difficult to grant a leave of absence after receiving Yi Sun-sin's letter a month earlier. However, he visited the Korean naval headquarters for an inspection. *Chechalsa* met Yi Sun-sin at Dangpo, near Hansando, and permitted him to leave for Yeosu. *Chechalsa* Yi Won-ik ordered Yi Sun-sin to inspect the military readiness of the inland provinces of Jeolla in preparation for a possible enemy invasion. Because Yeosu was the starting point for inspecting the inland military readiness, Yi Sun-sin had the opportunity to meet his sick mother, whom he had longed to see. After sailing all day from Hansando, Yi Sun-sin arrived in Yeosu around 10 p.m. and met his mother at Goeumcheon. Yi Sun-sin wrote about his feelings after meeting his mother in his diary on August 12, the lunar year. Yi Sun-sin slept by his mother's side that night and wrote in his diary, "My mother was delighted when I served her breakfast." Yi Sun-sin returned to the Jeolla Left Navy Headquarters in Yeosu from his mother's house the next day. From August 14, the lunar year, he set off on a long journey to inspect military facilities in the inland provinces and check the war preparedness. Yi Sun-sin returned to Yeosu headquarters after inspecting the inland provinces of Jeolla on September 28. Until he left for Hansando headquarters on October 10 from Yeosu headquarters, Yi Sun-sin's filial piety to his mother differed from other days. During his 10-day stay in Yeosu, he brought his mother to the headquarters and spent the day with her, taking care of her and enjoying her company. He also held a feast to show his filial piety, which he had not been able to do before.

He met and served her several times before leaving for Hansando on October 10. Did Yi Sun-sin know that the filial piety he had personally shown at this time would be the last in his lifetime? After that day, Yi Sun-sin never met his mother again in his lifetime. From October 10, 1596, when Yi Sun-sin returned to Hansando, to February 26, 1597, when he was arrested and transported, it was challenging to visit the Yeosu headquarters due to the situation of leaving the command post before and after the Japanese invasions of Korea. Yi Sun-sin was arrested and transported from Hansando to Seoul on February 26, 1597. He suffered a lot until he was released from prison on April 1 and went on the *Baekuijonggun* service.

On April 13, he heard the news that his mother had died on board a ship while traveling from Yeosu to Asan. Yi Sun-sin rushed to the sea and wept when he heard the news. He brought his mother's body to his house in Asan. Yi Sun-sin left on a long journey to the *Baekuijonggun* service without being able to hold his mother's funeral.

Chapter VII. Lessons from Yi Sun-sin and His Deep Love for Mother　　271

Figure 53: The Picture of Yi Sun-sin Meeting His Mother
*(Image Source: Yeosu City Hall)*

Figure 54: The statues of Yi Sun-sin in the Myeongryang Strait
*(The statue symbolizes Admiral Yi's deep contemplation before the Battle of Myeongnyang)*

# Bibliography

An, Y. B. (2018), *Jeongyujaeran (Forgotten war)*, Dong-a.

Bak, H. I. & Yi, Y. C. (1989), *Estimation of Trajectories for the Large General - Arrow Fired from the Early Korean Gun - Barrel Chonja and the Effective Gun Range from the Turtle Boat*, Chournal of the Korean History of Science Society, Vol. 1, No. 1, pp. 3-18.

Cha, S. K. (2021, July 4), "Yi Sun-Shin's disobedience during Jeongyoo War is false," Newsmaker.

Cho, W. R. (1987), The *Resistance of the People of Jeolla Province during the Naval Battles of the Imjin waeran*, Haenam County.

Choi, D. H. (1999), *The Translated Chungmugong Yi Sun-shin Collection* (6th), Wooseok Publisher.

Choi, D. W. (1975), *A Study on the Historical Relics of Gohado Island*, Master's Thesis, Chosun University.

Choil, Y. S. (2007), *A Holy Place of the Nation 'Goha-do'*, Doseochulpan-Hoon.

Ha, T. H. (1978), *The Translated Nanjungilgi: War Diary written by Admiral Yi Sun-sin from 1591-1598*, Yonsei University Press.

Hwang, I. S. (2022, January 6), "An Yi Sun-Shin's descendant who vindicated Yi's false reputation on disobedience," Newsmaker.

Jae, J. M. (2006), *Factors Contributing to the Joseon Navy's Victory in the Battle of Myeongnyang*, Haenam County.

Jung, J. S. (2012a), "The Causes of the Joseon Navy's Victory in the Naval Battles of the Imjinwaeran and Their Historical Significance", *Journal of Naval Military Studies*, Vol. 19, Naval Military Research Institute.

_____ (2012b), *The Authentic Theory about Admiral Yi Sun Sin Theory IV - Correct Understanding of the Turtle Ship*, Research theses of Yi Sun Sin, Vol. 17, pp. 143-169.

Jo, G. Y. (2021, April 26), "It's not true that General Yi Sun-Shin refused dispatch order from King Seonjo right before Jeongyoo War," Yonhap News.

Jo, S. D. (1970), *Yi Sun Shin – A National Hero of Korea* (written in English), Choong-moo-gong Society.

_____ (1974), *The Translated Nanjungilgi: War Diary written by Admiral Yi Sun-sin from 1591-1598 (originally written in Chinese, translated into Korean by Jo, S.D.)*, Korean Navy Headquarter.

_____ (1986), *Chungmugong Yi Sun-shin*, Namyoung-munhwasa.

Kim, B. L. (2010), "The Battle Formation and Naval Weapons Employment of the Joseon Navy," *Military History*, Vol. 74, p. 171.

_____ (2014), "Study on Weapon System of the Joseon's Navy," *Research theses of Yi Sun Sin*, Vol. 21, pp. 1-53.

Kim, D. J. (1995), *Janggye written by Lee Won-ik in Ori Teacher's Books* (Korean version translated by Kim, D. J.), Yeogang Publisher, pp. 507-531.

Kim, H. (2001), *Song of the Sword*, Tree of Thought.

Kim, H. G. (2015), *Yi Sun-shin (From Okpo to Noryang)*, Gyowoo Media.

Kim, I. S. (1991), *The Imjinwaeran & The Admiral Yi's Strategy*, the Research Papers on Admiral Yi, The Museum of R.O.K Naval Academy.

Kim, M. W. (2022, December 7), "Turtle Ship Restored through In-depth Historical Research: What are Differences from What We Have Known?," SBS News.

Kim, J. D. (2012), *Yi Sun-shin*, Gadian.

Kim, J. G. (1978), *Myth of the Turtle Ship*, Jungjeong Publisher.

_____ (1995), *Introduction to Maritime Strategy*, Naval Headquarters.

Kim, J. S. (2006), *The Translated Influence of Sea Power upon History*, written by Alfred Thayer Mahan, The World of Book.

Kim, S. W. (2001), *The State and the Aristocrats in the Mid-Joseon Dynasty*, Yeoksabi-pyungsa.

Ko, K. S. (2018), "A Critical Review of the Geographical Location of Anpyeon-do (Baleum-do) Written in the Nanjung Diary by Admiral Yi," *Journal of Navig. Port Res.*, Vol. 42, No. 6, pp. 469-477.

_____ (2020), "A Study on the Situation of Engagement & Hakik-jin in Yi Sun-shin's Forgotten Naval Battles/Jeolido Naval Battle," *Chournal of KNST*, Vol. 3, No. 2.

_____ (2021), "A Study on Yi Sun-Shin's Willingness to Follow the Order of King Seonjo to Dispatch the Navy in the Period," *Journal of KNST*, Vol. 4, No. 1, pp. 1-13.

_____ (2022), "The Verification Study on Yi Sun-Shin's Refusal of King Seonjo's Dispatch Order," *Chournal of KNST*, Vol. 5, No. 1, pp. 1-8.

Ko, K. S., & Choi, Y. S. (2021), *The Unknown Yi Sun-shin by Us*, Book Korea Publisher.

Ko, K. S., & Park, J. M. (2023a), "Reevaluation of Differences in the Forward Deployment Strategy of the Hansando Navy Before and After the Outbreak of the Jeongyujearan," *Chournal of KNST*, Vol. 6, No. 3.

_____ (2023b), "A Study on the Identification of the Effective Range and Blind Spot of the Battle Turtle Ship Cannon," *Journal of KNST*, Vol. 7, No. 1, pp. 001-010.

Kyujanggak Institute for Korean Studies, Seoul National University, https://kyu.snu.ac.kr.

Lee, B. S. (2018), *Yi Sun-shin (Astronomy and Geographic-Strategist)*, Gadian.

Lee, E. S. (1996), *Nanjungilgi* (Translated version of Yi Sun-sin's original work), Madang Media.

Lee, H. S. (1974), *The History of the Imjinwaeran*, SinHyunsilsa.

Lee, J. H. (2007), *An Understanding of Weapons*, angseogak.

Lee, K. B. (1999), *A New Discourse on Korean History*, IlChokak.

Lee, M. W. (2004), *Imjinwaeran (Japanese Invasion of Korea in 1592): History of Naval Battle (7 Year War, Record of Victory from the Sea)*, Chungeram-media.

Lee, S. I. (2011), *The Foundation of Industrial Mathematics*, Sanghakdang.

Lee, W. I. (1995), *Janggye written by Lee Won-ik in Ori Teacher's Books* (Chinese version), Yeogang Publisher.

National Archives, https://www.memorykorea.go.kr.

National Institute of Korean History, "Annals of the Joseon Dynasty, Seonjo Annals (Seonjo Revised Annals)," https://www.sillok.history.go.kr.

Naval Education Command (2004), *Admiral Yi Sun-sin*, Naval Education Command.

Naval Headquarters (2007), *Principles of Naval Warfare*, Naval Headquarters.

No, S. S. (2014), *The Translated Nanjungilgi: War Diary written by Admiral Yi Sun-sin from 1591-1598*, Book Publishing Yeohae.

Oh, S. J., Shin, J. H., & Park, H. J. (2015), *The Translated Jingbilog* (written by Ryu, Seongyong), Hongik Publisher.

Original Text of Imjin Jangcho, Yi Sun-sin, Munhajaecheong National Archives, https://www.memorykorea.go.kr.

Park, K. B. (2012), *The Translated Chungmugongjeonseo* (Written by King Jeong Cho in 1795), Vol. 3, Bibong Publisher.

Park, Y. H. (1973), *Admiral Yi Sun-shin and his Turtleboat Armada*, Sinseng Press.

Song, E. I. (2021), "Proposals for Current State and Assignment of Restored Imjinwar-Style Turtle Ships," *History & the Boundaries*, No. 120, pp. 31-76.

Sotooka Jinzaemon (1592), *Goryeo Seonjeon-gi*, http://www.gazo.dl.itc.u-to kyo.ac.jp.

Suh, Y. S. (2021, April 28), "Yi Sun-Shin's refusal against dispatch Order from King Seonjo is not true," The Asia Business Daily.

The Discovery of Admiral Yi's Naval Base (YouTube), https://www.youtube.com/watch?v=y363xJ3SZaY Classics (Comprehensive Korean Classics) DB, http://www.itkc.or.kr.

U.S.A. Naval Manual (1953), *Fire Control Fundamentals*, Bureau of Naval Personnel, Navpers.

Underwood, Horace H. (1933), *Korean Boat: Read before the Society*.

Yi, Sun-sin (1592-1598), *The War Diary Written by Yi Sun-sin*, Munhajaecheong.

# Chronology of Admiral Yi Sun-sin and Imjinwaeran

**1545**

March 8      Birth of Yi Sun-sin (April 28 in the Gregorian calendar)

**1565**

Marriage

**1576**

February      Passed military examination

December      First appointed as military officer at Donggubibo Fort, Hamgyeong Province

**1579**

February      Appointed officer at the Training Center

October      Appointed military officer under the Commander of Chungcheong Province

**1580**

July      Appointed as commander of Balpo, Jeolla Left Naval Station (first naval post)

**1582**

May      Reappointed to the Training Center

## 1583

| | |
|---|---|
| July | Appointed as a military officer under the Hamgyeong Province Commander |
| October | Appointed as officer at Gunwon Fort |
| November | Transferred to the Training Center |

## 1584

Returned home due to his father's death

## 1586

| | |
|---|---|
| January | Appointed as commander of Chosanbo, Hamgyeong Province |

## 1587

| | |
|---|---|
| August | Took on the additional role of overseeing Nokdun-do farms |
| October | Falsely accused by Commander Yi Il and demoted to serve as a common soldier |

## 1588

| | |
|---|---|
| January | Demotion lifted due to military achievements |
| August | Returned home |

## 1589

| | |
|---|---|
| February | Appointed as a military officer under Jeolla Province inspector Yi Gwang |
| December | Appointed magistrate of Jeongeup and Taeein counties |

## 1590

| | |
|---|---|
| July | Appointed as sub-military officer at Gosari Fort, then canceled |
| September | Appointed and canceled as sub-naval com-mander at Manpo |

## 1591

| | |
|---|---|
| January | Toyotomi Toyotomi Hideyoshi issues operational guidelines for the invasion of Joseon |
| February 2 | Appointed and then canceled as governor of Jindo County and subcommander of Garipo |
| February 13 | Assumed the post of Commander of Jeolla Left Naval Station |
| March | Joseon envoys Hwang Yun-gil and Kim Seong-il return and report their findings |
| December 1 | King Seonjo orders provincial governors to prohibit people from fleeing and halts defense construction |

## 1592

| | |
|---|---|
| April 12 | Yi Sun-sin conducts Turtle Ship firing drills |
| April 13 | Japanese forces invade Busan, marking the start of the Imjinwaeran Gyeongsang Left Naval Commander Bak Hong and Right Naval Commander Won Gyun desert their vessels and flee |
| April 14 | Busan Castle falls |
| April 15 | Dongrae Castle falls |
| April 26 | Japanese forces pass through Mungyeong Saejae |
| April 28 | Japanese forces occupy Chungju; General Sin Rip dies in battle |
| April 30 | King Seonjo leaves Hanyang (Seoul) |
| May 2 | Japanese forces cross the Han river |
| May 4 | Yi Sun-sin's first battle (with 24 vessels) |
| May 7 | Battle of Okpo (26 enemy vessels destroyed, enemy commander Todo); Battle of Happo (5 enemy vessels destroyed, enemy commander Wakisaka); King Seonjo arrives in Pyongyang |
| May 8 | Battle of Jeokjinpo (11 enemy vessels destroyed) |
| May 26 | Japanese forces cross the Imjin river |
| May 29 | Battle of Sacheon (23 warvessels and 3 Turtle Ships deployed); 13 enemy vessels destroyed, enemy commander Kamei; Yi Sun-sin is wounded |
| June 2 | Battle of Dangpo (21 enemy vessels destroyed) |
| June 5 | Battle of Danghangpo (Joint Fleet of 51 vessels); 26 enemy |

| | |
|---|---|
| | vessels destroyed; Joint Fleet of Yi Eok-gi and Won Gyun participates; Battle of Yongin (Wakisaka's force of 1,500 defeats the Joseon loyal army of 50,000) |
| June 7 | Battle of Yulpo (7 enemy vessels destroyed, enemy commander Kurushima Michiyuki) |
| June 9 | Joseon and Japanese forces hold talks at the Daedong river |
| June 11 | King Seonjo departs from Pyongyang and heads north |
| June 14 | Japanese forces capture Pyongyang Castle |
| June 17 | Katō Kiyomasa's forces invade Hamheung, Hamgyeong Province |
| June 19 | Ming Dynasty's Commander Cho Sueng-hoon and 1,300 troops enter Joseon |
| June 22 | King Seonjo arrives in Uiju |
| July 8 | Gwangju military commander Ko Gyeong-myeong and his sons die in the Battle of Geumsan; Battle of Hansan; Joseon fleet of 53 vessels defeats 73 enemy vessels, destroying 47 and capturing 12; enemy commander Wakisaka |
| July 10 | Battle of Angolpo (42 enemy vessels destroyed, enemy commander Kuki) |
| July 19 | Two princes, Imhaegun and Sunhwagun, captured by Katō Kiyomasa |
| July 25-29 | Militia leader Gwak Jae-u defeats Japanese forces in battles at Uiryeong, Hyeonpung, and Yangsan |
| August 1 | Yi Won-ik's forces fail to capture Pyongyang |
| August 29 | Battle of Jangnimpo (6 enemy vessels destroyed) |
| September 1 | Battle of Busan (74 Joseon warvessels among 173 vessels against 470 enemy vessels); 128 enemy vessels destroyed, General Jeong Un dies; Peace talks between Ming envoy Sim Yu-kyung and Japanese Konishi Yukinaga in Pyongyang, agreeing to a 50-day truce |
| September 7 | Katō Kiyomasa's forces withdraw from Hamgyeong Province to Anbyeon |
| October 6-7 | Japanese forces fail to capture Jinju Castle; General Kim Si-min achieves victory |
| December 25 | Ming General Lee Yeo-song and 50,000 troops cross the Yalu river into Joseon |

## 1593

| | |
|---|---|
| January 6-9 | Ming forces recapture Pyongyang Castle |
| January 18 | Konishi withdraws to Hanyang; King Seonjo travels to Uiju |
| January 27 | Ming General Lee Yeo-song's forces are defeated in the Battle of Byeokjegwan |
| February 6-8 | Ungcheon Landing Operation results in over 100 enemy casualties |
| February 12 | Battle of Haengju |
| February 18 | Ming General Lee Yeo-song withdraws to Pyongyang |
| February 29 | Katō Kiyomasa withdraws to Hanyang |
| March 7 | Ming-Japanese talks in Yongsan |
| April 7 | Hanyang-based Japanese forces receive orders from Toyotomi Hideyoshi to withdraw from Hanyang |
| April 18 | Japanese forces begin to withdraw from Hanyang |
| April 20 | Ming General Lee Yeo-song enters HanyangMay 23: Toyotomi Hideyoshi receives Ming envoys at Nagoya Castle. |
| June 21 | Yi Sun-sin relocates the headquarters of the Jeolla Left Naval Forces to Manghaeungpo, Hansando |
| July 14 | Yi Sun-si moves the headquarters to Dueulpo, Hansando July 22-29: Jinju Castle is captured by Japanese forces |
| August 10 | Ming forces begin to withdraw |
| August 15 | Yi Sun-sin becomes the Supreme Naval Commander of the Three Provinces |
| October 1 | King Seonjo returns to Hanyang |
| October 25 | Yu Seong-ryong is appointed Prime Minister |
| October 30 | Some Japanese forces begin to withdraw |

## 1594

| | |
|---|---|
| February 7 | Ming envoy Sim Yu-kyung brings peace negotiations to Hanyang |
| March 4 | Second Battle of Danghangpo (31 enemy vessels destroyed, enemy commander, Wkisaka) |
| March 18 | Remaining Japanese forces in Joseon number over 57,000 |
| April 6 | Yi Sun-sin establishes a military examination at Hansand |

| | |
|---|---|
| September 29 | Battle of Jangmunpo (2 enemy vessels destroyed) |
| October 1 | Battle of Yeongdeungpo |
| October 4 | Battle of Jangmunpo (no significant outcome) |
| December 1 | Won Gyun is appointed Commander of Chungcheong Province |
| December 30 | Ming officials Lee Chong-seong and Yang Bang-hyung are appointed as envoys for the peace mission |

**1595**

During peace negotiations, Japanese forces switch to a strategy of military provocation

**1596**

| | |
|---|---|
| April 3 | Ming envoy Lee Chong-seong flees |
| May 3 | Yang Bang-hyung is appointed chief envoy |
| September 2 | Toyotomi Hideyoshi receives Ming envoys at Osaka Castle; Ming-Japanese Peace talks break down |
| December 5 | King Seonjo gives Yi Sun-sin secret orders regarding preparations for a potential Japanese invasion |
| December 28 | Yi Sun-sin submits a report to King Seonjo |

**1597**

| | |
|---|---|
| January 1 | Japanese troops set fire to a military camp in Busan |
| January 2 | King Seonjo confirms Yi Sun-sin's request for an expedition (received on December 28, 1596s Yi Sun-sin and Kim Eung-seo to engage in battle (instructions given to *Chechalsa* Yi Won-ik) |
| January 13 | Katō Kiyomasa's forces arrive at Seosaengpo (over 150 vessels); Hwang Sin and Kim Eung-seo meet Yoshira in Uiryeong (Yoshira falsely claims that Katō's forces are stationed on Tsushima) |
| January 14 | Katō Kiyomasa's forces reach Dadaepo |
| January 21 | King Seonjo first learns of Katō's forces invading Busan waters (from Yi Won-ik's report) |
| January 27 | King Seonjo orders the impeachment of Yi Sun-sin and appoints Won Gyun as Supreme Naval Commander of the Three Provinces |

| | |
|---|---|
| February 6 | Yi Sun-sin is ordered to be arrested |
| February 10 | Yi Sun-sin, along with Kim Eung-seo, sets sail for the waters of Busan |
| February 12 | Yi Sun-sin learns about his impending arrest near Gadeokdo |
| February 26 | Yi Sun-sin hands over command to Supreme Naval Commander Won Gyun and is escorted to Hanyang |
| March 4 | Yi Sun-sin is imprisoned |
| March 12 | Yi Sun-sin is tortured |
| April 1 | Yi Sun-sin is released from prison (begins serving as a rankles soldier: *Tongjesa*) |
| April 13 | Yi Sun-sin's mother dies aboard a boat en route from Yeosu to Asan |
| April 27 | Yi Sun-sin arrives in Suncheon while serving as a rankles soldier |
| June 4 | Yi Sun-sin reaches General Gwon Yul's camp in Hapcheon, the final destination of his service |
| July 8 | A large Japanese force lands in Busan (over 600 vessels) |
| July 14 | Won Gyun's fleet suffers defeat near Jeolyeongdo (34 vessels lost) |
| July 16 | Joseon fleet is destroyed at the Battle of Chilcheonryang (Won Gyun, Jeolla Right Naval Commander Yi Eok-gi, Chungcheong Naval Com mander Choi Ho, Assistant General Bae Hong-rip, and others suffer heavy losses) |
| July 18 | Yi Sun-sin hears of the Joseon fleet's defeat and laments |
| August 3 | Yi Sun-sin receives his appointment as Supreme Naval Commander of the Three Provinces at Son Gyeong-rae's house (King Seonjo's appointment date was July 22) |
| August 19 | Yi Sun-sin holds a ceremony in Hoeryeong pojin, Jangheung County, Jeolla Provinc, to assume command of the Joseon navy; 12 vessels participate |
| August 20 | Moves from Hoe-ryeongpo to Ijinjin |
| August 24 | Moves to waters off Eoranpo |
| August 26 | Newly appointed Jeolla Right Naval Commander Kim Eok-chu joins with one ship at Eoranpo; the fleet increases to 13 vessels |
| August 28 | Retreats when Japanese vessels approach; no engagement occurs; moves to Jangdo (Hwangsan-myeon, Haenam County) |
| August 29 | Moves to Byeokpajin |

| | |
|---|---|
| September 2 | During the stay at Byeokpajin, Gyeongsang Right Naval Commander Bae Seol deserts |
| September 7 | Engages in two battles, fighting both times |
| September 15 | Moves from Byeokpajin to Jeolla Right Naval Station |
| September 16 | Battle of Myeongryang (13 Joseon vessels against Japanese vessels; around 130 enemy vessels participate in the battle; 31 enemy vessels destroyed, enemy commander Todo); retreats strategically to Dangsa Island by night |
| September 17-October 10 | Strategic maneuvers through remote islands in the West Sea, including Eoido, Beopseongpo, Wido, Gogunsan lands, and back to Beopseongpo and Eoido |
| October 11-18 | Lands on Anpyeondo; identified as present-day Anjwa Island based on *Ko Kwang-soob*'s 2018 research paper; used as a temporary naval headquarters; receives news of his youngest son Myeon's death on the 14th; stays for 18 days |
| October 29 | Moves from temporary naval base on Anjwa Island to Gohado, Mokpo, establishing a naval headquarters; begins rebuilding the Joseon navy; stays for 106 days |
| December 1 | Konishi completes the construction of Fortress |
| December 22 | Shimazu establishes Sa Cheon New Fortress |
| December 23 | Joseon and Ming forces fail to capture Ulsan Fortress |

**1598**

| | |
|---|---|
| February 17 | Yi Sun-sin moves the naval headquarters from Gohado, Mokpo, to Gogeumdo, Wando |
| July 16 | China naval commander Chen Lin arrives at ogeumdo, forming the Korea-China Joint Fleet |
| July 19 | Battle of Jeolido; 50 enemy vessels destroyed, large victory with the "Cranes Wing" formation (according to *Ko Kwang-soob*'s 2020 research paper) |
| August 18 | Toyotomi Toyotomi Hideyoshi dies |
| September 19 | Joint Korea-China forces commence coordinated offensive operations |
| November 17 | Joint Korea-China fleet conducts a blockade operation in Gwangyang Bay, destroying 30 enemy vessels; 39 Chinese vessels are sunk |

November 18-19   Battle of Noryang; over 200 enemy vessels destroyed; Yi Sun-sin dies in battle on the 19th (December 16 in th Gregorian calendar)

# Index

Adakebune 78
Alfred Mahan 256
Anjwado 35, 225
Annals of King Seonjo 233
Anpyeondo 35, 225
An Wi 215

**B**

Bae Heung-rip 193
Baekseoliang 247
Baekuijonggun 32, 185
Bae Seol 191
Balpo 249
Bang Jin 31
Battle of Busanpo 127
Battle of Chilcheonryang 34, 193
Battle of Jeolido 236
Battle of Myeongryang 212, 221
Battle of Noryang 37, 234
Bernard Law Montgomery 41
Bibyeonsa 42
Bigeokjincheonroe 143
Blockade Operations 242
Busan 49

Byeokpajin 212
Byeongsa 22

Chechalsa 33
Chechalsa Yi Won-ik 267
Chechalsa Yun Du-su 156
Chen Lin 37
Cheonja cannon 54
Cheonja-Chongtong (Heaven Cannon) 76
Chinese President Xi Jinping 255
Choi Ho 193
Chongtong 76
Chungcheong Province 31
Chung Ju-yung 80
Chungmugong 39, 254

**D**

Dadaepo 134
Dakyeongpojin 179
Dam Jong-in 152
Dangjinpo 249
Dangsado 35, 220, 222
Deng Zilong 250

Dodo Takadora  27
Dong Yil-won  241
Dowonsoo Kwon Yul  156
Dragon of the Seas  119
Duchijin  212
Dunjeon  164

**E**

Effective Range  59

**G**

G.A. Ballard  41, 121
Gadeokdo  130, 189
Gakseondo  58
Gamunpo  189
Gangyangrok confirms  228
General Manabe  119
generation of the Jangheung Ko  111
Geobukseon  52
Geojedo  140
Geumdangdo  238
Geumsan  111
Geumtopamun  152
Gimhae  130
Gi-nam, Yi  115
Gogeumdo  36, 232
Gogunsando  224
Gohado  35
Goheung Nokdo  178
Gomakwon  179
Goryeoseon Jeongi  69, 125
Gu Sa-jik  168
Gwak Jae-woo  110, 158
Gwaneumpo  252

Gyeongsang Province  22
Gyeonnaeryang  116

**H**

Hakikjin (crane wing formation)  113, 115
Hansan  117
Hansando  144, 148
Heungyang  233
H.G. Hulbert  121
Historical Evidence and Misconceptions  204
Hwado  116
Hwajung-umi  131
Hwangja cannon  54
Hwangja-Chongtong (Yellow Cannon)  77
Hwangjo Byeolmyo Shrine  255
Hwang Ok-cheon  44
Hwang Yun-gil  25
Hyeonja cannon  54
Hyeonja-Chongtong (Black Cannon)  76

Imjinwaeran  44
Imjin War  193

Janggae  43
Jangmunpo Landing Operation  155
Jeolla Jwasusa  32
Jeolla Left Naval Forces  145
Jeolla Left Navy  133

Jeolla Province  22
Jeolla Usuyeong  229
Jeolyeongdo  134
Jeong Geol  130
Jeong Un  135
Jeong Yeong-du  216
Jeongyujaeran (Jeongyu War)  202
Jeong Yun  133
Jeongyu War(Jeongyujeran)  33
Jepo  139
Jija cannon  54
Jija-Chongtong (Earth Cannon)  76
Jingbirok  39, 120
Jobangjang  150
Joint amphibious operation  161
Joint Tactics  71
Jo Seong-do  39
Joseongi  75
Jwauijeong  254

Kaesong  110
Kato  116
Kato Kiyomasa  26
Kato Yoshiaki  27
Ki  120
Kim Deok-ryeong  158
Kim Myeon-gwon  176
Kim Seong-il  25
Kim Tak  218
King Taejo  21
Kobaya  78
Ko Gyeong-myeong  110
Konishi Yukinaga  26

Korean-China Allied Forces  230
Korean-Chinese command  243
Korean Joint Fleet  155
Kuki Yoshitaka  27, 116, 242
Kuroda  26
Kwon Jun  133
Kwon Yul  34

landing operations  139

Maebong Mountain in Anjwado  226
Maengseon  73
Ma Gui  241
Manho  32
maximum range  60
Ming dynasty  23
Miracle of the Turtle Ship  82
Mirukdo  116
Mokpo  223
Molundae  131
Myeongjong Sillok  63
Myeongryang Strait  34, 200

**N**

Nakdong river  139
Nam I-gong  176
Nanjungilgi  30
Nankan  233
Narodo  243
Naval Academy Museum  57
Nelson  40
Nokdo  238

Noryang Sea 250

Oncheon Island (Chilcheon Island) 139
Oriryang 151
Ori Teacher's Collection of Works 204

**P**

Panokseon 53
Park Hae-il 61
Park Yi-ryang 115
Pochungsa Memorial Hall 111
President Moon Jae-in 255
principles of naval operations 256
Projectile Trajectory 66
Pyongyang 110, 138

**S**

Sahwarang 141
Sampowaelan 72
Saryangdo 138
Sato Tetsutaro 40
Sejong Sillok 63, 242
Sekibune 78
Seomjin River 178
Seon Geo-i 158
Seon Gye-yo 241
Seonjo 21
Seopyeongpo 131
Seunggun 47
Shin Ho 133
simulations 239

Songdo 140
Songjinpo 140
Song Yeo-jong 216
Son Won-il 38
Sorokdo 238
Susa 22

Tak, Jeong 176
Teppo 78
The 12 lessons left by Yi Sun-sin 263
The Admiral: Roaring Currents 219
The Battle of Angolpo 121
The Battle of Danghangpo 149
The Battle of Myeongryang 212
The Battle of Ungpo 138
The Five Spirits of Chungmugong 262
The Joint Korean Fleet 142
The Principle of Maneuver and Concentration 259
The Principle of the Offensive 258
The Principle of Vigilance 259
Tongjeoyeong 234
Tongjesa 33
Toyotomi Hideyoshi 24
Turtle Ship 48

Udo in Gwangyang Bay 248
Uldolmok 34
Ungpo 139
Ungpo Landing Operation 145
Unknown Island 225

Index

Usuyeong 225

Waegu 24
Waegwan 24
Waeseong 233
Wakisaka Yasuharu 27, 119
Wando 36
Wando Cheonghaejin 233
Wang Yu-geuk 244
Wido 223
Won Gyun 34

Yeongdeungpo 151
Yeonguijeong 39
Yeosu 44
Yeo Yeong-dam 150
Yi Bun 54
Yi Chungmugong Haengrok 50
Yi Chungmugong Yusa 250
Yi Eok-gi 34

Yi Eon-ryang 133
Yi Eun-sang 38
Yi Jeong 31
Yi Seong-gye 20
Yi Sun-sin 34
Yi Sun-sin's Historical Errors 205
Yi Won-ik 155
Yu Jeong 241
Yu Seong-ryong 39

**1 2 3**

4 Routes for Simultaneous Land-Sea Campaign 241
8,000 soldiers 234
12 ships 199
13 ships 200
40-Day Inspection 181
40-day retreat 234
40 days 223
53 warships 234
133 Japanese naval ships 220

The statue of Yi Sun-sin and the Turtle Ship at the Naval Academy
*(This Turtle Ship was restored in 2022 and is considered the most accurate representation of the Turtle Ship from the Imjinwaeran).*

Gwaneumru (above) and the Gwaneumpo Sea (below)
The sea off Gwaneumpo, where Yi Sun-sin fell in battle on December 16, 1598.

⬆ Hyeonchungsa Shrine (the shrine dedicated to Yi Sun-sin, located in Asan City, Chungcheongnam-do)
⬇ Yi Sun-sin's Tomb (Located within the grounds of Hyeonchungsa Shrine, Asan City, Chungcheongnam-do)

- ⬆ The "Mochung Gak" on Gohado Island, Mokpo (Admiral Yi Sunsin and the Korean navy stayed here for 106 days following the Battle of Myeongnyang, during which they strengthened the naval forces. In February 1598, they relocated the naval headquarters to Gogeumdo Island in Wando).
At Mochung Gak, Admiral Yi Sun-sin's achievements during his stay on Gohado Island are inscribed on a monument.
- ⬇ The area around Maebong Mountain on Anjwado Island, Sinan-gun, Jeollanam-do (This place was identified in 2019 by Professor Ko Kwang-soob as the temporary naval base where Admiral Yi Sun-sin and the Korean forces stayed for 18 days following their victory in the Battle of Myeongryang).

The above photo is of the Turtle Ship restored in 1999, which has been assessed to differ significantly from the one Admiral Yi Sun-sin deployed during the Imjinwaeran. The photo was taken by the author during his tenure as a professor at the Naval Academy. The photo below was taken in 2020 during a visit to his alma mater, Mokpo National Maritime University, after his retirement, alongside a firstyear student from the university's Naval AcademyDepartment

# About Author

**Professor Kwangsoob Ko** was born in Naju, Jeollanam-do, South Korea, and graduated from Gwangju High School. He then entered the Korean Naval Academy, graduating with honors in 1979 and ranking fourth overall in his class. While serving as a young naval officer aboard a destroyer, he was selected to pursue a career as a professor of navigation — a decision that led to a distinguished academic and military career spanning over four decades.

Professor Ko earned his Ph.D. in electronic engineering from Clarkson University in the United States and became a pioneering GPS navigation scientist. As an expert in navigation engineering, he made significant contributions to the development of Korea's satellite-based navigation systems and maritime safety technologies.

Alongside his technical and academic achievements, Professor Ko has devoted his life to the study of Admiral Yi Sun-sin and the Turtle Ship. Applying the rigor of a scientist to historical research, he used scientific verification and engineering analysis to uncover new insights into Admiral Yi's naval strategies and the operational principles of the Turtle Ship. His groundbreaking work has reshaped the understanding of Admiral Yi's tactics and corrected long-standing historical and scientific misconceptions.

This book represents a historic milestone: it is the first English-language publication on Admiral Yi and the Turtle Ship authored by a Korean scholar in over 50 years. It comprehensively presents newly verified facts and exposes historical and scientific inaccuracies that have persisted for decades.

Retired with the rank of Navy captain, Professor Ko has served as president of the Korean Society of Naval Science and Technology and has been honored with the Presidential Award and the Republic of Korea Order of National Security Merit. He now seeks to share Admiral Yi's legacy with the world and engage a global audience through this landmark publication.